A PASSION FOR Cats

A PASSION FOR

The Cats Protection League

Edited by PHILIP WOOD

DAVID & CHARLES
Newton Abbot   London   North Pomfret

British Library Cataloguing in Publication Data

A Passion for cats.
1. Cats
I. Cats Protection League
636.8   SF442

ISBN 0-7153-8971-8

Typeset by Typesetters (Birmingham) Ltd
Smethwick West Midlands
Printed in Hong Kong
by Regent Publishing Services Ltd
for David & Charles Publishers plc
Brunel House   Newton Abbot   Devon

Published in the United States of America
by David & Charles Inc
North Pomfret   Vermont 05053   USA

CONTENTS

See page 207 for key to chief contributors

FOREWORDS

There are a million stray cats in this country, doing their best to survive in a man-dominated environment. Each one is supposed to have nine lives but in reality it has only one and that life can often be harsh and painful. The frequently wretched conditions under which these unfortunate animals are forced to live should shame us all. Four thousand years ago we made a contract with the cat: you help us and we will look after you; you protect our food stores from mice and rats and we will care for you and protect you. This was a fair contract and both sides benefited. Out of it grew the domestic cat, more friendly, more kittenish than its wild ancestors and a valued servant in the home.

Those ancient cats were revered and to harm one in early Egypt was punishable by death. Then came the Dark Ages and the cat suffered centuries of torment at the hands of pious witch-hunters who stupidly labelled it as one of Satan's helpers. Only in recent times has the cat once again become a much loved companion animal in our homes. But even now it is maltreated by a cruel minority and all too often turned out to fend for itself. It is resilient and it somehow manages to scrape a living, but that is not good enough for so magnificent an animal. For the cat is full of fascination, a combination of physical grace and subtle, complex behaviour. To share a room with one is a special privilege and the better we understand the feline world the better our chances of honouring that ancient bargain we struck with the cat so long ago.

The royalties from this book will all go to an organisation that works ceaselessly to improve the lot of the less fortunate of our feline companions – The Cats Protection League. Without such bodies, there would be a great deal more feline suffering in this country and they deserve our appreciation and our respect for their labours. So thank you for having purchased this book, an act which will directly assist them in their continuing work.

As I write these words, an ex-stray is rolling on her back on the carpet by my desk. She arrived in my garden nine years ago, when I found her up a tree screaming, in a state of shock caused by some unknown drama. Taking her in, I gained a friend for life. She may no longer have mice to catch but she more than fulfils her half of the ancient bargain simply by the elegance of her daily presence. For this, the food, drink and warmth I provide are a ridiculously small price to pay. When you have read *A Passion for Cats* I hope you will feel the same way.

Desmond Morris

I'm so glad you've got together your book called *A Passion for Cats*. As you know, cats are one of my passions; but, really, people can be extraordinary. I know some families who have cats, and if they don't see them for days – it's usually one cat in this case, an un-neutered Tom or something – they wonder vaguely where they are, but they have no sense of achievement in bringing them up and looking after them and possessing them. Let me correct that, because you never possess a cat; you are allowed to be in a cat's life, which, of course, is a privilege. There are three around me at the moment – Jenny's sitting on the television, Dimly's straight in front of me and Cleopatra's seeing to some extraordinary parts of her anatomy, making sure they're awfully clean: I have no idea where she's going.

They're not easy to understand: in no way are cats subservient. Men tend to like dogs a lot, because if you whack a dog and bash it about and shout at it, it will come crawling towards you on its stomach, with its tail wagging; and I think, actually, that's what men expect us to do! I've never quite agreed with it – but there we are. 'Us', of course, meaning girls or ladies, or whatever. But cats are a totally different thing: each one has a different personality, a different and marvellous nature and a different way of treating you. You can get into disfavour with cats; for example, they don't like me getting zip-bags out and looking as though I'm going to Yorkshire to do a television or something – they hate all that, but they find me kind of irresistible when I come home. They play Hard to Get for about five minutes, then they're all rolling about the floor again.

But, as I say, they are remarkable animals; they're not like anything else – they're extremely good for anyone who is excitable or who has heart trouble or high blood pressure. If you live with cats, those are non-existent. They all have their extraordinary ways of eating, as we know: Patrick (named after Patrick Cargill), who, when he was alive, was King Cat or Leader of the Pack, had a passion for taking roses out of a vase and eating them. Or cabbage stalks – it was like Cabbages and Kings, really.

They are wonderfully soothing to be with, and they're very very restful. I'm so glad to know that people like Churchill must have got great satisfaction from the cats who reigned with him in Downing Street – Nelson, Margate and Jock – and that the cat who has just died, Wilberforce, who served under four prime ministers, had special perks – the police were instructed to ring the front door bell any time he made it known that he wished to enter. I get so much pleasure myself from things like the fact that, if I shout at Dimly in the garden, he does a sort of Commando get-away on his elbows – he crawls, and that makes me laugh very much indeed, but, of course, he *knows* it makes me laugh, and that's why he does it: he's no more upset by it than anybody else would be.

I think the wonderful thing is that people who do care for them *really* care for them and get a lot of pleasure out of their company. I'm delighted that this book has been written in association with the Cats Protection League, because they do some wonderful work and I was at one time the Vice President of that Association for a year and I did do a great deal of work for them at the time. My lovely Lulu came to me from Reading from them, and in her memory I'm more than happy to wish you the greatest success with the book; I'm sure they'll be very grateful for any money raised by *A Passion for Cats*.

When I told my Agent that I was going to write *The Cat's Whiskers* he said Oh – that's marvellous: so many more people like cats than like you! At the moment I considered having another agent, but he's very nice really – I'm sure he meant it in the best possible way – and in a manner of speaking, he's almost been proved right! Hope the luck holds for *Beryl, Food and Friends*!

Good luck with the book.

Love, **Beryl Reid**

1
MAKING THE MOST OF A CAT

These pages celebrate the cat, the whole domesticated species and your own individual. They contain a wealth of practical advice, anecdotes, sharing experience and a wide range of other ingredients mainly supplied by members of the Cats Protection League whose jubilee the volume marks. *A Passion for Cats* is a veritable work of love with its passionate and caring message that hopefully will instruct and entertain many thousands of cat lovers and make them better cat owners.

The true cat lover will already have noted that the title of this opening chapter is wrong. What it should, of course, say is: How to Enable a Cat to Make the Most of its Owner. For nobody should buy, accept as a gift or even give housing room to a cat that just arrives of its own accord one evening who is out to get the best bargain from it. You do not drive a cat, expect it to be in the least productive, reliable, co-operative, economical. Yet if you are (or might later become) an elderly person living by yourself, caring for a friendly cat might add so much purpose to your life that your days will be more fulfilling and therefore more numerous. There is growing medical evidence of the benefit of cats to humans, especially in reducing tension and blood pressure.

For this among other reasons the Cats Protection League is not a bunch of idiosyncratic individuals brought together through an obsession but one of Britain's most worthwhile charities. It indeed thrives partly through legacies left it by people thankful for the contribution a cat or cats have made to their own lives.

Most cats are great characters and of course we all think our own has the most splendid personality of all. And all cat lovers swap stories – of how a cat walked fifty miles back to its old home, how when two hungry strays came to dinner and one was frightened by a sudden noise the other would not eat until it had discovered its brother or sister and coaxed it back to the food, and how a mother as part of basic kitten training took successive litters up the curtain one side of the window, along the top and down the other. There are thousands of stories of friendships between cats and other animals and birds, of hunting exploits, of kittens being taught to threaten the goldfish as a means of securing attention and getting the door open, but being punished terribly if they actually caught one and so destroyed the power of the threat, and of cats, who have been

---

The woman's friend

The following tale is told among certain African tribes. The cat, conscious of his dignity and importance, resolved only to be friendly to the strongest and most powerful of living creatures. Having seen a hare put to flight by a jackal, he became friendly with the latter, only to scorn it when he saw it frightened by a leopard. His new friend, the leopard, was driven away by a lion, the lion frightened by a charging elephant, and the elephant killed and eaten by a man. Satisfied that he had, at last, found the 'lord of creation', whom no other living creature could withstand, the cat transferred his friendship to the man. For many moons they hunted together, then one day the man returned to his home, and entered, leaving the cat waiting for him outside in the sun. Suddenly a loud shrill sound of anger arose in the hut, and the 'lord of creation' rushed out, pale and trembling, followed by a volley of pots and pans. Curious to see the powerful being who could put to ignominious flight the conquerer of all other creatures, the cat walked into the hut and saw – a woman. Since that time, he has always remained her friend. – *The Cat*, 1936.

seen sitting patiently at the window waiting expectantly for their owner to return, immediately on catching a glimpse of him moving off to a chair and feigning complete indifference when the door is opened. Then, again, there are tales of cats who go to almost any length to attract attention, like bouncing a purpose-caught mouse against a window to stop a radio broadcast being recorded inside.

Many people especially like to tell of the things that cats have done for or with them, alerting them when there was a danger of fire, playing together with a ball. And that leads to accounts of cats described as acting with human rather than feline instincts. Anthropomorphic interpretations may be cute but are never accurate, and the cat lover who believes that he has tamed his four-legged animal into a small piece of humanity is bound to be puzzled and upset when the cat acts like a cat, and that puzzlement and upset will be felt more deeply by the cat itself.

Whatever the motivation for keeping a cat, the pleasure will be greatly enhanced if it is always remembered that it is a wild animal that has been more or less domesticated but is incapable of the thinking processes and values of men, women and children. It is obvious, yet few people thoroughly acknowledge it in their everyday living with their cat or cats. It is too easy to attribute human feelings to the feline, to be angry when it does something every self-respecting cat always will – like catch a mouse or bird – or to expect it to apply mankind's values of what belongs to whom. So rare is perfect understanding, that even the most caring owners, who believe they are very generous in their material and psychological offerings to their cat, in fact place repeated obstacles in the way of its enjoyment – and seek to change its behaviour in a self-defeating manner. What could be a valuable learning experience for children is often lost by the imposition of human discipline on the family cat.

A wild animal that has been – more or less – domesticated. There is much to understand, and the best way of setting about it is to watch your cat as steadily and patiently as it watches you

There is much to understand, and the best way of setting about it is to watch your cat as steadily and as patiently as it watches you. It will spend hours querying your intentions and reliability, tail twitches often indicating that it cannot quite make up its mind about something you are going to do, or its response to an action you have taken. The interpretation of a wagging tail is just one of dozens of aspects of cat behaviour that human mythology gets wrong; more often it signifies conflict rather than anger. A ten-year-old girl was once smacked for allowing a Siamese to approach her: 'They are very dangerous.' Every reader of these pages so far will have seen non-cat lovers making fools of themselves over something to do with our feline friends and few genuine cat lovers are as fully understanding as they should be.

Rule one is to remember that while the cat is a strong individualist and may spend years pitting its wits against you in order to gain a better diet or higher standard of living, or just more love, whatever its age, it will always cast you in the role of parent. For inevitably you control it as in nature only its mother

You do not drive a cat, expect it to
be in the least productive, reliable,
co-operative, or economical. Yet
caring for a friendly cat might add
so much purpose to your life that
your days will be more fulfilling,
and therefore more numerous

Right *Tiny, aged thirteen*

The hunting instinct is
irrepressible

did, you encourage, praise, admonish, prevent it having free access, and of course provide its food and drink. And while the cat may alternately please and irritate you, give you a happy half hour purring on your lap and then draw threads out of your best chair, welcome you home with great enthusiasm but spend the evening expecting you constantly to let it in and out, you are bound to appear far more perplexing to it. For example, just as it really relaxes and shows you how close it feels to you, and so starts treading or kneading your legs (the gentle motion accompanied by purring that it first did when exerting pressure at its mother's breast), you suddenly toss it off your lap. It is not to know that its claws are causing you pain. It is merely puzzled that having encouraged intimacy you have gone cold.

Biological facts do not go away because they are irritating or embarrassing. The cat may love the warmth of your fireside and your loving company, yet still be driven by instinct to check on what is happening in its territory, and to renew its scent to indicate to neighbouring cats that it is still around. The real irritation is that the home has doors which only the parent-figure can open. The hunting instinct is irrepressible, and while tossing the ping-pong ball around as a hunting substitute can be interpreted as delightful, few humans welcome presents of dead and even less live vermin, rabbits or whatever. It is doubly unfortunate that many owners least willing to cope with biological facts opt for neutered female cats who are the most likely to bring back live animals in suppressed motherhood and are puzzled and hurt when their owners protest. The confusing

Tickling the keys: a family cat will provide special moments in everyone's life

message is perhaps that there should have been a bigger animal.

Every good cat owner knows that keeping claws sharpened is a necessity of survival and that declawing is cruel. Most owners score less well on simpler matters. For example cats need an interest, and looking out of the window is one way of gaining it. So why did you need to clutter it with human paraphernalia? Is it the cat's fault that the vase on the landing strip was in the way and so got broken?

At which point we may begin to panic and wonder if any of us are really fit to be cat owners! Happily there are hundreds of thousands of very contented cats, proud of their owners and their homes. Cats, for example, who are so upset at being separated from their owners that upon being reunited will turn their backs on them (in human terms by way of punishment) only to become overwhelmed by emotion and rush into their arms. Cats who look forward to new experiences, who come and meet you at the bus stop, beg to be given another ride in the car or for you to bring out a favourite toy. Cats who become so close to their owners that they can safely laugh with each other.

Here are one cat lover's points of guidance:

★Always treat a cat seriously. Above all avoid a patronising tone of voice. Never laugh at a cat or risk the least touch of ridicule. You can of course talk arrant nonsense provided the tone of voice is right and another human does not laugh at you (with the cat feeling it is being ridiculed).

★When trying to make friends with a strange cat, place yourself in a receptive stance. Remember that at many times its height a tall human must seem pretty forbidding, so lower yourself. (Some cats ultimately stretch up to reduce the distance.) But do not approach the cat too rapidly or closely. Let the cat make the final approach. Try to prevent the owner picking it up and placing it on your lap. Friendships that might have flowered are cut short by such intervention. Don't try to make friends unless you have time and patience.

★Look a cat straight in the eyes, which again often means crouching or allowing the cat onto the table. When you have its attention, show that you are relaxed by blinking (when the cat is relaxed it will take long blinks with you) and by licking your lips. To be the cat's real equal you would of course need to lick it, but licking your own lips shows willing and will probably be repaid by the cat licking your fingers or kissing your nose.

★Develop your own technique for drawing attention to the fact that you would enjoy a moment of social intercourse with the cat up the drive or even on the opposite side of a quiet street. A high-pitched sound as you draw in air between moist lips may bring a response, though few self-respecting cats will rush to you in a straight line. Do not give an invitation unless you are prepared to wait while it gains time for contemplation with a bit of cleaning or scratching. We humans after all scratch our heads when we are not quite sure what to do.

Rescued cats are often the most characterful and affectionate

★To help make a new cat (or one you are going to spend some time with) feel at home, lower yourself all the way to the ground, lying on the carpet in a semi-circle. Many cats show their willingness to communicate by rolling over and exposing their weakest point, their underside. But you should not assume that this immediately gives you permission to tickle their tummy.

★Feeding time is of course vitally important. If you take your cat on a visit to another home, even a small treat will help settle it. On return from a visit away, a main meal in its own eating position will convey the message that things are back to normal. Even rival cats often eat happily together, the newcomer generally given a tough time being seldom harassed at meal time. Conversely the new kitten may be so unused to eating by itself that it may almost literally need its paw held to encourage it to eat. Cats who have been ill also sometimes benefit from companionship at meal times.

★Remember that we live in a class-ridden society and the food and values of one home are not necessarily replicated in another, or even by different people (like those who take care of your house while you are on holiday) in the same one. The cat used to a quiet life may be as upset by the television being left on loudly all day long as by a visiting dog. And if your cat was lonely for you while you were on holiday or in hospital, would you prefer to hear it had been sulking or pining? 'Nothing I can do; it's just sulking,' said one vet. 'I'm afraid it's pining and will need a lot of loving,' said another of the same animal with more time to spare.

★Cleaning after food is a biological necessity for cats. Even young children should be taught never to interrupt.

13

A sign of trust. If you could walk past without saying hello, you should not be reading this book!

Eleven-week-old kittens enjoying a mutual grooming session. If you have only one cat, it will need you to perform this role

This ginger and white tom, George, is now seven years old and a well and truly settled member of the family

(continued opposite)

Just one point of view

One often hears the question asked – 'Do you prefer cats or dogs?' It is not a sensible question: it is not even a reasonable question, because you cannot compare the incomparable.

'Would you sooner own a cat or a dog?' is a little more sensible, but the answer must almost invariably depend on the circumstances. If you are a man who shoots, you want a working gun dog; but if you are old and unable to get about much, a cat who exercises itself and who sits in front of the fire or on your knee, will certainly make a more suitable companion than a dog. You cannot compare cats with dogs. One might as well ask, 'Do you prefer eggs and bacon or a game of golf?'

The truth is – and it is not always recognised – that the more obedient a dog is and the better it is trained for its work, the more it becomes a 'slave' to its master, however willing that slave may be, and the more it loses its own independence of thought and action.

This never happens with a cat. Within very narrow limits, a cat can be taught a certain amount of obedience and it will invent games and pastimes for itself, but not at the behest of the owner. A cat can become just as devoted and affectionate as any dog, but never slavishly.

To get the best out of a cat demands constant and very careful study of its temperament and character. It is true that dogs vary in these characteristics but to nothing like the same extent that cats do. Cats will always maintain their independence of thought and action and, provided they are fed and looked after, they can make their own lives and get on very well without you.

On the other hand, if you will

★But that does not mean the cat is always right and that everything has to be arranged round its whims. The cat that needs its nightly loving on the lap but is too lazy to get started can well respond by having something like a newspaper gently thrown at it. The more matter-of-fact way such matters are conducted the better.

★Take great care, especially with kittens, in giving instructions. Ask how the cat will understand them. Thus an owner presenting a new chair that he did not want scratched to pieces showed it to the cat with great aplomb, stroking its texture gently, speaking in an appreciative voice and ultimately placing the cat on it. The cat took it to be a present, and for ever resented the owner taking precedence in sitting on it. The piano was being played when a kitten wondered about climbing up the chimney. A sharp smack on the back convinced it that every time the piano was played thereafter it would be smacked. Cats are bound to scratch to sharpen their claws and if they spend long hours indoors (and perhaps lack suitable wood or other surfaces outdoors) are bound to use fabric inside. Do not wait until the kitten decides what fabric it likes best before thinking of purchasing a special cat strip.

★Whatever you are known to be most upset by happening the cat will be sure to make happen when it needs attention. Suppressing your anxiety is just one clue. Most cats need most attention to be let through those wretched human devices, doors. Much frustration is saved when the cat can make its own way in and out, through a puss flap, window opening or doors left slightly ajar.

★If a cat lives with you, everything is equally yours. It is thus your fault if you leave a piece of prime steak unattended, and cats quickly learn that distraction caused by the telephone ringing can be used to advantage. And if there is a room where the cat is not welcome, it is of course entirely your fault if you fail to close the door securely. Making a song and dance about the cat being out of bounds is likely to increase curiosity. Most of us of course do not want a cat walking across our dining table when we are serving food. Serving the cat its meal at the same time – it has its eating place, you yours – can lead to a matter-of-fact understanding, which may be lost if the cat is then given a titbit by one of your guests. The matter-of-fact approach to eating is perhaps demonstrated by many cats having a stronger emotional tie to members of the family who do not feed them; at least food and love do not have to go together. Often it is indeed the least cat-loving person of the household who most dislikes the cat's plea for food and thus gives in and feeds it early. Hardly surprisingly the cat will then trade on this human weakness and demand ever earlier feeding. One person and one person only should be in charge of food.

★However much you may love birds, especially if the cat lives in a mouseless environment, it is going to start catching them. Apart from making sure that the bird table is out of cat reach (a simple precaution many nature lovers fail to take), you have to grin and bear it. The more neutral your approach, the less damage. Having the whole family shout and someone ultimately hit the cat will confuse and certainly do nothing to suppress biological instinct. It is however often possible to make an early introduction to chickens and even goldfish so that they become 'family' and safe from attack.

★Enjoy your cat's age. Everyone knows how rapidly kittens grow into cats, but horizons continue to widen for many years and experimentation in food as in other matters may pay handsome dividends. Look ahead: even if there is a relative to leave your cat with when you go on holiday (and some cats actually enjoy a change of surroundings) consider what might happen later on. You cannot suddenly send an elderly cat that has led a sheltered life and not been innoculated for a decade to a cattery. Old age brings its own challenge. Sometimes a younger cat may help, but more usually it will be resented. Cats are not good patients and mercifully spend a lesser proportion of their life in retreat than do humans, and when it becomes impossible to jump onto a favourite perch a helping hand is welcome, especially when dignity is protected. Never let a struggling cat catch you watching it. As the cat becomes less supple, privacy is increasingly important.

★Build up a dossier of photographs of your cat (perhaps based on the seasons which affect feline responses every bit as much as human ones) and do not be shy of sharing it with other cat lovers. Indeed reading and talking about your own and other people's cats, attending meetings and even the local cat show will make you a more appreciative owner. The Cats Protection League is always there with local branches throughout the country and its advisory services and magazine *The Cat*, from whose columns many of the anecdotes in this book have been drawn. Cats are serious business and let nobody mock the need many owners find to go into print to declare the love for their departed friend. The obituary the present writer did for his own faithful cat, published in a regional morning newspaper, brought an amazing response, and is also included in the pages that follow.

The range of the ingredients that make up the rest of this book is indeed wide, reflecting just how many-faceted are cats and cat care, and the wider interest in cats and even cat legend and artefacts. Read it, remembering that cats help us make the best of our lives!

take the trouble to make a real study of your feline friend and learn her methods of telling you when she wants to play or to be brushed and combed or to be made a fuss of, your reward will be great.

Above all, *talk* to your cat; it will not understand your words, but it will deeply appreciate the sound of your voice, as you will the sound of her purr. – *The Cat*

LIVING WITH A CAT

If there is an ultimate animal form it is surely that of the cat. Serene and enigmatic in repose, beguiling in sleep, agile and athletic in movement, fastidious in its habits and of a most appropriate size, it is the ideal pet and companion. Sadly, there are those who see the cat in a different light; as a predator of birds and mice, a garden pest, a disturbing noise in the night, or even as a shadowy link with the nether world, but, fortunately, these are very much in the minority, and, whilst cat lovers never change, there are many instances of those professing not to like cats eventually seeing the error of their ways.

The cat is the most adaptable of animals, as witness its ability to live wild or in such diverse surroundings as ships, hospitals, factories, theatres, railway stations, high-rise apartments, farms, stables and many other unlikely habitats. With this wide-ranging ability to fit into a variety of situations, the domestic puss will settle into almost any routine. Some seem to be like lodgers, having bed and board but otherwise following their own independent lifestyle; others are the feline versions of 'latchkey kids', left to their own devices during the day and taken into the family circle at night, whilst there are those cast in the role of peripatetic acquaintances, staying for a while, disappearing for a few days, and then returning for a further indefinite stay.

There is an American saying to the effect that 'smart people have smart cats', and, whilst this may border on the egocentric, it is a fact that one's relationship with a cat reflects very much what is put into it. Puss will respond to care and attention coupled with affection and understanding, and, once the trust is established, may even lift a veil or two and disclose to the privileged some of the many facets of cat nature.

The relationship is based on the appreciation that a cat is a cat: it is not a furry child, it is not a toy and it is not an idol to be placed on a metaphorical pedestal for worship. It is an independent creature with its own way of life, but one which is willing to become part of the family, given the opportunity, respect and consideration which characterises the harmonious household.

Cats are far too independent of spirit to be 'trained' in the sense that dogs are trained, but they can be led into acceptable patterns of behaviour as will be explained in later pages. They are well able to understand that certain things are done or, more often, not done, and will respond to stroking and talking and to the occasional offer of an especially favoured titbit. No physical action is ever appropriate for dealing with a problem; one hasty blow could ruin a relationship built up over many months. If some firm action is called for, a raised voice and a sharp tone are quite sufficient – and even this must be quickly followed by a stroke and a kind word in a normal voice.

The basic human essential is a sense of responsibility for the cat's requirements and this must be ever present if the relationship is to develop. Given this, and a generous measure of affection, the way is open to an enduring friendship with the most endearing and endlessly fascinating of God's creatures – the cat.

Philip Wood, The Cats Protection League.

2
ACQUIRING A CAT

It is a moot point whether most cats are acquired by people or whether, in reality, people are usually acquired by cats. Taking in the stray which appears on the doorstep is an impulsive act of compassion, but the conscious decision to set out to acquire a cat or kitten requires some careful thought.

Pedigree kittens are usually obtained from a recognised breeder and the best way of proceeding is to visit a cat show, possibly the doyen of them all, the National Cat Club Show, held annually at Olympia in London, or one of the other shows held in the larger provincial cities. The majority of breeds are to be seen at the larger shows and contact is easily made with the breeders who will be pleased to meet prospective owners. Failing this, there are many books and other publications on the subject of pedigree cats, which carry details of the specialist societies and clubs dealing with particular breeds, all of which will readily assist in making contact with breeders.

Most people, however, think in terms of the ordinary domestic puss – ordinary, that is, only in the sense that it will have no pedigree papers. Cats are obtainable from many sources, including friends and neighbours, pet shops, veterinary surgeons and animal welfare organisations, but, before taking the first steps towards adopting a cat, it is as well to give some thought as to what would be an ideal pet in the particular circumstances. Colour apart, the choice lies between kitten and adult cat, male and female and, indeed, between whether it is to be one single cat or more, many people holding that two cats offer much more than twice the pleasure of one!

Kittens are undoubtedly one of the most appealing of young animals and are almost irresistible to many people and particularly to children. However, every kitten will grow into a cat and, in the meantime, will require a lot of care and attention, so the charm of kittenhood alone is not sufficient reason for acquiring a kitten; it must be coupled with the intention of developing a caring relationship over a period of years. That said, there is something very satisfying about starting off with a kitten and watching it grow and develop into an adult cat, knowing that its whole concept of life is contained within the home which has been provided. Some people feel that an adult cat will be set in his or her own ways and that it may therefore be difficult to assimilate into the home, but, to the rather limited extent to which this is true, it may be regarded as an advantage in that any

A ten-week-old at play

19

The first steps in the new home. The adult cat can take a few days to adjust

Sexing kittens. Female left, male right

undesirable traits will already have manifested themselves to those who know the cat. For many prospective owners, such as the elderly and the very busy, for example, the rather more staid adult cat will be preferable to a kitten, even though it may take a little longer to settle in. The choice between male and female is a purely personal one and, assuming that the cat is to be, or has already been, neutered, is not really of great importance. Indeed, there are many who habitually refer to all cats as 'she'. There are also those who subscribe to the belief that neutered toms are very affectionate, whilst females are inclined to be aloof, but the truth is that cats are no different from humans in that some display great affection whilst others succeed in hiding it, if, indeed, it is there at all. Having decided on just what is wanted, a word or two of caution: many would-be owners have set out to acquire a tabby tom only to emerge with a black and white female – and her tortie sister!

Of the various sources from which cats may be obtained, undoubtedly the best are the animal welfare organisations such as The Cats Protection League, the RSPCA and similar groups. These will normally have a number of cats and, at certain times of the year, kittens which they will be only too pleased to place in good homes. Choice apart, there are other advantages in obtaining a cat from a rescue organisation in that it will have been looked over by a veterinary surgeon, or by experienced staff, and, furthermore, if the cat or kitten should not, for any reason, settle in at its new home, it can be returned without any problems arising. It may come as something of a shock to prospective owners to find that, despite their eagerness to home cats, responsible welfare societies do not part with them without careful investigation. However, no one should be offended at this, but, rather, should applaud the caring attitude of those who run such organisations and are not prepared to risk placing a cat in an unsuitable environment or, even worse, inadvertently permitting it to fall into the hands of the sub-human minority prepared to sell cats for the value of their fur or, in the past, for medical experiments. Welfare societies generally, and The Cats Protection League in particular, do not sell cats, but pass them on without payment, on the understanding that the new owner will not only take proper care of the cat or kitten, but that it will be neutered on reaching puberty and that, if for any reason it is not possible to keep the cat, it will be returned to the CPL for rehoming.

It is a good idea to take over the cat or kitten at a point where it is possible to spend some time helping it to settle in. It is a traumatic experience for a cat to find itself in unfamiliar surroundings with strange people, and a little gentle attention is required to help smooth the path. A box or basket should already have been installed in a quiet, warm and draught-free place, and the cat should be placed nearby and given time to get over the effects of the journey. Investigation and inspection from such extraneous sources as other pets or children should be discouraged until the newcomer has had time to settle down. The cat will probably want to make a brief inspection of its new quarters and this will likely be followed by a little washing while the new surroundings are assessed. This is a good moment to offer a little food or milk, after which the cat will want to explore its domain more thoroughly and take the first steps towards establishing a new routine.

The Cat that Walks by Himself
'The Cat keeps his side of the bargain . . . He will kill mice, and he will be kind to Babies when he is in the house, just so long as they do not pull his tail too hard. But when he has done that, and between times, and when the moon gets up and night comes, he is the Cat that walks by himself, and all places are alike to him. Then he goes out to the Wet Wild Woods or up on the Wet Wild Trees or on the Wet Wild Roots, waving his wild tail and walking by his wild lone.' – Rudyard Kipling.

Two brother and sister tabbies. Often two kittens in a litter become particular playmates, and it is naturally preferable if they can both go to the same home

Many adult cats retain a kittenish playfulness

Above right *This little brown tabby kitten is a perfect master of the art of relaxation*

A small troublemaker

Seven-week-old Peaches is completely exhausted

Below left *This furry individual was rescued by the CPL*

Two are much more fun than one, and won't suffer from loneliness while you are out – Rufus and Fergus

CATS AND CHILDREN

Introducing a baby into a household where a cat has lived in peace and contentment, or introducing a cat into a family household containing children, means that life is going to change for all concerned. There may be fears of jealousy, scratched children and the incidence of transferable diseases, accompanied by a vague overall doubt as to the wisdom of keeping a pet at all, and there will always be someone ready to recount stories of disasters. In fact, cats and babies have grown up together for hundreds of years, and all that is required is to establish a sensible routine in which all parties can live amicably together.

Many couples own a cat long before they start a family, and no caring person would feel that responsibility for the welfare of the cat was in any way diminished by the arrival of a baby, momentous event that it is. How the cat will react to the new arrival will depend on the nature of the cat and on a degree of foresight and planning on the part of its owners. The most difficult sort of cat is the timid, nervous animal, liable to run and hide when visitors appear and only really happy when the familiar routine of home and family is undisturbed. Rather less difficult to deal with is the family cat who always wants to join in, although it also follows that he is the most easily hurt if he thinks that affection has waned. However, being gre-

Children must learn that kittens and cats are not toys, but feeling creatures, sensitive to pain, which must be treated with as much care and consideration as they expect for themselves. Small kittens are especially vulnerable

garious, he will soon enlarge his circle to include the new baby – if allowed to. The easiest type of cat is the one who uses the house as a hotel, eating and sleeping there, accepting petting when it feels like it, but otherwise going its own way. This cat should be no trouble at all, providing accommodation and room service remain up to standard.

With ample time for preparation before the baby arrives, there are some practical steps to be taken in regard to the cat. The caring owner will always be concerned about the cat's health, but now, more than ever, it is advisable to be meticulous about grooming and to have the vet check that there are no fleas or worms present. Whilst he is about it the vet should also check the cat's teeth and ears to make sure no unpleasantness is developing there. If the cat has not been neutered, this should certainly be done prior to the arrival of the baby. Not only is a neutered cat an altogether nicer pet, but also the risk of disease and infection inherent in a wandering entire animal is very much reduced.

Apart from matters of health and hygiene, thought should be given to changes in routine necessitated by the new arrival. For example if the cat has normally had access to all parts of the house, the room or area intended for the baby's sleeping accommodation should be put out of bounds some weeks before the baby arrives.

It is likely that the baby will be about three months old before he takes any notice of the cat; puss, however, will have been aware of the baby from the moment of arrival, and, being a cat, will have carried out its own investigations. There is no harm in this. Very probably one sniff will confirm that the baby is neither feline nor a food-provider, and interest will wane. On the practical front, the use of a cot and/or pram net is to be recommended. In use, it must be kept taut if it is not to become a hammock for a nautically-minded cat, and, when the pram hood is up, it should be fitted securely across the opening.

It should be a matter of habit that the door to the baby's sleeping quarters is kept closed (and the room first inspected to make sure that the cat is not under the bed or otherwise hidden); if this gives a feeling of being isolated from the baby, the fitting of an alarm system is easily arranged.

It is as well to realise that babies and cats have a common interest in food, and it is essential that they do not develop communal habits. The baby's feeding utensils should be kept in a covered sterilising unit, and any spilt or leftover food or milk should be cleared up immediately.

In the midst of all the excitement and work of caring for the new baby, some time should be found to make a fuss of puss. The evening is often a good time (if the cat has not made other arrangements), and, apart from reassuring the cat that the bond of affection remains, there are few things more soothing than stroking a purring cat.

It is never too early to learn about cats, but it is important for the child to form a relationship based on respect, kindness, love and understanding, the true basis of companionship between a child and his or her pet. To this end, it is highly desirable that the cat or kitten is *not* introduced into the family as a birthday or Christmas present. It is asking too much of a young child to understand that a kitten is not a mobile toy with never-failing batteries, to be treated as other toys and discarded when boredom sets in. Time spent on teaching a child how to behave with a cat is never wasted, and attention should be drawn to the elementary points: that cats are easily frightened by sudden noise or movements, and that tails, ears and whiskers are not for pulling. It is probably better that very young children should be discouraged from picking up the cat, but, with older children, the correct and safe way of handling a cat should be carefully explained.

There are no miracles required for children and cats to live together. Mutual understanding, respect, love and kindness will ensure a happy family.

Heidi and Gemma have a strong family resemblance

CATS AND THE ELDERLY

There is a great deal of comfort and therapeutic benefit to be derived from having a pet, particularly for a person living alone. In the nature of things, contemporaries die, or find travel difficult, and the loneliness of later years can be substantially eased by the presence of a pet.

The acquisition of a cat requires some thought. An older cat, provided it has no difficult habits, will be easier for an older person to cope with than a kitten. Every cat welfare organisation will have a number of mature cats available for homing, and will be more than pleased to offer a choice of affectionate and placid companions, only too happy to settle into a peaceful domestic environment.

The establishment of a daily routine is dealt with elsewhere, but it is important, in the context of the older owner, that this pattern does not make undue demands on the human side. The last outing of the day should be completed reasonably early in the evening, in order to avoid late-night sorties with a torch, whilst a cat door (with fastener) will assist with the well-known feline trait of wishing to be inside when out and outside when in!

Cats often have a selection of sleeping places, but provision of a suitable basket or box will usually ensure that this becomes the preferred spot. The basket should be sited in a quiet and

☐■ IN EVENT OF EMERGENCY ☐

* *delete as appropriate*

* If I am admitted to hospital or am incapacitated I have arranged for

Mr./Mrs./Miss. ....

Address ....

.... Telephone No. ....
to care for my cats until I am able to do so myself. Please contact him/her on my behalf.

* If I should die, my Will contains instructions regarding my cats. Please contact my solicitor without delay, so that the cats will not be left to fend for themselves.

His name is ....

Address ....

.... Telephone No. ....

* I have made arrangements with The Cats Protection League to take the cats into care. Overleaf are the details of my cats. Please get in touch with The Cats Protection League, 17 Kings Road, Horsham, West Sussex, RH13 5PP. Telephone: Horsham 65566

EMERGENCY CARD

In case of emergency please contact:

Name _____

Address _____

_____

Telephone _____
who will take care of my cat

THE CATS PROTECTION LEAGUE

My name _____

Cat's name _____

Address _____

_____

Signature _____ Date _____

Thank you for helping my cat.

THE CATS PROTECTION LEAGUE   HORSHAM   WEST SUSSEX

DETAILS OF CATS OWNED BY _____

_____

1 Name of cat .... Sex ....

   Age .... Neutered/Spayed YES   NO

   Description ....

   Distinguishing features ....

2 Name of cat .... Sex ....

   Age .... Neutered/Spayed YES   NO

   Description ....

   Distinguishing features ....

3 Name of cat .... Sex ....

   Age .... Neutered/Spayed YES   NO

   Description ....

   Distinguishing features ....

   Signature _____ Date _____

The forms to be filled in by anyone concerned about their cat's welfare should the owner be taken ill. They can be obtained from The Cats Protection League

draught-free position where it does not form a hazard during any night-time walkabout, and, similarly, the cat should be discouraged from settling in potentially dangerous spots, such as on a particular step on a staircase, or on a mat behind a door. For the rest, it is largely a matter of including the cat in the usual commonsense precautions that most people take: an adequate reserve of food and other supplies against any shopping problems arising from illness or adverse weather conditions, a telephone number for use in case of emergency, and someone who can be relied upon if problems arise.

Undoubtedly, for many elderly people the most worrying aspect of having a cat is the question of what will happen to their pet if they should be ill, have an accident or, even worse, die. The burden of worrying about the cat's welfare can be avoided by establishing an arrangement for looking after the cat in an emergency, as soon as the cat is first acquired. There is usually a suitably reliable friend, neighbour or relative with whom an understanding can be reached, sometimes on a reciprocal basis. Of course, it is no good making such arrangements unless they come immediately to the notice of the emergency services or hospital staff, and this is best achieved by carrying a personal emergency card giving details of the arrangements. A suitable card is illustrated opposite, but you could also make one of your own.

It is also important that other people should be aware of the arrangements which have been made, and this can be done by completing a larger and more comprehensive card which is then displayed in a prominent position in the home. Copies of both these cards can be obtained, free of charge, by sending a stamped, self-addressed envelope to The Cats Protection League. Completion of the two cards should ensure that your cat is cared for without delay in the unfortunate event of an emergency arising.

The larger card covers the ultimate problem of what is to become of the cat in the event of the owner's death. This is an unpalatable subject, but, as with wills, the task of dealing with the temporal events which follow death is eased considerably if proper instructions are provided. From time to time the newspapers enjoy themselves with stories concerning eccentric pet owners who have died leaving large sums of money to their pets, but, whilst the individual who regards his pet as 'almost human' is a familiar figure, in the eyes of the law an animal is a possession, and, as such, cannot be the beneficiary of a will. However, there are various ways in which provision can be made for a cat to be cared for in the event of the death of its owner.

Probably the most usual course of action is to reach agreement with a son, daughter, or other relative or friend, to take over and care for the cat. This arrangement should work well, although, obviously, such a charge should not be laid on anyone lacking the necessary sense of responsibility. Even so, it is as well to set out the arrangements in your will, and to establish that the person concerned is the new legal owner of the cat. An extension of this arrangement, particularly appropriate where filial ties are not strong and friends scarce, is, by prior arrangement, to leave a sum of money, or the income therefrom, to another person, conditional upon their undertaking to provide a home for the cat for the remainder of its life. Here it is a good idea to provide alternative names in order to cover all eventualities. These arrangements, along with other alternatives, such as attempting to set up a trust for the maintenance of the cat, are not suitable subjects for the do-it-yourself form of will, and a solicitor should be consulted to ensure that they are incorporated in proper form in a duly executed will.

One further alternative is to enter into an arrangement with a suitable animal welfare organisation, to take over the cat, either for it to remain in care or, very much to be preferred, to be rehomed in a suitable environment. The Cats Protection League, for example, will become responsible for any cat or (within reason) cats, owned by a person at the time of death. This may sound rather impersonal, but it does have the advantage that a continuing and responsible charitable organisation, not subject to changes in family circumstances or other problems, will take over the cat and will do its very best to comply with whatever preferences are expressed. Full details of this scheme can be obtained from the director of The Cats Protection League.

It has been said that one sad aspect of pet ownership is that the pet's life span is so much shorter than that of its owner, but, when the time is reached that the position is likely to be reversed, these relatively simple precautions can ensure peace of mind in continuing to enjoy the pleasure of having a cat for company at any age.

3
BASIC CAT CARE AND FEEDING

In nature the cat is a very self-contained creature, well able to look after itself in regard to food and shelter and in the perpetuation of the species. In a domestic environment, however, the cat requires a certain amount of care, both for its own well-being and, equally, for the benefit of the other parties in the household. An unneutered cat, living rough on what it can catch in territory which has to be defended against intruders, is not likely to be regarded as a welcome pet in many homes, and hence spaying or neutering, proper feeding and care are necessary if the cat is to fit happily into the family.

Feeding is dealt with in detail on page 38, but, in the context of basic cat care, it is important as the primary means of developing a relationship with the cat and in persuading it to follow a desired routine, rather than doing its own thing. The nature of cats is such that there is no routine suitable for all, and much will depend on the cat itself, its environment, the time of the year and, of course, the routine of the household in which it lives. As a general guide, the day should begin with feeding, followed by an outing, although many cats like to reverse this arrangement and be let out first. Notice that the cat is let *out* in the morning, not *in*; the very best place for a cat at night is indoors, safe from the elements, traffic, cat thieves and all the other potential dangers of the small hours. The nocturnal way of life adopted by the cat in nature was determined by the need to hunt at night, but this has no relevance to a way of life in a domestic environment. The rest of the day is taken up with a mixture of outings, watching the world go by, hunting, playing, sleeping and, ideally, spending some time in the company of the cat's human friends. The second meal of the day should be given in late afternoon or in the evening, followed by an outing before being called and kept in for the night. The individual nature of your cat will soon become apparent and the routine can be adapted accordingly; for example, many cats are accustomed to popping out for a few minutes last thing at night, whilst others, if once let out in the late evening, would require endless coaxing to persuade them to return to be shut in for the night.

Cats are naturally clean animals with a comprehensive washing procedure and careful attention to the disposal of waste products. However, a kitten will need to be house-trained and should be provided with a smooth-surfaced plastic toilet tray, obtainable from any pet shop. Although an ordinary plastic

Opposite When is the next meal coming? Meal times would not be meal times without all the expectancy. Stay in control, and don't let your cat talk you (or your weaker second half) into ever-earlier meals

Confrontation: Two warm and well-fed characters with all the time in the world – or are they being paid for a cooker commercial?

Silver Tabby. Come and talk to me! Sometimes the cat will make the approach. Here, clearly, it's the human's turn to make the next move.

seed tray, lined with polythene, can be used in an emergency, it is preferable that the tray be as large as possible, say not less than 38cm (15in) square, and partially filled with dry, sifted earth, peat, cat litter or wood shavings (*not* sawdust) and permanently sited in a quiet easily accessible place on a washable surface. The kitten should be taken to the tray after meals and on waking up from sleep, and it will soon realise what is expected of it. There is no need to change the litter every day; faeces should be removed immediately and flushed down the toilet, whilst wet patches can be removed and placed in polythene bags for disposal with the household rubbish, if commercial cat litter is used, or put on the garden compost heap in the case of earth, peat, or wood shavings. Periodically the entire contents of the tray should be disposed of and the tray thoroughly washed in warm water containing a little suitable non-toxic disinfectant. Once the kitten is introduced to the outside world, a small patch of soil should be forked over and shown to it and it will soon take to this method of attending to its needs. The toilet tray should be retained and made available at night, or if the cat is to be shut in the house for any length of time.

Cats vary in their behaviour and some will be out of the house for most of the day, particularly in fine weather, whilst others are inclined to be in and out at frequent intervals as fancy takes them. Depending on the circumstances, it may be helpful to fit a cat door so that the cat can come and go as it pleases, although some means of fastening the door is desirable, so that the cat remains in when required, for example at night or, for that matter, out, as when food is being prepared or the kitchen floor cleaned. Cat doors come in various forms and are usually fitted to an outer door (on the hinge side, of course, more than an arm's length from any bolts), but could be fitted to the lower part of a window if this were more convenient. The older type of cat door required the cat to lift the flap by putting its nose under an upturned edge in order to gain entry. The cat had to learn the art of lifting the flap from the outside, and hence passing cats were unlikely to gain access. This type of door is no longer easy to obtain, and most of those now on sale operate on the principle of a single, or double, swinging flap which the cat just pushes against to go in or out. These vary in design, some even incorporating a transparent panel so that the cat can see what is on the other side (rather like the door into the kitchen used by waiters!), but, as they are so easy to use, there is always the possibility of finding the cat complement of the household unwittingly increased, although this can be dealt with by fitting a door which incorporates a magnetic catch, the 'key' to which is fitted to the cat's collar. A cat door can be very useful in allowing the cat access when the house is unoccupied, or even just to save having to provide the doorman service which most cats seem to regard as a basic right.

With the cat out and about it is very desirable that it should

A long white coat like Toby's needs regular attention to keep it looking at its best. A matted coat will cause the cat acute discomfort.

Eating is a serious business

wear a simple collar with its owner's name and telephone number or address; a collar without identification is useless, and the cat's name is of interest only to the owner – and possibly the cat. Many people seem to regard it as unnatural for a cat to wear a collar, as indeed it is, but only in a tiny minority of cases does the cat object, and the advantages of wearing a collar are considerable. In the first place, the cat is identified as belonging to someone, but, far more important, if the cat should stray or be involved in an accident, there is every prospect that contact will be made and the cat returned. Anyone who has worked in cat welfare will testify to the frustration of knowing that a lost cat has come from a caring home, but not from one which cared enough to provide the means of identification which would enable the cat to be restored to its owner.

Part of the problem arises from the unsuitable nature of many of the collars which are commercially available. These tend to be made of leather or plastic, with a short insert of elastic, and are sometimes provided with a disc for engraving, a bell or, rather incongruously, a row of fancy studs. The bell is apparently intended to warn prey of the presence of the cat and is about as effective as providing puss with a hunting horn to blow. The elastic insert is, admittedly, better than nothing, but is often of inadequate size to allow an easy means of withdrawal for the cat's head if the collar should get caught up on a fence or branch. The very best form of collar is fully elasticated, with the ends joined in such a manner that they will break under light strain. There are various ways of achieving this, including fastening the ends together with a small elastic band, but one simple method is to use a length of 7mm (¼in) flat white elastic, cut to provide a comfortable fit around the cat's neck. The ends

It's important to support a cat properly when you carry or hold it

32

should overlap about 1¼cm (½in) and be joined by a short length of 25mm (1in) adhesive plaster. The completed collar should be stretched over a small book, or something suitable, so that a firm writing surface is provided, and the details relating to the cat then written on the elastic with a waterproof biro pen. In use the collar will easily stretch to release the cat's head if it should get caught up or, with a little further pressure, the elastic will pull out from the plaster. Indeed, the cat will probably return without the collar from time to time, but it is easily replaced and its use will remove the anonymity which can cause so many problems. It is desirable that the collar be removed at night so that the cat can include this area in its wash and brush-up routine and also, especially with longhaired cats, to avoid a mark developing around the neck.

Indoors, the cat should be provided with its own sleeping quarters although, rather perversely, it may have some ideas of its own on the subject. Cats sleep on beds, in airing cupboards, on armchairs and in many other places, but it is best to encourage the use of a basket or box if possible. The traditional form of basket is draughtproof and durable, whilst a stout cardboard box, from the local supermarket, is equally draughtproof and easily replaced from time to time. A piece of old blanket, or other soft material, will provide suitable bedding, and this should be topped with a piece of easily washable material. The box or basket should be kept in a quiet and warm spot, out of draughts, where the cat can sleep undisturbed. A substantial part of a cat's life is spent in sleep, kittens and older cats, especially, sleeping for up to two-thirds of the twenty-four hours, although not all at one time, of course. A cat is interested in eating, hunting, playing and taking notice of anything that

---

Respect the cat

'Respect the cat, I beg you, for he is unique. Respect him, for he is deserving of respect. Respect his lineage lost in obscurity, his Egyptian ancestry, the reverence accorded him in temples of the East. Respect him for his grace and elegance, his soundless movements, his waving tail, his composure, self-assurance, independence, eyes deep as a pool or lustrous as jewels. Respect him for the services he renders, for killing rodents, snakes, wasps and flies. For keeping us company, playing with our children, making us laugh.

Respect the cat for the place he occupies in the animal kingdom. Consider the conclusion drawn by Mivart, that on the physical level the cat rather than man is the best fitted among mammals to make his way in the world. Respect him as God's creature; the Lord, St John of the Cross reminds us, bestowed upon all things touches of himself: 'The creatures are traces of God's passing, wherein he reveals his might, power and wisdom.'

Respect the intelligence of the cat. Respect his discernment. A dog and a cat, Russian legend tells, were posted as sentinels at the gate of Paradise. The Evil One tried to sneak in, disguised as a mouse. The dog let him pass. The cat pounced and slew him.' – Elizabeth Hamilton, *In Celebration of Cats*.

33

Even the best-fed puss may help itself to an occasional titbit in order to prove its independence

Opposite
The dynamic energy of the well-fed cat

might be going on, but, in the absence of any of these, and given a warm quiet spot, indoors or out, according to the season, it will happily pass the time in sleep.

Apart from cats which have lived rough or been subjected to ill-treatment, most will respond to being handled, provided that it is done in a proper manner. Contrary to popular belief, a cat or kitten must never be picked up by the scruff of the neck. The correct procedure is to hold the cat with one hand under the chest, with the weight supported by the other hand. Kittens, particularly, must be handled very gently as their bones are fragile. Movements towards a cat must be made slowly; the cat is likely to interpret a sudden grab as a potential blow and will react accordingly. It is a good idea to extend a hand slowly for the cat to inspect and sniff, and then to stroke the cat gently before picking it up, holding it in the prescribed manner, firmly, but not so that the cat feels constrained, and, of course, putting it down gently at the first sign of discomfort.

Many people, who groom their other pets as a matter of course, seem surprised at the thought of grooming a cat. Show cats are groomed as part of their normal routine, but, although cats are fastidious at keeping themselves clean and smart, most will welcome a little help with the process, particularly in the case of longhaired cats, and with all sorts at moulting time. It is a kind gesture occasionally to hold up your cat's tail very gently by the tip, thus enabling it to get a good firm lick, a manoeuvre which is not always easy for it to achieve. A bristle brush and a metal comb with rounded points to the teeth, obtainable at any pet shop, are all that is required to give an occasional brushing and combing which will remove loose hair, dirt and dust and help to prevent the build-up of fur balls in the cat's stomach. The cat should be gently combed from head to tail, along the back

34

The hunting instinct is strong, but so is the 'family' one. With careful introductions so that it is clear what is family, cats live happily with many creatures large and small

Opposite We all need some uninterrupted peace. Disturbing a cat grooming after feeding is even worse than waking it up

and flanks and then down the chest and along the underparts. This can be followed by similar treatment with the brush, except that the first brushing should be the 'wrong way', that is from tail to head, followed by firm strokes the 'right way', from head to tail. In the general way of things cats do not need bathing, but if the paws or coat have become contaminated with tar, oil, paint, or some other substance, it will be necessary to find some means of cleaning it off. It must be remembered that a cat will lick such soiled areas, and hence whatever is used for cleaning is likely to find its way into the cat. A cloth wrung out in plain hand-hot water is a good beginning, whilst stubborn substances may respond to rubbing with cooking oil or butter, followed by the hot-cloth treatment. Mud should be removed, as far as possible, with a tissue or piece of kitchen roll and then left to dry, when it can be brushed out of the coat. If the contamination is extensive, or if it involves an obviously noxious substance, the advice of a veterinary surgeon should be sought immediately.

One problem which sometimes arises, even with cats which have access to a garden, is a tendency to claw furniture, furnishings, or even wallpaper. This can be very annoying, as well as expensive, but it is important to understand the cat's motivation before getting too upset about it. A cat's claws are not only essential to its tree-climbing ability, they are also its primary means of defence, and hence care of the claws is as instinctive to a cat as regular washing. The common idea of a cat 'sharpening its claws' is not altogether accurate, as what it is actually doing is cleaning them and removing the loose bits of the outer shell of the claw; the effect, however, is the same. The answer to the problem is most certainly *not* to consider declawing the cat and, indeed, the vast majority of veterinary surgeons in Britain would not consider undertaking such an operation purely for the convenience of the owner, but only if necessitated by a medical condition. Even if only the front claws are removed, the cat is left virtually defenceless, and there is always the risk of post-operative complications. Justification for the operation is sometimes sought in the assertion that the cat's current lifestyle provides it with a totally safe environment, but it is surely a truly remarkable owner who can forecast the entire future course of his cat's life.

The solution is to provide a scratching post, and, from an early age, to encourage the cat or kitten to use it. There are some elaborate commercial models available, but an offcut of thick carpet is perfectly satisfactory and is easily renewable from time to time. The carpet can be fastened to a wall or behind a door, or, alternatively, tied tightly around a convenient table leg, say in the kitchen, in simulation of a tree trunk. Any piece of furniture, which has previously been favoured as a scratching post, should be covered or removed, and the cat or kitten shown the carpet pad. It will soon grasp its purpose. The extent of the problem should not be exaggerated; most cats with access to a garden or yard will soon select a favourite tree or post outdoors.

36

It is not only kittens that are playful; most adult cats enjoy games for as long as they are active. The old jibe about the difference between men and boys being the cost of their toys does not apply either, for, although there is a truly remarkable range of playthings available commercially, kittens and cats will play happily with the simplest things. All cats are fascinated by things which move and the ubiquitous piece of string, either on its own or with a piece of card or paper tied to the end, will be pursued for as long as someone is willing to pull it around. It might be mentioned in passing that, the game over, it is preferable not to leave the string with the cat or kitten as it may well become entangled and hurt, or chew it, and string is not the most digestible of substances.

Another great favourite is a table-tennis ball which, being light and very mobile, responds most satisfactorily to a blow from a paw. It is even more fun if it can be knocked under furniture or down a flight of stairs. Away from things which attract by movement, many cats enjoy diving into a large paper (*not* plastic) bag and will soon reduce this to a crumpled ruin. On a more ambitious scale, and given the space, in a loft or outhouse, a cat maze can be constructed out of a number of cardboard boxes. These require openings cut in the sides (and the tops, if a two-tier structure is the aim), and they are then glued, or otherwise fastened together, so that there are any number of ways into, out of and in between the various boxes. This construction is ideal where there is more than one cat or kitten, and will keep boredom at bay for hours on end. On which note it is appropriate to recall the old saying – the best plaything for a kitten is another kitten!

Cats are usually healthy creatures, although their adventurous nature sometimes leads to mishaps, and occasionally they do fall sick. These subjects are dealt with elsewhere, but there are some health matters which are not in the nature of illness or accidents, but rather more a matter of routine care. The kitten's first visit to the veterinary surgeon should be at around ten weeks, for vaccination to guard against the usually fatal feline infectious enteritis and cat flu. Booster injections will be required at yearly intervals, and it should be remembered that no reputable establishment will accept a cat or kitten for boarding without a current vaccination certificate. The fact that the cat is unlikely to be boarded in no way lessens the need for vaccination; the viruses are not found exclusively in boarding catteries, although the risk of infection is obviously greater where there are concentrations of cats. Incidentally, the annual visit for a booster injection provides a good opportunity for the veterinary surgeon to have a look at teeth and ears, two areas which are often neglected until problems become all too obvious.

At around five months, depending on the size of the kitten and the views of your veterinary surgeon, the time will have come for neutering. Some people have an emotional hang-up on this

Try goat's milk
So many cats and kittens seem to be upset by cow's milk so why not try goat's milk which is far better for them anyway? It is particularly useful for kittens in need of bottle feeding. Goat's milk keeps well and can be frozen and kept in blocks; when required, simply chip off a piece and thaw it out to body heat. You can usually obtain goat's milk from a health store if you have no goat handy! – *The Cat.*

A convenient scratching post

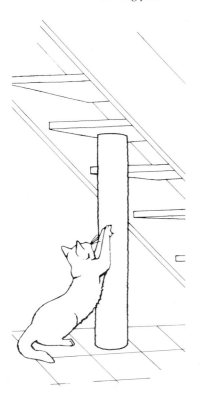

subject, but practical considerations overwhelm the philosophical arguments. The blunt facts are that an entire tom will grow into an aggressive fighter, absent for long periods, and with a powerful-smelling urine which he is liable to spray around both indoors and outside, whilst an unspayed female will produce a dozen or more kittens a year, with all the problems of disposal or homefinding that this involves. The neutering operation on a male cat involves removal of the testicles and is relatively simple. Once recovered from the anaesthetic, the cat will quickly return to its normal state. Spaying a female cat is a much more serious operation, as it involves making an incision and removing the ovaries. The cat will need to be kept as quiet and peaceful as possible for a few days after the operation, and it will probably be necessary to pay a return visit to the veterinary surgery for the removal of the stitches. Although neutering is best carried out before puberty, the operations can be performed at a later stage as, for example, when a fully grown cat is rescued and homed into a caring household. However, there is no justification for the old-fashioned view that a female cat should be allowed one litter before being spayed. Indeed, some veterinary surgeons believe that the operation is more serious if carried out after a pregnancy, as the organs are larger and a bigger incision may be required. If there are lingering doubts on the wisdom of neutering, thought might be given to the fact that one female cat and her descendants can be responsible for 20,000 kittens over the lifetime of the original cat; the neutering of those fortunate enough to find responsible owners will never lead to the extinction of the species.

Feeding
The cat's natural food is its prey, mainly mice and other small forms of animal life, which provide not only raw meat, but also roughage in the form of skin, fur and bones. Unlike some animals, cats usually eat most of any prey taken for food, apart from some of the internal organs, but they instinctively restrict the intake of bone and roughage to meet their requirements. This approach to natural feeding provides a pointer to the needs of the domestic cat's diet, which should aim to provide a varied intake rather than making the common mistake of feeding the cat entirely on one form of food. From an early age, as wide a variety of food as possible should be provided, thus avoiding the emergence of the feline food fad.

A visit to any supermarket will confirm that domestic cats eat their way through many millions of tins of commercially prepared cat-food every year. All the familiar brands are there, together with 'own name' products in the case of the larger supermarket chains. The nature and content of the cans vary, the cheaper varieties tending to be bulked up with cereal, while some are paste-like in consistency and others chunky. Any recognisable brand will have been hygienically prepared and will be a perfectly satisfactory food. While cats, just like humans, often show a preference for one particular brand, it is a good idea to vary the supply, if only to guard against the formula changes which manufacturers seem to find necessary from time to time.

Dry and semi-dry foods are also very much in evidence, both in branded packet varieties and in loose form. Such foods may contain some or all of such ingredients as fishmeal, meat, bone-meal, various cereals, yeast and vitamin supplements, and whilst the fat content is often low, they do at least provide the cat with an opportunity to use its teeth. There has been much discussion in recent years as to whether dry cat-foods are a possible cause of feline urological syndrome, a term which covers cystitis and other urinary-based complaints, but, whilst no definite conclusions appear to have been reached, such foods should never form the only, or even the staple, part of a cat's diet and should never be given without free access to an adequate supply of clean drinking water.

Commercially produced food apart, there is a wide range of other food which can be fed to cats. All meat and offal sold for human consumption is safe to serve raw to adult cats. It should be cut into narrow strips, thus ensuring that the cat uses its teeth to tenderise the meat. All suitable foods can be chopped and mixed together, raw food with cooked food, commercial canned food with cooked and chopped liver, and so on. Some cats like a topping of dry cat-food with their meal, but this can have an emetic effect on some cats, when it should, of course, be avoided. Minced meats such as beef or lamb, cheap cuts of lamb or beef, boned and diced rabbit, poultry in most forms, and offal, such as kidney, liver, heart, lights, melts and tripe, are all suitable foods and can be given as a supplement to the usual tinned food. For a change of diet, both white fish, such as coley,

Visiting cats or newcomers to the household may be met with hostility elsewhere, but almost invariably, feeding is seen as mutual, necessary territory

huss and whiting, and oily canned fish, such as sardines, pilchards and herrings, are usually welcomed. Canned fish are cooked prior to sale, and the bones can be mashed in with the fish to provide a valuable source of calcium. All bones from other fish, meat and poultry must be removed before the food is served, as they can be extremely dangerous to the cat.

Although plant-based foods form no part of a cat's natural diet, many are well liked and easily digested by most cats. Ready-cooked crunchy breakfast cereals, like wheatflakes, puffed rice and puffed wheat, or cereals cooked in water or milk, such as oat flakes, pearl barley or rice, along with such vegetables as peas, broad, runner and haricot beans, cabbage and carrots, are all suitable diet supplements. The vegetables should be cooked in the usual manner, cut up or shredded, and added to the serving of meat, fish or canned food.

Cats and milk are inseparable in the minds of most people, but milk should only be given in small quantities to adult cats, as over-indulgence can give rise to digestive problems. Milk is more akin to a food than a drink, and is certainly no substitute for water, although it must be said that some cats take very little water and that mainly from puddles, garden ponds or the bird bath! Generally speaking, cats are not great drinkers, relying on the liquid content of their food to provide their needs, and hence it is important to include the liquor arising from the cooking of meat, offal or fish in the cat's diet.

Apart from the basic fare, cats often enjoy other things, such as cheese, yoghurt, eggs, butter, the skin off custard, potato crisps, sausage, beetroot, digestive biscuits and much else, and, given as an occasional titbit, these will do no harm. Cats also need access to grass, and, whilst those having the benefit of a garden will usually find a suitable patch, house-bound cats will appreciate a supply from some other source. A convenient park, or a friendly garden owner, will provide the means of picking a few blades to be kept in water until required. Alternatively, cocksfoot grass (*Dactylis glomerata*) can be grown in a pot on a windowsill indoors. Seeds of this variety can be obtained by sending a stamped, self-addressed envelope to The Cats Protection League.

Whilst it is scarcely a food, cats also enjoy the availability of catmint (*Nepeta mussini*), a handsome plant with aromatic greyish leaves and lavender-coloured flowers. It is readily obtainable from any garden centre or nursery, easily grown in almost any type of soil and, being perennial, requires little attention. Most cats love catmint and will chew the shoots, sit on it, roll in it and generally enjoy themselves. Just what the attraction is has long been the subject of much conjecture, but all cat-owning gardeners should certainly plant some.

In the matter of food adult cats are one thing, but kittens are something else. As with babies, they require special treatment, although, fortunately, not over so long a period. From birth kittens will be fed by their mother, but, at about three weeks, they should be taken once a day and fed individually with a small amount of either goat or cow's milk, enriched with a little cream. Initially the kittens will know nothing of lapping, and a finger should be dipped into the milk and the kitten's lips moistened. It will soon learn to lick the finger and thus progress to lapping. Under no circumstances should a kitten's mouth be dipped into the milk, as some of the liquid might be sniffed up its nose, frightening the kitten. After a few days the feeds can be stepped up to twice daily, and one of the meals can now be gruel rather than plain milk. In this way you can progress to three, and eventually four, meals a day.

At this stage (about six weeks, although kittens vary in their rate of progress) a little food can be given in place of a milk meal, perhaps cooked white fish, pounded to a paste, or very finely minced raw meat, at about one teaspoonful per kitten per meal. Milk and meat, or milk and fish, should not be given at the same time, as this is likely to cause digestive and other problems. By about eight weeks the kittens will be used to taking solid foods, but it must be remembered that they have very tiny stomachs, and, as they will be growing rapidly, the rule is to feed little and often, say two teaspoonfuls at a time, and maybe five or six times a day. The quantity fed at a meal can be increased steadily, whilst the number of feeds is gradually reduced, so that, at around four months, the kitten is being fed three times a day, and, on officially becoming a cat at nine months, is established on a routine of two meals per day.

The pattern of feeding should ideally be one of regular and adequate meals, and most cats thrive on the suggested twice-daily programme, with the first meal around breakfast time and the other in late afternoon or early evening. Cats being cats, there may well be convincing demonstrations of con-artistry, with performances of the 'I'm a hungry cat' routine around lunch time or at night, when a small feed of dry cat-food or some titbit might be given.

Quantities of food required daily will vary, there being no such thing as the average cat, but, as a rough guide, something like four heaped tablespoons of food, like minced meat, fish, rabbit or offal, or half as much again of canned food, per cat per day, is a useful starting point. The aim should be to achieve a balance between satisfaction and thwarting the ambitions of the puss who wants to be a fat cat. Where there is more than one cat, care should be taken to ensure that each gets its proper share, both for the benefit of the timid or slow eater, and to foil the clearing-up efforts of the greedy. To this end, all uneaten food should be removed, and either kept under cover for subsequent use, or disposed of as appropriate.

Commonsense is the main requirement for a healthy diet; cats will soon indicate their likes and dislikes and the provision of preferred items, with a little hardening of the heart to avoid over-indulgence, should ensure that there are no problems with feeding.

Recipes

Gruel

This is very useful for introducing kittens to something a little more solid than milk, or for feeding to a convalescing cat.

You will need 1 tablespoon fine oatmeal and ½ litre (1pt) milk.

Mix the oatmeal to a fine paste with a little milk; bring the rest of the milk nearly to the boil and stir in the oatmeal. Cook for about ten minutes, without boiling, stirring from time to time.

Crunchies

These are a wholesome substitute for bought, dried cat-food and make a useful snack for those odd occasions when a proper meal is inappropriate.

You will need crusts from wholemeal bread and some Marmite.

Cut the crusts into cubes. Dissolve the Marmite in hot water to provide an amount suitable for moistening the cubed crusts, without making them too soggy. Space out the cubes on a baking tray and cook on the bottom shelf of a low oven until dried. Allow to cool, then store in an airtight container.

Canadian Cat Relish

This requires a certain amount of preparation but is much appreciated.

You will need: 500g (1lb) liver
500g (1lb) white fish
1 cup dry cat-food
½ cup tomato juice
1 teaspoon cod liver oil

Simmer the liver and fish gently in water until cooked. Soak the dry cat-food in the tomato juice. Drain the liver and fish, remove the bones, but save the liquid. Place all the ingredients in a food processor, using the metal blade. Use the saved liquid to adjust the consistency of the mixture to the cat's liking.

A well-chosen cat can be a superbly affectionate and charming companion, and surprisingly little trouble, though it may be preferable to choose a mature cat rather than a kitten

A PORTFOLIO OF CATS

The magazine of The Cats Protection League, *The Cat*, keeps thousands of cat lovers in touch, and has a level of audience participation that is the envy of editors of many other periodicals. Here is a small selection of the readers' own words, in which they share their passion for their own cats.

Trophies

Oliver, a handsome, long-haired red with white trimmings, has just presented me with his third mousetrap, complete with very deceased occupant. This has led me to wonder what trophies other cat owners receive.

One of my friends has a highly intelligent Siamese called Pepe and he loves footwear, bringing home socks, lightweight slippers and a baby's bootee. However, his greatest prize was a Yorkshire pudding – still warm and dripping gravy.

My grandmother's cat, Pip, was an incorrigible thief and suddenly appeared, one lunch time, atop the neighbouring fence, with a whole plaice in his mouth; it was cooked one side and battered and breadcrumbed the other, obviously removed from a frying pan. This was confirmed a few seconds later by an anguished shriek from next door as to the whereabouts of her lunch. Gran never had the courage to enlighten her, so it must have remained to her as weird a mystery as the disappearance of the *Marie Celeste*! How Pip managed to extract the fish from a hot frying pan and remain unscathed was an equal mystery.

Oliver's greatest treasure is a thick rope handle from a large carton or basket found on the road. He came rushing down the drive with one end in his mouth and the rest streaming behind him. My late husband, seeing him through a window, shouted, 'Quick, quick! Oliver's caught an eagle!', causing all to rush out to investigate amid gales of mirth.

Oliver still loves his 'eagle' and, if we lived in the Scottish Highlands – or wherever eagles abound – I would not be surprised to find one on the doorstep, next to the mousetrap!

Rescued Cats

The two little white kittens – a male and a female, not related – always ran hopefully to meet visitors. The mother of the female stared wistfully from the Belfast Shelter run. Many prospective new owners stopped to admire the snowy trio, and tell them how beautiful they were. The cats didn't respond to these human voices. Sadly, all three of them were stone deaf. Like the old Victorian ballad of the Blind Orphan Boy, when people learned of the creatures' handicap, they took some other cat instead, and the pathetic deaf ones were left behind.

Until the day the Kind Person came. She had a safe, quiet place in the country, and foresaw no problem with a cat who lived in a silent world. The little male went happily home with her. Next week the Kind Person was back. Her kitten was pining for his playmate. So, off went the pretty white girl. The mother cat cried to see her daughter closed in a basket. Now she was quite alone. But, ten days later, the Kind Person rang the Shelter doorbell yet again. Both kittens had settled splendidly, and she couldn't bear the thought of the poor unwanted mother when there was room at her fireside for another moggy. The joy on the white cat's face as she was cradled in loving arms was worth a crock of gold.

With luck and patience, there'll be someone, somewhere, for a disadvantaged cat which needs a very special brand of caring.

Cats and Burglars

Woozie was one of the feline victims of the 1941 blitz. In search of help he mewed outside the door of a flat, perhaps guided by that uncanny intuition that leads Aeluros to friends, was taken in, nursed and adopted. In March 1946 he repaid his debt of gratitude by giving warning of the presence of a burglar. His owner was out and Woozie was enjoying the air in the yard. He sensed the proximity of an unauthorised visitor and 'gave tongue'. His loud mewing attracted the notice of a cleaner on the premises. 'He seemed to want me to follow him', was her comment in telling the story. Woozie led his companion to the window of the flat where he began to scratch furiously at the window pane. Looking through it, the cleaner saw the burglar busy at work. Finding he was discovered, the man ran away, having succeeded in stealing only a few articles of little value, thanks to the observant Woozie.

This was by no means an exceptional instance of feline vigilance; our files are full of true stories of cat home guards who in fires, floods, burglaries and other unusual happenings have given the alarm and saved their owners or their belongings.

. . . And down came a spider!

My mother once had a little long-haired tabby cat called Possum. She used to give it its food and milk on a newspaper in the scullery. It was an old house with a flagged scullery floor and beside Possum's 'dining table' was an old, built-in wooden cupboard. One day, my mother mentioned that Possum was off his milk; he would drink some of it when

(continued overleaf)

she poured it out for him, but would never come back later to finish what was left as he used to do. So, she would tip it away, wash the saucer and refill it in case he felt thirsty. Days passed, but he would never touch it unless he saw her pour it out for him in a clean saucer. This faddiness was quite new.

One day, when it was twilight time, I happened to come into the scullery very quickly in stockinged feet. I glanced at Possum's dining table; there was the half-full saucer of milk and, clinging to the rim, was a huge, black spider!

We had to find Possum a new 'dining table' and always pour out his milk in front of him. Never again did I go into the scullery in stockinged feet, although I never saw the intruder again. But, what I would like to know is . . . did Possum once find the spider perched on his saucer or did it leave some unpleasant smell behind? And, was Possum afraid of it . . . or merely indignant?

The Icing on the Cat

Our first Siamese cat was a roguish young tom called Mingyar; he always wanted to be into everything, no matter what. The Christmas season was upon us and, one afternoon, I decided to ice the Christmas cake. Once my masterpiece was complete, it was placed in a large container to dry, the lid partially covering it, and I went off to visit my mother in hospital.

I was gone about two hours; on my return, I was met by a rather iced-up cat. Mingyar had had a whale of a time; he had knocked the lid off the container and had walked all over the cake, covering his feet with wet icing. Then he had tried to wash it off and some had stuck to his chin and whiskers. The icing had dried and so had his footprints on the cake!

Tabitha

How many cats do you know who insist on going through the pussy flap when the door is wide open?

I regret to say that Tabitha is not noted for her intellectual prowess, although she is not without a certain feline cunning. Finding herself temporarily of no fixed abode, the enterprising creature took a post as an assistant in a butcher's shop. In due course the ungrateful tradesman viewed his plummeting profits with some dismay and whisked the green-eyed sausage eater off to the Josephine Fryer Sanctuary, where she selected us as her future owners.

To our little accident-prone half-Burmese, Spooki, she brought comfort and sisterly affection and to us, her humans, the sudden bubbling purring that is the reward for taking on a rescued adult cat.

Shadows of a haunted past still flicker briefly in those enormous eyes when visitors arrive and prove less than satisfactory, ie they have not brought a tin of pilchards or, if they have, it is not big enough. On such occasions, Tabitha will retreat into her 'cat from the wrong side of the tracks' role until she forgets herself and launches into song. Tabitha's speciality is singing; she is a veritable Maria Callas with regular musical accounts of her activities:

'I am opening all the kitchen cupboards . . . I wonder if it would sound better in Italian?'

Some cats travel remarkably well

4
HOLIDAYS, TRAVELLING AND MOVING HOUSE

The general living pattern of most families today includes taking one or more holidays each year, and for the cat-owning household this involves making provision for the cat's welfare during the family's absence. There are four approaches to this matter: the cat can remain at home; it can be booked into a boarding cattery; or, in suitable cases, it can join the family on holiday. The choice of one of these three solutions will depend on a number of factors, but arrangements must be entirely satisfactory if the holiday is not to be clouded by recurring worries as to the cat's well-being.

Lucky is the cat owner with the fourth option of a completely reliable friend or relation willing, and able, to move into the house and look after not only the cat, but the house itself. This arrangement is probably the best of all, and, if it can become an established routine, provides the simplest and easiest way of having puss cared for in the family's absence, with only a few basic matters requiring attention. It will be necessary to arrange for adequate supplies of food and other requirements, for both cat and cat-sitter, to be available, or to be delivered periodically, whilst the telephone numbers of the vet, the absent owner and anyone else likely to be needed should be readily to hand. The cat may spend a while looking around for absent friends, but will almost certainly settle back quickly into its routine in familiar surroundings.

A somewhat less satisfactory variation of this arrangement is to leave the cat in residence and to have a friend or neighbour call in for feeding, cleaning up, shutting the cat in at night and letting it out again in the morning. This requires some dedication on the part of the person concerned, and the cat will, of course, lack the company and attention that it normally enjoys. However, any tendency to seek solace elsewhere should be overcome by the availability of food in familiar surroundings, and the arrangement should work satisfactorily, at least for short periods.

Boarding catteries are rather like hotels in that some are really excellent, the majority are satisfactory, and some are distinctly mediocre. Recommendation is often at one's peril in that the standards tend to vary in most establishments, quite apart from changes of ownership. The basic advice is to start with the nearest, pay an unannounced visit during working hours, and let commonsense be your guide. No cattery owner

Keep on good terms with your neighbours, in case your kitten gets into trouble next door . . . Some young cats have a remarkable tendency to wander. In fact one of the writers of this book had a cat that brought home the neighbours' Sunday lunch!

Bosscat finds waiting can be exhausting . . .

Why can't you take me too? Some cats will expectantly jump into a basket – even their own cat basket – when you prepare to go out

should mind a visit of this sort, and, indeed, should in fact be pleased to show a prospective customer around. The nearness of the establishment is helpful as you can seek local opinion, as well as reducing the amount of travelling involved, although many catteries operate a local collection and delivery service. This facility may be eschewed by many owners who would prefer to see their pet comfortably installed in holiday quarters before their own departure, but it can be a useful arrangement for those without their own transport.

As already mentioned, the assessment of a cattery is largely a matter of commonsense. The accommodation should be in an excellent state of repair, clean and tidy, light and airy, and there should be neither any objectionable smell nor any strong smell of disinfectant. The pens should be of ample size and should open into a safety corridor. The owner should be recognisable as a cat person, that is one caring for cats with affection rather than solely for profit, but, that said, satisfactory cat-care does not come cheaply and boarding cattery expenses are no more immune from the ravages of inflation than any other type of expense.

Many owners, particularly those with pets of a nervous disposition, will prefer establishments devoted exclusively to cats. If the kennels cater for both cats and dogs, it is essential to

The village cat

It was a few days after moving in that he first appeared, sitting just inside the back gate and keeping a watchful eye on the door into the house. He was undoubtedly scruffy, off-white with patches of smokey-grey, his ears serrated from many a battle and, as the saying is in this part of Wiltshire, a manky tail. He looked like an old gentleman of the road, down on his luck, but philosophical about it, and he ate the proffered handout slowly and methodically, rather like a travel-guide inspector on his first visit to a restaurant.

Most days he takes a walk along the village street, hopping into the verge if traffic appears and stopping off at his regular ports of call to see what is on offer. On rare occasions, particularly during spells of warm weather, he will sit around for a while, responding to a little chat and a stroke with a silent miaow and sometimes even with a purr, somewhat akin to an ill-tuned diesel engine. Opinions differ as to how long he has been around. First thoughts that it was about ten years have given way to recollections that he was about on this or that occasion at an earlier date and he is obviously set fair to become the feline equivalent of the oldest inhabitant.

Long may he continue! – Philip Wood.

They must be coming home soon: Shall I feign indifference, or do I really need them?

ensure that the cat-boarding is not regarded as a mere ancillary operation to the dog-boarding business. All reputable catteries will require the production of a valid certificate of vaccination against feline infectious enteritis and cat flu, and will reserve the right to refuse admission to any cat which appears to be ill. Furthermore, it will be understood that if the cat should develop any symptoms of illness during its stay, which, in the opinion of the cattery owner, require veterinary advice, then this will be obtained. The cost of this will naturally fall upon the owner of the cat, although some establishments offer an insurance scheme whereby the cat can be covered for veterinary attention during the period of boarding. An establishment which fails to insist on these precautions produces only one recommendation: find another cattery.

Inevitably, with many hundreds of establishments in being, there are some where conditions are on the borderline, if not below it. Dark and cramped quarters in buildings obviously in need of repair, rusting wire mesh or netting, a casual attitude to the fastening of doors, and what might be described as a general lack of vocation, are all worrying signs which it would be well to heed. By virtue of the Animal Boarding Establishments Act of 1963, all boarding catteries must be licensed and controlled by the appropriate local authority. Licences are renewable annually, on payment of a fee, and the onus for regular inspection is placed upon the local environmental health officer, to whom any complaints should be directed.

Having decided upon a suitable cattery, reservation should be made well in advance of the holiday. Nearer the day of departure, the actual time of taking the cat, or of having the cat collected, should be agreed, together with any particular arrangement as to food or other requirements. Although most catteries provide sleeping accommodation, it is preferable that the cat's own bed should be taken along, together with any favourite toy. If the cat is used to wearing a collar, it is desirable that a new one be fitted, giving the address and telephone number of the cattery, so that, in the unlikely event of the cat getting out, it can be returned to the safety of the cattery, rather than to an empty house. It is also sensible to leave your holiday telephone number just in case any problems should arise; although little can be done from a distance, it does provide a point of contact.

The next option, of taking the cat on holiday, must rest in the wisdom of the cat owner. There are many examples of cats going along with the family, particularly in caravans and on boats, and whilst hotels which welcome pets usually turn out to mean dogs, self-catering accommodation, or staying with friends, offers fewer restrictions. However, it has to be recognised that taking a cat into a strange environment, where the actions of other parties cannot be controlled, and where the natural curiosity of the cat will come to the fore, is to expose the animal to a degree of danger, the level of which will vary with the circumstances. The caring owner will obviously assess the risks involved, and, before embarking on this course of action, will establish that concern for the cat's welfare is the prime motivation for the decision, rather than personal convenience, self-interest or saving money.

Finally, you may be fortunate enough to have someone in the family, or even a cat-loving friend, who would be pleased to have your cat to stay while you are away. This must, of course, depend totally on the cat. It is often said that cats are more attached to a property than to an owner, and in some cases such a change could indeed be traumatic. Certainly it will be so if the cat is not made thoroughly welcome and treated properly. Many cats seem to enjoy a change as much as humans and quickly exploit the possibilities of their own 'country cottage'. This is especially true of Siamese and Burmese who, upon seeing the cat basket, often jump straight in in excited anticipation.

Especially if the other house is nearby, and perhaps the cat occasionally walks or is taken there loose in the car, the use of a cat basket, even for a short journey before and after a holiday, will help to make it clear that this is a temporary transference of home. Taking a familiar feeding bowl and providing a favourite meal on arrival might also help. Often such visits work out so well that the cat owners are soon asked when they are next going on holiday! Not that that prevents an enthusiastic reunion between cat and owner. It is just that many cats positively benefit from a change, and, if they can enjoy the comfort of a second, caring home, the absence of owners is made less

Mouse first

One of the more soothing things in life is watching a cat meticulously grooming itself after eating a meal. Folklore has it that the cat once followed the human practice, known to generation upon generation of small boys, of washing before eating but that it abandoned this procedure after an experience with an unusually clever mouse. The little animal, well aware of the fate awaiting it, commented that the least the cat could do was to have a wash before starting. The cat complied but during the elaborate washing procedure the mouse quietly stole away. The cat, cleaner and wiser, vowed that henceforth washing would be a post-prandial operation.

49

The Cheshire Cat

'. . . we're all mad here, I'm mad. You're mad,' said the Cat.

'How do you know I'm mad?' said Alice.

'You must be,' said the Cat, 'or you wouldn't have come here.'

Alice didn't think that proved it at all: however, she went on: 'And how do you know that you're mad?'

'To begin with,' said the Cat, 'a dog's not mad. You grant that?'

'I suppose so,' said Alice.

'Well, then,' the Cat went on, 'you see a dog growls when it's angry, and wags its tail when it's pleased. Now I growl when I'm pleased, and wag my tail when I'm angry. Therefore, I'm mad.'

'I call it purring, not growling,' said Alice.

'Call it what you like,' said the Cat. – Lewis Carroll, *Alice in Wonderland*.

traumatic than being left in an empty house or being transferred to a cattery. However, do remember that if a cat regularly moves to and from a second home, and if you fail to give it the inoculations that a cattery would correctly insist on, the option of sending to a cattery, should your friends or relations cease to be available, really rules itself out.

Leaving holidays aside, there will be other occasions when the cat has to travel, perhaps to the vet (if only for a routine vaccination), to a boarding cattery, or in the course of moving house. Even the shortest journeys are best undertaken with the cat safely ensconced in a suitable carrying basket. It is not unusual to see cats travelling loose in cars, but this practice is not to be recommended, either from the road-safety aspect, or from the viewpoint of the cat's own protection. There is always the chance of the unexpected happening – an accident, the lowering of a window to meet a sudden need for ventilation, or if stopped by police or traffic census officials, for example – and a cat could jump out of the car very quickly indeed.

There are many forms of carrier, not all of which meet the basic requirements of comfort, hygiene and safety. A cardboard carrier is useless, other than for dire emergencies. Apart from being airless and claustrophobic, it will disintegrate if the cat should urinate under the stress of travel. It is also possible for a determined cat to rip its way out in something under two minutes. If it becomes necessary to use one, it should be enclosed in small-mesh, plastic, garden netting to provide some degree of reinforcement.

Similarly, the use of a bag with a zip fastener has nothing to recommend it, as it is unhygienic and the zip fastener can come undone all too easily.

Apart from the traditional wicker basket, now generally provided with a plastic-coated wire-mesh door, there are other models available in plastic, glassfibre and other materials, all of which are durable, easily cleaned and capable of being fastened securely. The basket should be of ample size, bearing in mind that young cats grow bigger. The bottom of the basket should be lined with waterproof material such as polythene, topped by a layer of something replaceable and suitably absorbent, such as newspaper, and a piece of old blanket, or something similar, for the cat to lie on.

The cat basket must *not* be put in the boot of the car, which is dark, airless, noisy and smells of petrol fumes, but rather inside, on the floor, in front of the rear seats. If the car is of the hatchback type, it is a good idea to fold down one or both of the rear seats to provide more room. Care should be taken to place the basket in such a position that an emergency stop will not cause it to shoot forward, whilst the driver must bear in mind at all times that he has a potentially nervous passenger aboard. Do not place the cat basket close to a radio speaker and do remember when switching on the car radio that the cat's ears are much more sensitive to noise than your own.

50

The insatiable need to explore can lead some adventurers further and further afield

Clever cat

In the early days of the war, single German bombers used to fly over London, some to drop bombs, some flying over to other cities. Every time a German plane went over, my cat went under his chosen 'air raid shelter' – the electric cooker! If a British plane passed overhead, he took no notice at all. How did he know the difference? Indeed, he used to hear the German planes at least half a minute before I did. – *The Cat.*

The postcat

Mash, a very friendly black and white cat living in Hornchurch, waits every morning for the arrival of the postman and then rides with him the length of the road, sitting on the postbag on the front of his bicycle and jumping off to return home when the postman continues his round into the next street. Needless to say, the postman is known in the area as Postman Pat! – *The Cat.*

If the journey has to be undertaken by public transport, and involves anything other than a short bus trip, the first move should be to obtain details of the rules and regulations of the railway or coach operator concerned, noting particularly those relating to whether or not the cat may travel with its owner, or whether it will be required to travel elsewhere. Coach operators will normally allow a cat to travel with the passenger, provided it is securely housed, but this is often left to the discretion of the driver, and, with this in mind, as well as the overall desirability of a peaceful journey, it is obviously preferable to travel during quiet periods, if at all possible. On trains the letter of the law is usually ignored in favour of the spirit, and it is normally possible for the cat, in its basket, of course, to travel with its owner. If the cat should be required to travel in the luggage compartment, the question of access will need looking into, mainly from the aspect of reassurance. Unless the journey is of considerable length, it is better not to feed the cat whilst travelling in case it is sick, although drinking water should be made available. Some carriages containing luggage compartments are so constructed that passengers may walk through, and, in this case, care should be taken that the basket is placed out of reach of passersby.

In the general concern for the actual journey, it is easy to overlook the fact that travelling by public transport usually requires quite a lot of walking, and a fully grown cat can feel very heavy after a few hundred yards. Trollies are sometimes available at major railway stations, whilst, away from the main termini, it might even be possible to find a porter, but, as a precaution, it is worth considering the use of one of the small folding trollies used for suitcases.

All this assumes that the cat and owner are travelling together, but circumstances may arise where the cat has to travel unaccompanied. This situation should be avoided if at all possible, because the cat will pass through many hands on its journey, and, at times, especially if a change of trains has to be made, may well not be the responsibility of anyone in particular. If unaccompanied travel is totally unavoidable, the cat must be securely housed, equipped with a collar with the address and telephone number of its destination, and the container itself should be more than adequately labelled, not only as to destination and collection details, but also as to the fact that it contains a live animal, and, if this is not obvious from the nature of the container, an indication of the right way up. The cat should be accompanied until the last possible moment, ideally being handed over to the care of the guard, always assuming the train is watched over by one of this disappearing breed. Departure and anticipated time of arrival should then be telephoned to the person responsible for collecting the cat at its destination.

The other form of transport which now features more often in the lives of many people, is travel by air. Indeed, whereas in Europe air travel often means international travel, in America,

Australia and elsewhere it is a normal means of domestic travel. For obvious reasons airlines are strict in the application of their regulations in regard to the transport of animals, and the details should be studied carefully. It is worth remembering that even the shortest journey by air seems to require a lengthy wait on the ground, so that the overall time involved is going to be much longer than might be first thought on reading the flight times. Some airlines, particularly on domestic flights, will permit a properly housed cat to travel in the passenger cabin, but more usually it will be required to travel in the heated and pressurised section of the cargo hold, to which there is no access during flight. If the cat is travelling unaccompanied, it is essential to make foolproof arrangements for the flight to be met without delay on arrival, as only a handful of major airports are equipped to provide even overnight accommodation for animals. Apart from the consideration of travelling arrangements, international travel requires compliance with the rules and regulations regarding vaccination, health certificates and quarantine procedures including – a point often overlooked – those applicable on re-entry, if the cat is to return to the point of departure. Information on current requirements can be obtained from the

Waiting and wondering . . . some cats actually look forward to a holiday or a change themselves

Jamie

The weary process of clearing up after the bazaar had just begun when someone heard a faint noise from one of the cardboard boxes heaped up by the door ready for collection by the refuse department lorry. Box after box was opened and then there they were; five little forms hardly recognisable as kittens just a few days old. The initial reaction of fury and loathing for the perpetrator of such a deed soon gave way to more practical thoughts and the kittens were taken off to the CPL sanctuary at Haslemere where they could be given the round-the-clock care and attention which their age and condition required.

With the passage of time the pathetic little bundles turned into delightful kittens and the process of home-finding was begun. One of the kittens was reputed to be identical to our Crispin, recently fatally injured in a road accident, and it was arranged that he would be kept for us and he was accordingly named Crispin Two – or, possibly, Crispin, Too. Eventually the day came when he was ready to join us and off we went to Haslemere to collect him. He was a dear little chap, black and white with bright beady eyes, and he sat in his basket all the way home without saying a word. We decided there and then that he was not Crispin and so he became Jamie.

Susie, our resident matriarch, was not impressed with the new arrival although the theory had been that she would need a companion in place of Crispin. In particular, she did not intend to show him her best hunting grounds and and secret hiding places which she had discovered over the years and when Jamie took to following her she would remain firmly seated until he grew bored and went his own way.

(*continued opposite*)

embassy or consulate of the country concerned or, in the case of entry into England or Wales, from the Ministry of Agriculture, Fisheries and Food, and in the case of entry into Scotland, from the Department of Agriculture and Fisheries for Scotland, at the addresses given on page 206. All requirements must be strictly observed; failure to do so exposes the cat not merely to refusal of entry at its destination, but also to potential refusal of re-entry on return to the point of departure, and even, possibly, to an order for destruction.

Moving house can be a traumatic experience for all concerned, but particularly so for pets who do not understand precisely what is going on. The inevitable disruption of normal routine will soon make it obvious to puss that something is afoot and time should be found to devote some reassuring attention to the cat. By far the best idea is to arrange for the cat to be booked into a boarding cattery, either one normally used, or one conveniently located near to the new house, for a period of two or three days before, during and after the actual move. This procedure ensures that the cat does not disappear in the course of the upheaval, nor require concentrated attention when there is so much else to do.

If it is not possible to arrange for temporary boarding, a lockable room or shed should be cleared of everything involved in the removal operations, and the cat installed there early on moving day, complete with its own bed, toilet tray, food and water. The room or shed should then be locked and the key kept safe, preferably on a string around your neck. The removal men should be told that the room is empty and that a cat is in residence. Once loading is complete and the removal van has departed, enter the room carefully and transfer the cat to its travelling basket. Sedatives or tranquillisers should not be given unless specifically advised by a veterinary surgeon; most cats find the process of moving worrying enough without the added problem of being partially doped. On arrival at the new home, a similar procedure should be followed, with the cat locked in a safe place, complete with its basket and so on, and the key retained.

When the removal men have gone, and the house put into some sort of order, the cat can be let out from its place of safety, or fetched from the cattery, and introduced to its new home, all doors and windows being firmly closed, of course. The people, and probably much of the furniture, will be familiar and the cat will almost certainly turn its attention to a room-by-room inspection of the house. Allow it to do this until it is satisfied, when a small meal will confirm to it that this is now home and all is well. Opinions differ as to the best method of introducing the cat to the outside of the house, but some period of acclimatisation to the new indoor surroundings is certainly desirable. Once the cat appears to feel at home – and this point will depend very much on the cat's temperament – there is no reason not to let it out.

54

The cat should be accompanied on its first few outings which should be in daylight and of short duration. It is a wise precaution to fit an elasticated collar bearing your new address and telephone number, just in case some strange sight or sound should alarm it. There is no reason why the cat should want to wander from familiar persons and things, except to the extent that natural instinct will require that it explores its new territory. Some cats are wanderers by nature, but this trait will already be known and due allowance made in the period of familiarisation before letting the cat out. In the early stages the cat should be recalled at shortish intervals to ensure that it does not wander too far, and meals should be given after an outing rather than before. It is well worth while establishing an early rapport with the neighbours, so that they will know that the 'strange' cat in the garden belongs to the new folk at 'Chez Nous'. It is also wise to identify the best-recommended local veterinary surgeon and boarding cattery. With a little luck and application, feline domestic harmony will soon be re-established.

However, with much hard work, they were persuaded into a state of mutual toleration, if not admiration, until the sad day when Susie fell gravely ill and Jamie was left with everything to himself.

Jamie is a gentle, highly intelligent cat, with most impressive whiskers, who will rattle the doorknob if he wants to come in and who discovered at a very early age that lying on his back with his legs in the air was guaranteed to attract the attention of any human in sight who could then be persuaded to open the door, put down food or perform any other little service which might be required. As an encore he will stretch front and back legs to their fullest extent thus providing a full metre of upside-down black-and-white cat. Middle-aged now and a little portly, perhaps, he is still quicker off the mark than many of the local mouse and rabbit population. He has a wide circle of admirers (some of whom even send him Christmas cards although he does not reciprocate) and he is altogether a very special and cherished puss. – Philip Wood.

Left *Jamie and* below *Susie and Crispin*

GONE MISSING

Most cat owners are familiar with the numb feeling of panic when their pet fails to respond to a summons, or does not appear at a mealtime. It is natural enough to assume that something untoward has happened, but a little reflection will usually bring to mind a number of previous occasions which proved to be false alarms. Some cats, particularly those which have not been neutered or spayed, are natural wanderers and may go off for days at a time, but even the most docile of cats occasionally shows signs of being a card-carrying member of Cats' Lib, by spending a few hours out of sight. It may have found something intensely interesting to watch, or there may be a stray cat around, which situation requires a long period of each pretending to be unaware of the other, and where to leave early would involve loss of face. It may even be that puss has been overcome by a desire to sleep, and, having found a quiet and comfortable spot, has settled down there, oblivious to any amount of calling.

However, with the passing of time and the continued non-appearance of the cat, some action is required. Looking for a cat is easier in daylight, but if, as often happens, it is dark before you really begin to worry, a powerful torch is indispensable, and the quiet of night makes it easier to hear any sound from the cat, whilst the darkness will make eye reflections easy to see.

The first thing to do is to recall when and where the cat was last seen. This is simple enough in the one-person household, but where other people are involved it is less easy, and it is worth having a good look indoors to start with; many a weary search has taken place in the garden while the cat has been comfortably asleep on a chair under the dining room table. The cat's favourite haunts should be inspected, followed by a thorough look around the house. Cats are adept at pushing doors open, but often have difficulty in pulling one back to get out from the other side, whilst any doors fitted with self-closing mechanisms or magnetic catches (as on cupboards and refrigerators) are virtually impossible for a cat to open. Rooms are best inspected by getting down on the floor, thus bringing the searcher down to cat height, and rendering visible all those nooks and crannies under beds and furniture which cats find so attractive. In the bedrooms the bed coverings should be turned back to ensure that puss has not taken up residence under the eiderdown and the tops of wardrobes and cupboards should be checked; a sudden noise, such as a low-flying aircraft, or a loud bang, might have caused the cat to take refuge in an out-of-the-way place.

If the search inside the house fails, attention must be turned to the outside. Choose a quiet moment for calling, or tapping the food dish with a knife, and listen carefully for any response. The garden should be searched, along with neighbouring properties, paying particular attention to local hazards such as sheds, garages, coal bunkers, greenhouses, cold frames and other enclosed areas where the cat might have become trapped. With the thought in mind that the cat may be injured, either as the result of a fight or an accident, front gardens, roadside hedges and similar areas should be searched, as the cat's natural instinct will be to hide away to recover. Checks should also be made on whether any strange cars or tradesmen's vans have been parked in the immediate vicinity since the cat was last seen, as it could just happen that the cat found a warm spot for a sleep in a car, or was exploring a van when it was driven away.

If none of this produces a result, the next move must be to widen the search, and here the more publicity that can be obtained the more likely it is that information will be forthcoming. Children are a splendid means of spreading the word, whilst the postman, milkman and newspaper delivery boy will be visiting most houses in the area and can be asked to keep eyes and ears open for any news. It is worth contacting the local police station as the police are out and about in the neighbourhood, and are often aware of things which are not strictly their concern. It is also sensible to give details of the cat to the local RSPCA inspector and to nearby veterinary surgeons, as good-hearted souls often take injured cats for treatment, which may then face destruction if the owner cannot be traced. In a few areas animal welfare organisations maintain a register of lost-and-found cats.

Notices should be placed in local shops and pinned to any convenient trees, telegraph posts and fences. Depending on the area, the local papers and radio station may be willing to help with publicity. Leaflets can be prepared and delivered by hand to houses in the neighbourhood, whilst the local pub can also be a useful point for spreading and picking up news. People sometimes offer a reward for information, but this should not be done without thought.

If these measures produce no result, there is little more that can be done. Cats have been known to reappear after long absences, but this is an outside chance, and comfort must be taken in recalling times in the long and happy relationship, rather than the sadness of departure.

5
WORKING FOR OUR CATS' WELFARE

There is an old story to the effect that if ten Britons find themselves together in some out-of-the-way place, they will immediately form a club. This devotion to banding together is not an exclusively British trait, but certainly there can be no interest or activity in the United Kingdom which does not have one or more societies to further its aims. Animal welfare in general, and cats in particular, are no exceptions, and a number of organisations exist for the care and protection of animals.

The oldest and largest of the organisations devoted exclusively to the welfare of the cat, came into being at a meeting held at Caxton Hall in London in 1927, under the chairmanship of Miss J. Wade, at which it was resolved, '. . . that a society be formed to be devoted exclusively to promoting the interests of cats and that its name be The Cats Protection League'. Clearly defined objectives were established: to rescue stray and unwanted cats and kittens, rehabilitating and rehoming them where possible; to inform the public on the care of cats and kittens; and to encourage the neutering of cats not required for breeding. These objectives remain the same today.

The first organising secretary was Mr A. A. Steward, and the headquarters were established at Slough. Early achievements of the League included the introduction of an elasticated collar for cats, the development of a simple cat door, the setting up of a clinic at Slough, and the provision of shelters to accommodate cats, pending rehoming. Progress was held up by World War II which brought its own difficulties of cats rendered homeless by bombing or family separations, colonies becoming established

South London tearaway cats in Peckham

Felix, who found a happy home through the CPL

on bombed sites, and the general worry of finding cat-food in a severely rationed economy. In the aftermath of the war everyone had their own problems to contend with, but, in the 1960s, the League began its major expansion, becoming Registered Charity No 203644 in 1962. The most important of the initial moves was the pioneering of the spaying of female cats, then regarded as a very contentious matter, but considered by the CPL as an essential concomitant to the neutering of male cats if the cat population was to be contained.

Now celebrating its sixtieth anniversary, The Cats Protection League has eight large shelters, administered from the headquarters in Horsham, and some 150 groups and branches compared with just over twenty in the early 1970s. There is a large band of devoted members, supporters and workers helping tens of thousands of cats to a better life every year.

The oldest, and certainly the best known of the general animal welfare organisations, is the Royal Society for the Prevention of Cruelty to Animals, which came into being as long ago as 1824, acquiring its Royal prefix at the instigation of Queen Victoria in 1840. The RSPCA concerns itself with the welfare of all animals, and its inspectors are to be seen in cattle markets, pet shops, street markets, farms and everywhere that animals are involved. The Society has an excellent record of bringing prosecutions against perpetrators of acts of cruelty, and has many branches

58

and an active junior section which encourages a caring attitude in the young.

Another organisation which cares for most pet animals, but which has narrower and more specific aims than the RSPCA, is the People's Dispensary for Sick Animals, set up in 1917 by Mrs Maria Dickin, with the objective of providing free veterinary treatment for sick and injured animals where the owners were unable to afford the usual fees. The PDSA has well-equipped animal treatment centres in many towns throughout the United Kingdom, supplemented by an auxiliary service provided by veterinary practices in areas where the PDSA does not have its own facilities. The original precept is still followed, in that the provision of treatment is generally restricted to pets whose owners are in receipt of state benefits, or otherwise clearly unable to afford private fees. Urgent cases, however, receive initial treatment, irrespective of the owner's financial position. Apart from its traditional activities, the PDSA also offers guidance to pet owners on animal care, and runs an active educational programme.

Apart from the CPL there are other welfare organisations which concentrate exclusively on cats. The Feline Advisory Bureau is a registered charity, founded in 1958, which is particularly concerned with promoting the knowledge, understanding and treatment of feline diseases. It has established a scholarship, at the University of Bristol Veterinary School, which pays for a veterinary surgeon to specialise solely in feline medicine. The FAB produces a wide range of publications on cat diseases and other cat matters, including comprehensive material on boarding-cattery construction and management.

A relative newcomer to the cat welfare scene is Cat Action Trust, a registered charity founded in the 1970s to deal with the problem of feral cats. The broad policy of the Trust is to trap cats living in feral colonies, to find homes for the kittens, and to neuter and return to site those which are too set in their feral ways to become domesticated. Feeding rotas are established to care for the cats on site, and to keep a watch for new arrivals. This policy has led to the acceptance of such colonies, particularly in institutional and industrial surroundings, which, previously, in their uncontrolled state, were regarded as little better than pests.

There are many other groups with the welfare of cats at heart, ranging from the Cat Survival Trust, which cares for and breeds endangered species of wild cat, to the many local welfare groups which struggle on, often against fearful financial and practical difficulties, to make their contribution to improving the lot of the cat. All these organisations are in need, not only of money, although that is always welcome, but of practical help of all kinds. At the sharp end there are those who do the trapping, cleaning and feeding of the cats, but there are plenty of other jobs too, from fostering to fund-raising. All caring people should give their support to these splendid organisations.

Cats in music
It is surprising that the grace and beauty of the cat has given relatively little inspiration to classical composers. Rossini's *Duetto buffo di due gatti* is familiar and when sung by competent artistes produces what can only be described as a delightful caterwaul whilst, on the instrumental front, Prokofiev's story of *Peter and the Wolf* uses the clarinet to convey, in the most believable form, the stealthy movements of the cat. At the opposite extreme from these comparatively well-known pieces is the opera *The English Cat*, with music by Henze and libretto by Edward Bond which, although broadcast by the British Broadcasting Corporation, has yet to have its stage première in Britain. There are other items such as Scarlatti's *Cat's Fugue*, the cat in Ravel's *L'Enfant et les Sortilèges* and a few appearances in ballet but musically there is nothing like the rapport which, as has often been remarked upon, exists between writers and cats.

Becoming Involved

At one time nearly every locality had its 'cat lady', known throughout the area as the person willing to help with any cat problems, from taking in dumped kittens to caring for the cat 'orphaned' by the death of its owner. Many of these kind souls continue with their devoted work, unsung and often ridiculed, but deriving great satisfaction from the knowledge that they are making some contribution to alleviating the suffering of the underprivileged members of the cat population. However, the ravages of inflation, the growth of high-rise accommodation, unsuitable for pets, the development of municipally owned property which is subject to restrictions on the keeping of pets, and other factors, have made the task of the would-be rescuer ever more difficult, and, as with many other forms of service, the tendency in cat welfare work is towards what might be described as a group practice.

There are obvious advantages in like-minded people banding together, mainly because working alone is often difficult and, at times, downright impossible, but also because it permits members of the group to contribute their individual skills and to follow their own particular bent. There is a further advantage, although it is treated rather like Cousin Willie who was persuaded to take up residence abroad and thereafter rarely mentioned, in that the group practice tends to thwart the growth of what is known in the cat welfare world as a 'collector'. These kind-hearted folk can never say 'No' when asked to help, but rarely say 'Yes' when the opportunity arises to home a cat and, as a result, their cat family greatly outgrows the facilities available, to the consternation of neighbours, the local authority and, eventually, the cats themselves. The group is able to take a more rational approach to the utilisation of available resources and should be able to prevent this situation, with all its attendant problems, arising.

Inevitably there are some potential disadvantages with a group acting together, but these are easily avoidable with a little commonsense. The group's finances must be in the hands of a totally reliable individual who will not only collect the money and issue receipts, check bills and attend to their payment, but will also ensure that the group's expenditure does not exceed its income. If a member of the group does not wish to take on this role, it is often possible to find a husband or friend of a member who has no wish to be actively involved with cats, but who is not averse to a little administrative work.

The other potential problem is the incompatibility of members, and this is dealt with by ensuring that all decisions are taken in open discussion and that all concerned accept that the primary object of the group is to contribute to the welfare of as many needy cats as the group's resources in money, time and people will permit.

The setting up of a rescue group will require a spark of initiative from someone who, in the early stages at least, will take on

Opposite Misty is still cautious as to what may lie the other side of the door. No sudden noises, please

60

the role of co-ordinator, organiser, chairman, or whatever title seems appropriate. He or she will need to be able to motivate people, to work amicably with those inside and outside the group, and to be able to say 'No' in a suitably disarming manner. Apart from the treasurer, whose duties have been outlined above, it will be necessary to appoint a secretary, who will attend to correspondence and keep notes of meetings, a welfare/homing officer, who will be responsible for taking cats into care and for seeking out (and inspecting) potential homes for cats, a fund-raiser, whose duties are obvious enough and which are covered in detail elsewhere, and a public relations officer, who will seek publicity by all means possible, both to raise money and to assist with homing. In addition to these identifiable tasks, there are many others, including the all-important fostering or otherwise accommodating cats pending rehoming, providing transport for cats to and from the veterinary surgery or to a new home, and for food and other items to foster homes, or, indeed, for collecting goods for bazaars. Depending on the ambitions and resources of the group, and the locality, there are other areas of activity which can be developed, such as maintaining a lost and found register (ideal for a house-bound member with a phone), taking temporary care of cats where the owner is involved in an accident or other emergency, feeding feral cats on site, and much else. If all this seems rather daunting, it must be remembered that, as with many counsels, this is one of perfection, and, certainly to start with, each of a handful of willing helpers can play several roles until, provided enthusiasm does not outrun resources, the work can be spread as the group becomes known in the locality.

The first and most essential requirement is some facility to house cats whilst homes are being sought. Many groups function on the basis of parking them in a member's house but this should be a last resource, because of the many problems of the possible spread of infection (particularly where there are pets in residence), of security, and the upset to the cat itself, not to mention domestic harmony! Purpose-built chalets or pens in the gardens of members provide ideal facilities, or it might be possible to make arrangements with a local boarding establishment to provide temporary accommodation at a reduced rate, although there may be problems here over the lack of inoculation certificates. In rural areas it is always possible to find some sort of accommodation, but in town, where inevitably the need is greater, a satisfactory solution may not be so easy.

Records should be kept of each cat helped, not only for the group's own purposes, but also as a safeguard in the event of problems subsequently arising over ownership or identification. The latter point requires something more than the average 'black and white tom' description; a photograph is ideal if one of the members' interests lie in this direction. On the question of ownership, it sometimes happens that a 'stray' turns out to have a home and there is annoyance, to put it mildly, that the cat has

Valuable fur

The fur arising from the grooming of healthy cats should not be thrown away. In the nesting season it can be spiked on convenient bushes in the garden where it will be appreciated by the birds as nesting material. Alternatively it can be sent to The Cats Protection League at 17 Kings Road, Horsham, West Sussex RH13 5PP, which sells it in bulk to a pharmaceutical company which uses it to produce a vaccine for the treatment of people who are allergic to cat fur.

been 'rescued', but adequate records should enable this, fortunately rare, occurrence to be sorted out.

Homing is satisfying but demanding work, and requires development of the philosophy of doing what is possible in the prevailing circumstances. There is no substitute for the time-consuming personal visit (and for a follow-up visit after homing), and resentment at such a proposal might be a warning sign. Regrettably, there are not endless homes with the red carpet out awaiting the arrival of puss, and it is a personal decision whether something less than ideal is better for the cat than a long stay in a shelter. Obviously thought will be given as to the suitability of the cat to the surroundings, and vice versa; a nervous or deaf animal would not do very well living on a main road, a boisterous kitten may not be ideal for an elderly or infirm person, and so on. It goes without saying that all cats homed must be in good health – nobody will benefit from passing on a

Looking after someone else's cats can be quite a handful, but definitely fun. They will almost certainly seek favours not normally granted

63

sick cat – and it must be understood that if all does not go well, the cat must be returned to the group and not handed on else-where. With an eye to future problems, the group would be well advised to neuter (or seek undertakings to neuter in the case of kittens) all cats before placing them in new homes.

A final word on the subject. Even in these enlightened days, there are still those whose interest in cats is financial or research-orientated and vigilance is required to ensure that a cat is not inadvertently placed in the hands of a supplier to the fur trade, or to laboratories (this is illegal as of January 1987).

The group's work will be helped by establishing a friendly relationship with the local veterinary practice, and with other animal welfare organisations in the area. Although they are, by the nature of their calling, caring people, veterinary surgeons should not be expected to provide their services free, or even at reduced rates. They are professionals with a very expensive training to recoup, and must be expected to charge accordingly. The most likely welfare presence in the area is the RSPCA, and their inspectors are not only willing to help, but also have access to the resources of a large organisation and a fund of knowledge. It is also worth becoming known to the local police (not in a legal sense, of course!) who occasionally have a cat problem, as when an accident victim is found to have a cat requiring care or rehoming. Their reciprocal help may be useful one day. There should be no element of friction or competition with other welfare organisations; if all of them work to capacity there will still be plenty of needful work left undone.

As an alternative to working individually, or as an indepen-dent group, the possibility of becoming the local branch of one

A rescued cat can be the most rewarding of all. Understanding and respect will grow daily

of the national charities might be considered. The feasibility of this depends on various things, including the location of existing branches, and requires, of course, adherence to the policies and practices of the charity concerned. On the other hand, practical, and possibly financial, help will be forthcoming to assist in the establishment of the group. By way of illustration, The Cats Protection League has some 150 groups and branches throughout the United Kingdom, from the Shetlands to Cornwall, and beyond to the Channel Islands and Dublin. The League's policy is to provide initial funding, equipment and advice, and continued support thereafter, although the group is expected to be largely self-financing. However, whether as individuals, independent groups, or as part of a national organisation, all contribute towards this very rewarding work.

Cat to the rescue
Answering the door, a middle aged Californian woman was roughly pushed to one side as a stranger forced his way into her home. As the woman screamed, the would-be rapist punched her and threw her to the floor, tearing at her clothes. In the nick of time, through the air came a spitting, clawing mass of fur, straight onto the man's back, sending him off in panic. The family cat had come to the rescue! – *The Cat.*

Fund Raising

In cat welfare, as in all other good works, the financial aspect is a prime determinant of the amount of activity which can be undertaken. However, those whose hearts and minds are concerned with the needs of animals in distress often find money matters a great problem, and it is well worth trying to find a numerate sympathiser who will take over this aspect of the work.

Everybody concerned with fund raising knows of the two traditional sources, the jumble sale (now usually dignified with the name of bazaar or bring and buy sale) and the coffee morning (with its up-market offspring, the wine and cheese party). Although commonplace, they play a very useful role, and, with a little thought and care, can be developed into a social occasion and a means of widening the circle of supporters. Those who have long experience in such matters will know that, simple as they appear to be, such events do not happen of their own accord and newcomers to fund raising might therefore welcome a few comments.

The success of a bazaar depends on having the right things to sell at the right price at the right place at the right time. In some areas the choice of place is limited to the church hall or village hall, but, elsewhere, particularly in towns, there is often a wide choice of venue and it is worth doing some research, not only on relative costs, but also as to their popularity, as evidenced by their use by other fund-raising organisations. The question of size sometimes creates a problem; the very small hall tends to lead to a breathless and crowded atmosphere which may be off-putting to potential buyers, whilst a large hall, sparsely occupied with stalls, will give the impression that the event is not going very well. If there is space to spare it can be offered to other organisations, particularly those which are too small to promote an event of their own, and which would welcome the chance to have a single stall without the problems of organisation. There is sometimes a fear that 'outsider's stalls' will detract from the funds raised by the sponsoring organisation, but this is false

Cat figurines

The earliest figures of cats are those found in the tombs of ancient Egypt, where the cat was a sacred animal; later representations of cats appeared in the Middle and Far East as votive objects. The western porcelain and pottery industries began to develop at the end of the 18th century at a time when cats were still being persecuted in Europe, and hence there are few early cat figurines. With the turn of the century, and a more enlightened era and the growth of the ceramic industry, models of cats became more in evidence, from Meissen, Chelsea, Derby, Rockingham, Worcester, Staffordshire, Delft and many others. Having regard to the fragile nature of their products, and the fact that there are many individuals and museums collecting antique pottery, many of these early items are now extremely scarce and valuable. Nowadays you can buy all kinds of attractive cat figures, such as those from the Royal Doulton company, who produce two different sets of kittens, a cheerful black and white seated cat called Lucky and a larger seated figure in flambé ware. There are also a great number of imported cat figures, as well as glass and wooden cats – all the way down to stone garden ornaments or cat silhouettes to hang in the garden to scare away birds!

thinking; all buying at bazaars is on impulse, and the more stalls there are, the more people are likely to stay around and spend money. In passing it might be mentioned that the reverse situation should also be considered, should the opportunity arise to have a stall at someone else's event.

The nature of the goods to be offered will depend on the area and the number of supporters who are able and willing to help. It is usually possible to get people to make cakes or jam or other produce ('home-made' items are always good sellers), whilst others can do the rounds to acquire the traditional jumble-sale items. This requires some care and a lot of tact in treading the path between offending would-be supporters and having the event become the depository for everybody's rubbish. In some areas there are certain very well-known items which have been going the rounds of the white-elephant stall and the jumble-sale circuit for years!

It is worth giving some thought to creating an unusual feature, for example, a stall with items all of one colour. This is not as difficult as it sounds, and a stall piled up with blue stationery, kitchen towels, toilet rolls, china, soaps, materials, and so on, will attract a lot of attention.

The selection of the right day for the event can contribute greatly to the success. A check should be made on any competing local events (although in areas with only one suitable hall this largely takes care of itself), and, even more important in these days of mass participation via television, a further check should be made on whether any major national events are scheduled for the proposed date; attendance is likely to be thin on Cup Final Day!

The actual running of the event is largely a matter of commonsense, plus a little luck. As much publicity as possible should be sought by notices in shop windows, announcements on local radio, leaflets through letterboxes and so on. There are two schools of thought on the merits of charging an admission fee, but, on balance, it is probably unnecessary in rural areas, while a useful control on keeping out undesirables in urban areas. The expectation of people looking in at a bazaar is that there will be bargains to be had, and pricing should be done accordingly. Refreshments are a very desirable feature, as they attract casual passersby, and persuade people to stay around for a second look after having a cup of tea.

A final and, unfortunately, necessary word on the subject. Financial success can be diminished if a sharp eye is not kept on both the stock and the takings. If the money is kept out of reach behind the stall, turning away, to obtain change, exposes the goods on display to what is euphemistically known in the retail trade as 'shrinkage', whilst keeping the money on the stall has its own hazards. Many people like the idea of aprons with large pockets which neatly solve the problem of stowing the cash in a safe place and keeping an eye on the goods at the same time.

Coffee mornings and wine and cheese parties can be held in a hall, but a distinctly better atmosphere prevails if someone is willing and able to hold the event at home. Once again, they need some organisation if they are to go well, but they do provide the opportunity, not only to raise money, but to establish a rapport with potential supporters. Apart from the usual bring and buy stall and the sale of cakes and other home-made items, it is usual to have a raffle or tombola, or, particularly at wine and cheese parties which are normally held in the evening, a silent auction.

Which of these money-raising activities is most appropriate depends on the scale of the event and the number and nature of the prizes available. For a small local coffee morning, a few donated prizes of boxes of chocolates, a bottle of wine and a cake or two will support the sale of a hundred or so tickets at the event itself, but a more ambitious raffle, with tickets sold in advance, will require rather more ambitious prizes. Incidentally, and obvious though it may seem, if cash prizes are offered, it is essential that the money really is available; there have been occasions when the sale of tickets failed to produce sufficient funds for the prizes.

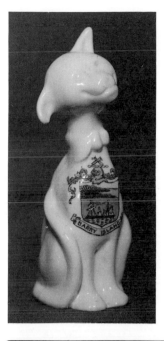

A tombola requires a lot of prizes of moderate value. The general approach is to number each prize, often in a five, ten, fifteen sequence, and to put the number of tickets equivalent to the highest-numbered prize (eg if the sequence reaches 300, then 300 tickets) in a drum or container. The tickets are then offered for sale and all numbers ending in five or zero win a prize. The ratio of tickets to prizes, and the cost of tickets, may be varied, but it is essential to give buyers a good prospect of a win.

If better class items are available, and if space and the number of helpers permit, wine and cheese parties provide a good opportunity for a silent auction. The items (which can be made up from small contributions by, for example, assembling a box of groceries) are displayed on a table, each accompanied by a form with space for names and amounts bid; a reserve price at which bidding starts can be included. The idea is for someone to start the bidding for each item by entering their name and amount bid, and then for others to overbid by adding their name and amount. It is often useful to get one of the helpers to bid for a few items to get the ball rolling. The closing time for bids should be prominently displayed, and warning of its approach given to encourage some last-minute bidding. Closure should be signalled with a bell or whistle, when the successful bidders are identified and united with their lots in exchange for the money.

Two smaller alternatives to the usual bazaar are the garage sale and the car-boot sale. The garage sale is an import from North America where the traditional method of disposing of unwanted items is to display them in the garage on Sunday morning, having publicised the sale beforehand by the usual means. The car-boot sale is usually arranged by an organisation which rents parking space at a suitable location and then sells

spaces, with the right to display and sell a car-bootful of goods. This often gives rise to some very curious vehicles which appear to be 90 per cent boot and 10 per cent passenger accommodation, but nobody seems to mind, and some locations offer excellent prospects for readily saleable items.

There are many other ways of raising money, and no one should miss the chance of adopting successful ideas from other fund-raising organisations. Some have done very well with sponsoring participants in marathons, cycle rides, fun runs, swimming events, and even losing weight, whilst the opportunity to participate at fetes or carnivals should also be followed up. In this connection, some novel or striking feature is a great help. Two ideas which have been used with great success are young ladies in cat suits, with collecting boxes if possible, and, on a static basis, a model cat with a moneybox, of which The Cats Protection League's Thomasina, a 3ft high tortie puss, designed and made by Mrs Valerie Stiller, is a splendid example.

The money having been collected, it is vitally important that it is accounted for in a meticulous manner. A very convenient way of dealing with funds is to open an account with the National Girobank. This costs nothing to run, provided it is kept even £1 in credit, and has the advantage that cash can be paid in at any post office, whilst cheques can be credited by sending them to head office in post-paid envelopes which are provided free of charge. Withdrawals of cash can be arranged at appropriate post offices, and payments can be made by cheque, or by credit transfer if the other party also has a National Giro account. A statement is sent automatically by post after every payment in, or after every ten payments out, so it is easy to keep a continuous check on the account. A brochure, setting out details of the services offered by the National Girobank, can be obtained from any post office. Any amounts of money over and above those required for immediate use, should not be left in the cash box or on current account, but should be placed in an interest-bearing account, care being taken, however, to ensure that withdrawal is possible at short notice without penalty.

Many people yearn for the perfect world where money would play no part but Utopia is always around the corner and if it were to exist then, by definition, there would be no needy cats.

If the cats go after the birds, there is nothing you can do to stop them

THE EXPERIENCES OF A
CATS PROTECTION LEAGUE CAT-SITTER

The idea of registering as a CPL Cat-Sitter appealed. I had already 'cat-sat' for a friend and my sister and, having answered an ad in *The Cat*, had done so for a charming family of four lovely cats whilst Mum and Dad took a holiday in Spain. Not long after I registered, I received a phone call from a lively lady and hubby who lived on the Kent/Greater London border.

'We haven't had a proper holiday for five years because we have twelve cats.'

I gasped. Four was one thing. But – twelve? However, in for a penny, in for a pound – and very soon, we had arranged for me to spend a short weekend with them. By then, two more kittens had joined the family. I spent most of the weekend trying to put names to furry bodies and win feline confidences so that they would not run a mile when next we all met.

My new-found friends gleefully booked a week's holiday in Cornwall and bought in cat food, almost by the ton, including frozen chickens and coley.

The first day, I got through the 5 o'clock feed with alacrity. Three or four plates, deposited in the garden (as the weather was fine), in the kitchen and on newspaper in the dining room, took care of most of the pussies. Another plate just outside the front door, under cover, took care of Goldie, a golden tabby who had once been attacked by Buzz, a neutered cat who did not realise it and who had bitten the unfortunate Goldie who was not standing for that sort of treatment and would not come either indoors or into the back garden.

That night someone – I think it was Timmy, the only marmalade cat – slept on my bed and someone else – Tabbies, I believe – crept *inside* for a while.

The next morning began early. Various felines came and went on the bed and a plaintive miaow from downstairs made me realise that it was feeding time in this cat hotel. I washed and dressed, watched by several inquisitive pairs of eyes and went to make my way downstairs but, at the top of the stairs, I stopped, amazed. Below was a milling mass of different coloured fur, whiskers and tails. Hoping *all* the natives were friendly, I cautiously made my way into their midst. Fine – they dispersed like magic into the kitchen and dining room. I opened the back door and caught up the cat flap with string (dropped down for the kittens at night to keep them indoors, as they had not yet worked out how to open it for themselves). By the way, by now yet another kitten had been added to the family, a pretty, white, smooth-haired puss with black markings and named Bobby.

Before they left I asked Marie just how many cats she had now. 'God knows', she breathed. So, I decided to count. There was big black and white Willie who now resembled a Manx, having had his tail docked due to an accident; Susie, a 15 year old tabby who spent most of her time in a box in the living room; Buzz, another tabby whom I have mentioned; Snorkie, also tabby and Snuffles, a tiny tabby girl with a funny little mouth that caused her little pink tongue to show. She took a shine to me and her tongue would come out further with excitement when she was stroked – a real sweetie. Then there was a gorgeous big black, resembling my own cat Seebee, who answered to Bill; Peter, a soppy black and white; Buttons, a truly enormous tabby male who lived outside in a shed unless the weather was really bad; Timmy, the marmalade; Goldie who lived out the front; Tabbies, an elderly tabby with hardly any teeth and whom I spoiled, cutting her food finely and feeding her separately from the mob; Tiggles, another tabby lady, very affectionate, and yet another tabby girl, Sparkie, who would only eat on top of the fridge. Then, of course, the three imps, the babies, Bobby, Bonnie, a prettily marked tabby and white girl, and Silvie, an almost silver tabby named after me.

Now, if you count that lot, as I did, you will find it comes not to twelve or fourteen, but to *sixteen*!

The babies were a pain to get in at night. Bobby was the worst culprit; no matter how stealthily I crept up on him (calling him was a waste of time) that kitten scampered up the damson tree and on-to the shed roof, to disappear into next door's garden. At midnight one night I gave up, closed the cat flap and, as there was a nice warm box lined with blankets in the greenhouse, I left the sliding door open just enough for a small kitten to get through, with water outside to drink, and went to bed. That little cat was there, quite unconcerned, next morning, scoffing down his breakfast at a rate of knots with the others in the garden.

We soon settled to a routine. I arose early. You try sleeping when three boisterous kittens are running up and down your spine like express trains on a main line! As the week went on and they realised I was not just a meal ticket but would make a genuine fuss of them, brushing them all every day, I found wearing old jeans in the evening compulsory to save my clothes as first one and then others decided to show their appreciation and sit on my lap, or curl up on the arm of the chair.

During 'time off', I was able to explore new territory, one of the perks of cat-sitting. But the real reward was getting to know all the cats' different personalities as the week progressed.

6
WE HELP IF WE CAN

Tabitha and her lifelong friend Elizabeth were happy in their modest council maisonette. The morning Elizabeth died, strangers had to wrench poor bewildered Tabitha from her mistress's body.

Sweep was a familiar character in the little mining village, but the pit closed, and Sweep became a luxury his desperate family could no longer afford.

Melissa and Tarquin, the Siamese brother and sister, were super fun for the children until they clawed the lounge furniture – frightfully 'naff' behaviour in a Mayfair apartment.

Pixie, antecedents unknown, was innocently pottering near a car bomb in embattled Belfast. She lost a hind leg and her tail, but her spirit and dignity remained intact.

Tabitha, Sweep, Melissa, Tarquin and Pixie are a microcosm of the thousands of cats which, every year, come into the care of The Cats Protection League. Since its foundation, this oldest of voluntary cat charities whose motto is, 'We help if we can', has expanded into a nationwide network of branches and groups.

In an ideal society, there would be a waiting list for each newborn kitten. As matters stand, the pathetic, wriggling scrap has more chance of being chloroformed out of a world its tiny blind eyes have not yet even glimpsed, than of enjoying a cosy fireside.

To produce an accurate tally of the number of unwanted cats in the United Kingdom alone would stump the most sophisticated computer, but the sum total is a grim chronicle of human tragedy, cruelty and fecklessness. Since cats breed thirty-five to forty times more frequently than people, every queen is a potential population explosion, and every tom a megadynasty founder. That is why the League sends all its strays, over six months old, to the vet for sterilisation.

The basic requirements of these feline victims are food, warmth and tender loving care. 'TLC' is recognised by the veterinary profession as a significant plus factor, and it is on round-the-clock offer at the CPL. Accommodation varies, but standards of care do not. Bigger branches have custom-built catteries with a live-in superintendent, whilst others make shift with portable huts and wire runs in members' gardens. Small groups with minimal facilities are, however, undaunted; there is always the secretary's guest-room, or a snug corner in the treasurer's airing cupboard.

Katy, one of the many thousands of cats who might never have had a happy home but for the CPL

Whoever your cat may be, it will be an individual with its own way of looking at the world

Tiger has a particularly uninhibited way of expressing himself

Emma was a little cat who needed a great deal of tender loving care when she first arrived at the shelter

A terrified black tom rescued from a blaze

No matter how crowded the shelters, their inmates are never handed out lightly. There is a routine drill for rehoming, designed to ensure, as far as reasonably possible, that a cat rescued from hardship is guaranteed a better deal for the rest of its nine lives. Prospective new owners are welcome to book a pet, but cannot take it until a League volunteer has paid a check-up visit. Genuine animal lovers appreciate this precaution and experience has proved the system's worth. Not only people, but places, are assessed and danger signals noted. Is there murderous traffic? Do packs of dogs roam unsupervised? Could the balcony of a high-rise flat spell disaster for an over-curious moggy? Again, things are not always what they seem. A father brought two well-behaved children to choose an eight-week-old kitten. When the CPL visitor waded through January snows to the family's door, the man showed her where the kitten would be kept – in a wire-fronted rabbit hutch at the bottom of the wintry garden! His wife, he explained, became hysterical if a cat came near her. The rabbit hutch remained empty.

Equally vital is the follow-up visit, usually a week to ten days after the cat has been homed. Any problems of behaviour, feeding, or toilet manners are discussed and the appropriate advice offered. If, on a subsequent call, it is clear that cat and adopters are still at odds, an amicable parting is arranged. Should the standard of care be unsatisfactory, the same principle applies. One volunteer had a nasty shock. The tabby which she had left purring in a pleasant house, with a charming middle-aged couple, was not to be seen when she dropped by again. Determined questioning winkled out the truth. The cat had been acquired to act as a ratter and was now crouched forlornly in the filthy rain-soaked yard of the husband's building firm. The visitor whisked the shivering puss into her car and drove back to the shelter. 'Maybe we should invest in a lie-detector,' she said wryly to the superintendent. But such cases are rare and most adoptions are happy and permanent.

Authority to repossess a cat or kitten is a safeguard written into CPL rules. Gratuitous donations are welcome, but no cat is ever sold, and so, in theory, they all remain the property of the League. If, for any reason, a cat can no longer be kept, it must be returned to League custody, not shunted onto someone else. All this is explained when the new owner collects the cat, and he or she is required to sign a form agreeing to these conditions. The form also incorporates an undertaking to have kittens spayed or neutered by a specified date; adults will, of course, have already been attended to. Anyone who objects to feline sterilisation has their offer of a home politely, but firmly, refused.

Animal lovers are often accused of being indifferent to the needs of people, a charge as groundless as it is unfair. Seventy-two-year-old Lucy, the sole surviving resident in an urban redevelopment street, braved a busy trunk road to buy her

The Cats Protection League shelter at Haslemere. The people who work at the shelters are all dedicated cat lovers. No matter how crowded the shelter, the inmates are only given out when the right home has been found

weekly shopping from the supermarket. One Saturday afternoon she was knocked down by a motor cycle. Helpless in hospital with a broken thigh, she was frantic about grey Smokey, locked in the house with nobody to feed him. The hospital almoner telephoned the CPL and two members brought Smokey to their shelter. As senior a citizen, in feline terms, as his mistress, Smokey looked distinctly moth-eaten and had difficulty in eating. Investigation revealed acute flea eczema and a massive dental problem. By the time Lucy came home, Smokey was a new man – courtesy of the CPL. The joy of their reunion was ample recompense for the vet's bill.

Regrettably this kind of extramural assistance cannot be made as freely available as the League would wish. In common with most charities, it has a constant cashflow problem. Legacies and donations are a major lifeline, providing an immediate cash injection, but, with a bewildering array of worthy causes vying for public support, these bonanzas are sporadic and unpredictable. Animal welfare organisations lack the 'there but for the grace of God' dimension which boosts appeals for the relief of human suffering. To imagine oneself a starving Ethiopian is frighteningly easy; to think oneself inside the skin of a starving cat is not. Each individual branch or group must therefore be self-financing, even though membership subscriptions, at affordable levels, cannot begin to make ends meet when cat-food, veterinary and maintenance bills are counted in thousands of pounds. Committees are always at full stretch organising and manning the time-honoured money-spinners of sales, coffee parties, auctions, open days and any other novel functions ingenuity can devise, but the chill wind of economic recession now blows through many a church hall, and stallholders in work-starved areas are finding that customers have increasingly lean purses. With each successive year, branches and groups are having to run harder and harder just to stand still.

What kind of people sacrifice so much of their time, money and energy on work which is emotionally and physically exhausting, and earns no applause? Tradition laughs them off as a gaggle of dotty old ladies in quaint hats, forever boiling herrings and boring the vicar to prayers for deliverance with tales of Kittywinkle's latest trick. The reality is rather different.

Behind the dignified portals of his law practice, Charles does not look the stuff of which heroes are made. Precise, bespectacled, thinning on top, the usual height of his aggression is walloping a golf ball at weekends. But when, on taking a short cut to a London carpark, he chanced on a gang of mindless hooligans playing football with a ginger kitten, Charles discovered a James Bond inside him thirsting to burst out. It did not matter that the odds were six to one, or that he might invite a knife in his ribs, all Charles saw was that orange bundle being booted through the air. He charged into the attack, flailing briefcase and umbrella. In sheer amazement at the ferocity of this

Tabitha has forgotten all about being a domestic pet for a while .

Rufus reminds his friend Fergus that it's time to play

Farm kittens playing together

Making friends. Two cats greet each other, sniffing and intertwining whiskers

pinstriped city gent, the gang scattered in disarray, and Charles was gone with the kitten before they could gather their wits and return. Good CPL members both, Charles and his wife, Daphne, were already owned by four rescued moggies. As he collapsed into his car, shaking with delayed shock, Charles reflected philosophically that one more mouth to feed would not make much difference.

School-cleaner Pat, known locally as 'the cat lady', was so busy figuring out how to reach the squeaking kittens twenty feet below pavement level that she forgot she was 'on the sick', recovering from a slipped disc. The small girl, who had knocked on her door to tell her about the bag which somebody had thrown into a derelict basement, hopped anxiously from foot to foot.

'It's an awful long way down, Miss,' she said, 'I'd better fetch me dad.'

'Don't bother, love,' said Pat, hitching her nylon clothes line to a broken metal railing, 'I'll manage.'

She did, and found excellent homes for the five terrified, but unhurt, kittens as well.

Retired civil servant Eileen was walking her dog, Susie, in Barnett's Park, on the outskirts of Belfast. At the centre of the picturesque park stood Barnett House, a fine period residence, now turned into a museum of Irish history. Among other treasures, it contained a unique collection of original costumes. Suddenly there was a shattering roar. Horrified, Eileen saw the house erupt in flames, ripped apart by an IRA bomb. Sirens blaring, emergency services raced along the tree-lined paths. Eileen watched the museum caretaker and his wife, personal friends of hers, being rushed out injured. Then a sickening thought made her heart lurch. Blossom! Blossom was the deaf, white, spayed female her friends had adopted from the CPL the previous summer, because she needed a traffic-free environment. She was gentle and shy in her silent world and only

So many kittens are born every year – the CPL has all strays over six months old sterilised to help curb the population explosion

Gentle, shy, exquisitely beautiful: it's hard to imagine that this cat was a victim of cruelty and neglect

ventured out when the museum closed. Almost certainly she would be hiding somewhere in the caretaker's flat. Already flames were licking through the roof. Eileen lashed Susie's lead to a tree and ran. Handkerchief clutched to her mouth she was inside the smoke-filled entrance hall before anyone noticed her. Five minutes later she staggered out, faint and choking, with Blossom in her arms. A fire officer was just fitting her with an oxygen mask when the roof of Barnett House caved in. Eileen was astonished, and more than a bit embarrassed, to find that she had hit the headlines in the Belfast papers. Her only consolation, she said ruefully, was the spin-off of donations to The Cats Protection League Ulster shelter.

Charles, Pat and Eileen are ordinary men and women who just happen to love cats. Sharing League membership with them are many other cat lovers of all ages, classes and creeds, willingly coping with the thousand and one assorted chores entailed in making living creatures safe and comfortable. You will not find their names in honours lists, though sluicing out a stack of malodorous toilet trays demands its own brand of courage. Glory is not their goal; to the CPL members the supreme accolade is the purring of a ragged stray transformed into a sleek, contented family pet.

In this, its Diamond Jubilee Year, how does the League see the way ahead? Among today's young people there is a growing upsurge of concern for the suffering of animals. The CPL hopes to attract a significant number of them to its ranks, for they are, after all, the future in the flesh.

Some day a Utopian age may dawn when humane and enlightened attitudes make animal charities redundant. Until then, with unpretentious dedication, The Cats Protection League will continue to help if it can.

Humans sometimes leave ladders to help in the process of exploration. This tabby gains a vantage point for his curiosity, then sets off to explore from a lower level

BEHAVIOUR OF CATS

The cat is an unfaithful domestic, and kept only from the necessity we find of opposing him to other domestics still more incommodious, and which cannot be hunted; for we value not those people, who, being fond of all brutes, foolishly keep cats for their amusement. Though these animals, when young, are frolicksome and beautiful, they possess, at the same time, an innate malice and perverse disposition, which increase as they grow up, and which education learns them to conceal, but not to subdue. From determined robbers, the best education can only convert them into flattering thieves; for they have the same address, subtlety, and desire of plunder. Like thieves, they know how to conceal their steps and their designs, to watch opportunities, to catch the proper moment for laying hold of their prey, to fly from punishment, and to remain at a distance till solicited to return. They easily assume the habits of society, but never acquire its manners; for they have only the appearance of attachment or friendship. This disingenuity of character is betrayed by the obliquity of their movements, and the duplicity of their eyes. They never look their best benefactor in the face; but, either from distrust or falseness, they approach him by windings, in order to procure caresses, in which they have no other pleasure than what arises from flattering those who bestow them. Very different from that faithful animal the dog, whose sentiments totally centre in the person and happiness of his master, the cat appears to have no feelings which are not interested, to have no affection that is not conditional, and to carry on no intercourse with men, but with the view of turning it to his own advantage. – Georges Louis Leclerc Buffon, *The Cat.*

Thomas Huxley's cat

A long series of cats has reigned over my household for the last forty years or thereabouts. The present occupant of the throne is a large, young, grey Tabby – Oliver by name. Not that he is in any sense a Protector, for I doubt whether he has the heart to kill a mouse. However, I saw him catch and eat the first butterfly of the season, and trust that the germ of courage, thus manifested, may develop with age into efficient mousing.

As to sagacity, I should say that his judgement respecting the warmest place and the softest cushion in a room is infallible, his punctuality at meal times is admirable, and his pertinacity in jumping on people's shoulders till they give him some of the best of what is going, indicates great firmness. – Thomas Huxley (1825–1895).

The secret ways of cats

Everyone is aware that a perfectly comfortable, well-fed cat will occasionally come to his house and settle there, deserting a family by whom it is lamented, and to whom it could, if it chose, find its way back with ease. This conduct is a mystery which may lead us to infer that cats form a great secret society, and that they come and go in pursuance of some policy connected with education, or perhaps with witchcraft. We have known a cat to abandon his home for years. Once in six months he would return, and look about him with an air of some contempt. 'Such,' he seemed to say, 'were my humble beginnings.' – Andrew Lang.

The well-bred individualist

There is, indeed, no single quality of the cat that man could not emulate to his advantage. He is clean, the cleanest, indeed, of all animals . . . He is silent, entirely self-reliant, beautiful, and graceful. He makes his appearance and his life as exquisite as circumstances will permit. He is modest, he is urbane, he is dignified. A well-bred cat never argues. He goes about doing what he likes in a well-bred, superior manner. If he is interrupted he will look at you in mild surprise or silent reproach but he will return to his desire. If he is prevented, he will wait for a more favourable occasion. But like all well-bred individualists, the cat seldom interferes with other people's rights. His intelligence keeps him from doing many of the fool things that complicate life. Cats never write operas and they never attend them. They never sign papers, or pay taxes, or vote for president. An injunction will have no power whatever over a cat. A cat, of course, would not only refuse to obey any amendment whatever to any constitution, he would refuse to obey the constitution itself. – Carl Van Vechten (1880–1964), *The Tiger in the House.*

7
THE PEDIGREE CAT

Cats are delightful creatures, whether pedigree or pet, and all have different personalities, very much like humans. The majority, whether pedigree or mongrel, live as pets, but most people tend to refer to the mongrels as moggies, or pet cats, to distinguish them from those with pedigrees.

Mongrels are the result of mixed matings between unknown parents, and can be any colour or mixtures of colours and coat patterns. The pedigree cats, the aristocrats of the cat world, are those whose parentage has been known and recorded for many generations. Their colourings and coat patterns conform to certain set standards, and they have registered pedigrees, or birth certificates, giving the names of their parents, grandparents, great grandparents and great great grandparents, all of whom were usually of similar appearance.

The domestic cat's origin is very much conjecture, but it is generally assumed cats may have originated more than three thousand years ago in Egypt, possibly from the wild Kaffir cats which were tamed and used for hunting. In Egypt cats guarded harvested corn from the ravages of rats and mice, were worshipped in the temples and were much loved. On the death of a cat, the whole family shaved off their eyebrows as a sign of mourning, and the cat's body was embalmed and placed in an exotic mummy case.

The early Romans are usually given the credit for introducing cats into Britain. They were much prized, being considered very valuable, and quite distinct from the resident wild cat which was hunted for its fur. By the Middle Ages, however, cats fell into disfavour when tales of witchcraft became rife and cats, particularly black ones, were thought to be familiars of the Devil, many being destroyed along with their so-called witch owners. By the Victorian period, they had returned to favour once again and were often portrayed by famous owners, such as writers and artists, in poems, stories and paintings. Most homes seemed to have a cat, either as a pet, or to keep away vermin. What must be looked on as the beginning of the vast trade in cat-food began then, with the cat-meat man going around the streets selling a halfpenny's worth of meat at many houses, and often followed by hungry, mewing cats. Cat-meat men were so much appreciated that in 1901 a big Christmas dinner was held for them, which was even attended by the Duchess of Bedford who gave them each a tin of tobacco.

Sacred and profane cats
Cats have been connected with religion from ancient times, in Egypt, Babylon, Burma, Siam and Japan. The true cat goddess, Bast, signified to the Egyptians the fruitful powers of the sun, '. . . the Soul of Osiris', and was worshipped as such, with an annual festival at the city of Bubastis. The cat was sometimes thought to be entrusted with the souls of the dead, leading them to Paradise. There was, however, confusion between Bast and the lion-headed goddess Sekhmet, who symbolised the sun's destructive powers, so the nature of the cat was seen to be ambivalent. Perhaps because of its sinuous shape, its changing eyes and its tendency towards independence and the fact that in Hebrew and early Christian beliefs it was regarded as a part of devil or idol worship, the cat became man's enemy instead of his friend. – Margaret Ellis.

*Penny a Longhaired Silver Tabby,
very much in a class of her own*

*Polo, a beautiful and affectionate
male Abyssinian*

In 1871 Mr Harrison Weir had the idea of organising a cat show that would bring to everybody's notice '. . . the beauty and attractiveness of the cat'. This was held in the Crystal Palace in London and attracted so much attention that at times it was difficult even to see a cat because of the crowds. Nobody could have foreseen that this was the beginning of the Cat Fancy throughout the world today. More shows followed, not only in Britain, but also in America and, eventually, in other parts of the world. This, in turn, increased the interest in 'fancy' cats and it began to be realised that, by planned breeding, it could be possible to produce cats with coat patterns and colourings to order.

Over the years resident domestic cats had their numbers increased by unusual cats brought to this country by sailors and other travellers from all over the world. (There were, of course, no quarantine restrictions until comparatively recently.) These interbred with the resident cats and introduced new colourings and coat lengths.

Cats with long fur had been seen in Europe as early as the end of the sixteenth century. These were the Angoras from Turkey, soon to be followed by other longhairs from Persia. At the first cat shows in the 1870s, the majority of cats were shorthaired, but, as the longhairs became increasingly popular, they began to take over the shows. This trend continued for some years until the arrival of the Siamese from Siam (now Thailand), and soon these were almost status symbols. However, as more was learned about breeding, many more longhairs, with various coat colours, appeared and they came into their own once again. In comparatively recent times the Burmese have been introduced from America, and they are now taking over in the shorthairs and appearing at the shows in greater numbers than the Siamese. It is almost incredible to realise that, in the short period of a little over a century, by planned matings, over eighty varieties of colour variations and coat lengths have been produced, all of which may now be seen at shows.

Cats are registered according to their type and coat length, colours and patterns. They are divided more or less into four sections: the Longhairs; the British Shorthairs; Foreign Short-hairs (including Burmese); and the Siamese. All have their set standards for which 100 points are allocated and apportioned between the various characteristics required.

The Longhairs

These are often popularly referred to as Persians, and should have long, flowing fur, with a ruff or frill framing the face, and short full tails. The heads are broad and round with small tufted ears, short broad noses and big round eyes which vary in colour according to the variety. The bodies are cobby, on short sturdy legs. The varieties with fur the same colour all over are known as 'selfs'. These include the Blues, with fur any shade of blue and eyes of deep orange or copper; the Blacks, with raven-black

The ancient Egyptian cat, post 600bc, possibly the ancestor of our own

81

Gadger, a female Red Abyssinian, a companionable pet

coats and eyes of orange or copper; the Whites, with pure white fur and eyes of deep blue, orange or copper, or, in the Odd-eyed variety, one eye deep blue and the other orange; the Creams, with pale cream fur and deep copper eyes, and, lastly, the Red Selfs, with fur a deep rich red and deep copper eyes. Very striking varieties are the Smokes, which are known as the cats of contrasts, with white undercoats and varying-coloured tippings. There are several possible colourings, but the most popular are Black, the Blues, the Red and the Cream. An unusual feature of the Smokes is that from a distance the coats appear to be self-coloured, and only as the animal moves does the white undercoat appear.

The Tabbies are striking; the Silver having a ground colour of silver with dense black markings and the eyes green or hazel; the Red, with deep red coat, deep rich red markings and eyes deep orange or copper, and the Brown, with a rich copper-brown coat, dense black markings and orange or copper eyes. It is also possible to have a Blue Tabby, but they are comparatively rare.

The markings on the Tabbies, whether long- or shorthaired, should conform to a very definite pattern. The forehead should be marked with a letter 'M', with pencillings on the cheeks and lines running over the top of the head to the shoulders, where the markings resemble a butterfly, whilst there should be oyster-shape markings on the flanks. The legs and tail should be ringed.

There are the female-only varieties, with any males born invariably proving to be sterile. The female-only include the Tortoiseshells, with their distinctive patched coat in three colours, black, red and cream; the Tortoiseshell and White, having the same three colours but with the addition of white, and the Blue-Creams, with the fur blue and cream softly intermingled, and eye colour of deep copper or orange.

There are longhairs with two-coloured coats, known as Bi-Colours. They may be black, blue, chocolate, lilac, red and cream, all with the addition of white. The colour should be quite distinct from the white. The type is as for other longhairs.

Considered to be one of the most striking pedigree cats is the Chinchilla, with pure white coat, delicately tipped with black on the head, ears, sides, back and tail, giving a silvery appearance to the fur. The eyes differ from many other longhairs in that they are a striking emerald or blue-green colour. The Chinchilla is usually a somewhat lighter-bodied cat than many longhairs, but is in no way delicate.

A very popular variety is the Colourpoint (known in America as the Himalayan). This is a manmade variety, produced about thirty years ago through the efforts of a well-known breeder. He was in a position, and had the knowledge, to reproduce a cat to order, which had long fur, but the coat pattern of the Siamese, that is a pale body colour with darker mask, legs and tail, known as 'points'. Producing a new variety takes years, as various matings have to be tried and many kittens in such a breeding programme have to be given away as pets until, eventually, some are produced with the coat and eye-colouring required. This is a long and costly procedure, as there have to be at least four generations of pure breeding, that is all the kittens born in each generation are the same in appearance as the parents, before they are recognised by the Governing Council of the Cat Fancy, and their standard approved.

A difficult factor in breeding for Colourpoints was that the eyes had to be brilliant blue and not the orange or copper seen in many other longhairs. This was accomplished by using Siamese, but there was also the problem of getting the long fur required. However, this was eventually achieved, and today the Colourpoints are one of the most popular of the longhairs, with a range of point colour including seal, blue, chocolate, lilac, red and others. As an offshoot from the original breeding programme, it was realised that it was also possible to produce cats with self-coloured coats of chocolate, lilac and also lilac-cream and chocolate-tortie.

Another attractive variety, introduced into Britain from France some years ago, is the Birman. The heads are round, but not quite as broad as most other longhairs, the ears are

Max, the original blue-eyed ball of Persian fluff

Cats on Inn Signs
There are three pubs in the country called 'The Cat and Custard Pot' – perhaps from the habit of giving the cat the custard bowl to lick after use. Several other signs featuring cats started off as heraldic beasts, for example 'The Rampant Cat' at Burford, which has a distinctly leonine look about it. In the village of Croyden in Cambridgeshire, 'The Downing Arms' has an heraldic lion on the sign, but for some reason is known to everyone as 'The Scratching Cat'. Another unusual inn name is 'The Cat i'th' Well', which has two signs, one showing the cat falling into the well, and the other the cat climbing out. This inn is in the village of Wainstalls near Halifax, and the resident cat is well known for demanding crisps from customers, who ignore him at their peril!

'The Cat Inn' at West Hoathly in Sussex has an attractive sign depicting a crouching tabby. The origin of the name is uncertain, but is thought to have a
(*continued opposite*)

medium-sized, rather than small, the chin slightly tapering and the eyes almost round and bright blue. They have a similar coat pattern to the Colourpoints, but the long and silky fur is pale beige with seal points, or bluish-white with blue points. An unusual and distinguishing feature is the white marking on the paws, the front paws having little white gloves, and the back ones having white markings which cover the front of the paw and taper to a point at the rear. The bushy tails are of medium length. Other point colours are possible and are being produced. The Birmans are now appearing at shows in ever-increasing numbers.

Discovered in Turkey over thirty years ago, and later introduced into Britain, the Turkish Van cats are still a comparatively rare variety. The type is similar to that of the original Angoras, with short, wedge-shaped heads, large ears, longish noses and light amber eyes. The bodies are long, and the legs of medium length. The fur is chalk-white, not so luxurious as many other longhairs, but easy to groom. The heads have auburn markings on the faces and the tails are auburn in colour, with faint rings. When they first came to Britain they were known as the swimming cats, as, in Turkey, they were known to enjoy swimming in streams and warm pools.

Cameos, a new and only recently recognised variety produced by cross-breeding, have tipped coats, and there is a red series and a cream series. The type is as for other longhairs. In the Reds the undercoats are white, with the tips shading to red or tortoiseshell, whilst those with the fur lightly dusted with rose pink are known as Shells. There is a further variety where the coats are evenly shaded with red, giving the appearance of a red mantle, and these are known as Shaded. There are also the Red Smokes. The Cream Cameos have similar tippings, but the coats are dusted with cream instead of red. In the red series there is a female-only variety known as the Tortie Cameo, with the tipping being black, red and cream patches, whilst the cream series also has a female-only variety, the Blue-Cream Cameo, with the blue and cream tipping being softly intermingled. All the varieties have broad heads, snub noses, large, round, deep-orange or copper eyes, cobby bodies and short bushy tails.

There are one or two varieties which have not yet achieved championship status, such as the Golden Persian, with an undercoat of apricot colour deepening to gold, and the fur tipped with seal brown or black, giving the coat a golden appearance. The big round eyes are green or blue-green. There is also a Pewter, with a white coat, evenly shaded with black, like a mantle, and orange or copper eyes. In both cases the type is as for other longhairs.

The British Shorthairs
These cats are much liked, with their broad heads, big round eyes and noses which are broad, but not as snub as those of the longhairs. They are very sturdy, with strong, short legs. The

coats are short and dense and the tails thick and of medium length. The colours are similar to those of the longhairs, with self-colours of White (with three eye colours), Black, Cream and Blue. The Tabbies come in Silver, Red and Brown, with the classic pattern of markings similar to those of the longhairs, but, because of the short fur, the markings are more striking. It is possible to have a Mackerel Tabby, so called because the markings are said to resemble those of the fish. There are also Spotted Tabbies, the markings on the head being the same as those for the classic Tabbies, but with the body and legs having distinct spotting, standing out from the body colour. The tail should have narrow rings or spots.

The British cats are known for their charming personalities and make delightful pets. At the moment the British Blue is the most popular, with kittens being much in demand. The coats should be light to medium blue, but should be the same colour all over, and the eyes may be copper, orange or deep gold. The Britishers are very easy to groom, with hard hand stroking helping to remove any loose hairs. A soft brush can be used sometimes, but a wide-toothed comb is not recommended as it will open the fur and leave track marks.

As in the longhairs, there is the female-only Blue Cream, with the coat a mixture of blue and cream, evenly intermingled. It is very difficult to breed without some patching which is regarded as a fault. There are also the female Tortoiseshells and the Tortoiseshell and Whites, with coats of black, rich red and pale red intermingled for the former, and patches of black, red and white for the latter. The Tortie and White coats, in particular, are very striking, with the patches appearing very bright in the short fur. The kittens are much sought after, but, as they are not easily bred to order, few are available at any one time.

There are Bi-Colours, with coats of any self-colour with white patching, and the Smokes, their silver undercoats tipped with any of the accepted British colours, so that, from a distance, and until they walk, they appear to be self-coloured cats. One of the newest varieties is the British Tipped, similar to the Chinchilla, but with short dense fur and with the pure white undercoat tipped with any of the British self-colours, giving a sparkling effect.

One shorthair differs from all the others and that is the Manx, said to have originated in the Isle of Man. Very few are seen at shows these days, although they do have many admirers. These cats should be completely tail-less, with hollows at the end of the backbones where, in other cats, the tails would begin. (It is also possible to have a Stumpy, with just a few inches of tail.) The Manx coat should be double, with a thick undercoat and slightly longer top coat. Any colour or coat pattern is allowed. The heads are largish and round with prominent cheeks, the noses of medium length, straight and broad and the ears tallish. The eyes are large and round and of a colour in keeping with the fur colour. The sturdy bodies should have rounded rumps and

connection with the cat o' nine tails, and the inn was the haunt of smugglers in the 16th century. Another mystery name is 'The Mad Cat' at Pidley in Cambridgeshire, which has had several signs in the past, including one with eyes that lit up in the dark – perhaps too much of a hazard for motorists!

A very attractive sign is that of 'The Burmese Cat' in Melton Mowbray. It has an ornate surround, suggesting a temple, and the painting of the cat is very true to life; there's also an attractive stained glass window in the entrance showing a pagoda and three temple cats. The 'Black Cat' at Lye Green in Buckinghamshire was originally called 'The White Horse', but one of the landlords was the owner of a huge black cat and he persuaded the brewery to change the name.

There are three 'Squinting Cats', in Harrogate, Leeds and New Clipstone. The last named has an amusing sign of a cat lapping some spilt beer, which appears to be the cause of the squint, although, again, the origin of the name is obscure.

Research into inn signs featuring cats has revealed a great many which have interesting origins, but even more whose beginnings are extremely obscure and which would merit further research of your own, should there be one in your area.

Siamese like Tobi usually have plenty of character: adventurous, cuddly, very much part of the family – and seldom quiet

the back legs should be slightly longer than the front ones. This, and the shortish bodies, gives them their characteristic 'rabbit' gait, more like a hop than a walk. They are difficult to breed, as even if two Manx cats are mated, they may not produce Manx, but possibly some kittens with tails, some with stumps and, maybe, a Manx.

Foreign Shorthairs

A number of groups of pedigree cats with short coats are referred to collectively as 'Foreign', as there are certain similarities in that the heads are wedge-shaped, the bodies longish, the legs long and relatively slim, and the tails long, or fairly long and tapering. The various groups do differ, usually in coat colouring, but some differ also in outline.

The Russian Blues are charming, quiet cats which have short, soft, seal-like fur, medium to dark blue in colour, but the same all over. They have slender bodies, short wedge heads, with flat skulls and large pointed ears, the skin of which is almost transparent. Their striking eyes, almond in shape, are vivid green. The legs are long with small, dainty, oval feet. It is known that, many years ago, similar cats came to Britain on ships that traded between Archangel, in present-day USSR, and Britain and these were known as Archangel cats. The Russians of today cannot claim such ancestry; the variety died out long ago and today's Russians have been produced by selective breeding over the years. Their elegant appearance and calm dispositions have made them very popular as pets. A White Russian is now being bred in Britain.

Abyssinians have moderate wedge-shaped heads, with comparatively large pointed ears, often tufted. Their large beautiful eyes may be amber, hazel or green. The bodies are of medium length, with longish tapering tails. The coats are unique, being short and fine with double or treble ticking, each hair having two or three bands of colour. There are now several varieties, but the original was registered in Britain in 1882 and appeared at the Crystal Palace shows in 1884. They were said to have been brought to Britain originally by a British lady, but experts now say that the Abyssinians known today are the result of careful breeding. The strange thing is that they resemble very closely the cats seen in mural paintings and statues in Ancient Egypt. The original variety is now known as 'Usual', but they have had various names, including 'Bunny Cat', because the fur resembles that of rabbits. The Usual should have a body colour of a rich golden-brown, ticked with black, and with the base hair rich apricot or deep orange. One, previously known as 'Red', but now referred to as Sorrel, is the variety with a body colour of rich copper red, ticked with bands of chocolate and with base hair of deep apricot. The type is as for the Usual. It is possible to have a Blue Abyssinian, with blue-grey fur, ticked with deeper steel blue, and the base hair pale cream or oatmeal. There is also a Silver, with the coat clear silver, ticked with black, with base hair

Grey and white and brown and white tabbies

pale cream. Other varieties are possible, including the Sorrel/ Silver and Blue/Silver, their fur being mixtures of the two colours. The Abyssinians are very friendly cats and highly intelligent. They love to be admired, dislike close confinement and are attractive house pets and show cats. They are not prolific breeders, and a kitten may have to be booked well in advance as there is quite a demand for them.

Occasionally, over the years, an Abyssinian would produce a litter and in it would be a kitten with longish fur. Little notice was taken of these at first, although breeders thought them very attractive. Then a breeding programme came into being and the Somalis, as they are now known, now have many admirers and their own classes at shows. Apart from the medium fur length, the characteristics required in the standard are the same as for the Abyssinians. The coat should have at least three bands of ticking and the tail be a full brush, very thick where it joins the body and slightly tapering. The colour is as for the Usual and the Sorrel.

The Havana is a manmade variety, produced in the first place from matings with Siamese. It was first known as Chestnut Brown Foreign, but, by general approval, the name was changed to Havana in 1970, as it was said that the colour was like that of Havana cigars. The type is that of the Siamese, with a long body on slim legs with small oval paws, the head long and wedge-shaped, the nose straight, the oriental-shaped eyes of vivid

87

green and the tail long and tapering. The short fine-texture fur is a rich chestnut brown, and the kittens, even when first born, are the same colour. Gentle cats, they love affection and are home-loving.

Over the years, by similar breeding involving Siamese, other self-colours have been produced. These include the Lilacs, with distinctive frosty-grey fur, having a pinkish tone, and the type the same as for the Havana, and the Foreign White, with a striking, pure white, short and silky coat, brilliant blue almond-shaped eyes and a type as for the Siamese. There are also the Foreign Black, with jet black fur and green eyes, the Foreign Blue, with light to medium blue coat and green eyes, together with Red and Cream. Again by cross-matings involving Siamese, a number of cats have evolved with wonderful coat patterns and markings, all having the distinct Siamese type and being known as Orientals. They include the Oriental Spotted Tabbies, in various colours, Oriental Classic Tabbies, Oriental Tortoise-shell, and many others. The choice is numerous.

The Korats are attractive self-coloured cats which came to Britain via America, having been imported to that country from Thailand. The coat is short and lies close to the body, with a definite silver sheen on the blue. The large, luminous eyes are brilliant green in colour and are set in a heart-shaped head. The ears are large with rounded tips, the body of medium size, and the tail of medium length with a rounded tip.

The Cornish and Devon Rex varieties differ from all other cats in that they have short wavy and curly coats. In the 1950s a cat with wavy fur appeared on a farm in Cornwall. He was mated to his mother and kittens with similar fur were born. A carefully planned breeding programme was carried out, involving the mating of the kittens from Cornwall to other pedigree breeds. Eventually it was found possible to produce curly-coated kittens to order and they were recognised and became known as Cornish Rex. The heads are medium-wedge with flat skulls, large ears, straight noses and oval-shaped eyes. The slender bodies are long and straight, the tails long and tapering and covered with curly fur. The coat is short and plushy, very soft and without guard hairs. All colours are allowed, including the Siamese pattern.

In Devon, a few years later, a similar kitten was found and was presumed to be related to the Cornish Rex. However, after various matings were tried, it was realised that it was a different variety. The head shape is different, being wide-cheeked with a short muzzle and a definite stop to the nose. The large low-set ears give the cat a 'pixie' look. The fur is very short and fine and is usually wavy rather than curly. The tail is covered with short fur. All colours and coat patterns are recognised. The Rex have outgoing personalities. They can be very demanding, constantly seeking attention from their owners. It has been found that whereas some people are allergic to cat fur, they may be able to live happily with a Rex, but this is not always the case, and, if

88

possible, tests should be carried out before purchasing a kitten.

Burmese cats were introduced into Britain in the 1950s and have now become one of the most popular shorthaired varieties. The original Burmese had rich warm seal-brown fur and these are still seen in the greatest numbers at shows. As a result of careful matings and further imports from America over the years, there are now Burmese with ten different coat colours. All varieties should have similar type, not British or Siamese. Their heads should have slightly rounded tops with wide cheek bones, and be medium wedge-shape, the slightly rounded, tipped ears should be medium in size, never too large, and have a slightly forward tilt. The noses have a definite break. The wide-apart large eyes may be any shade of yellow, from chartreuse to amber. Green eyes are a bad fault. The bodies are of medium size, with strong chests, and the legs should be slender with the back pair slightly longer than the front. The tails are straight and of medium length with rounded tips. The short fine fur should be satin-like in texture, giving the glossy sheen look which is characteristic of the Burmese. In all colours the underparts are lighter than the backs.

The colours now available are Brown, with a rich warm seal-brown coat; Blue, with a soft silver-grey coat; Chocolate, having a warm milk chocolate coat; Lilac, with fur a delicate dove-grey with a slight pinkish tinge; Red, with coat a light tangerine colour, and possibly slight tabby markings on the face; Cream, with the coat a rich cream, and again possibly with slight tabby markings on the face. There are also the Brown, Blue, Chocolate and Lilac Torties, with varying mixtures of colours, but all requiring to be of good Burmese type.

The Burmese are delightful friendly cats, very intelligent and great extroverts. They are full of energy and seem able to open any doors and cupboards, even fridges, with ease. They make elegant house pets and at shows the kittens attract attention with their amusing antics. There is a Burmese Cat Club which has a very large membership, with representatives in many parts of Britain. They are always ready to help and advise would-be owners. A large show is held annually, usually in June, where anyone particularly interested in the Burmese may visit and see the various coat colours for themselves.

Siamese

It is difficult to trace the origin of the Siamese. The first known in Britain were shown at the Crystal Palace show in 1871, but similar cats were known in Thailand (then Siam) centuries before. P. S. Pallas, a noted naturalist and explorer, described in his writings several cats that he had seen in Russia in 1793. He said that these cats had light-brown body colour with dark points. In 1884 a pair arrived in Britain, sent by the then Consul General as a present for his sister. Apparently they came from the Royal Palace in Siam. They were bred from and exhibited with their progeny at the show in 1885, but died very shortly

Kim, a beautiful Burmese

afterwards, probably from infection which was rife at shows in those days. Other imports followed and always there were stories that they had been given by the King of Siam, or that they came from other royal palaces and temples. As their numbers increased, their exotic appearance, brilliant blue eyes, and the air of mystery surrounding them, all helped to make them top favourites in the cat world in a very short time.

Siamese make wonderful pets, being very intelligent, loving companionship and disliking being left on their own. They are extremely lively and very talkative and can be quite noisy at times, especially a queen when calling. They like toys to play with and readily take to walking on leads. If the owner is to be out a great deal it is better to have two kittens to keep one another company. The kittens are white when born, with no signs of points for a week or more.

They are medium-build cats with long svelte bodies on fine legs with dainty paws and with the tails long and tapering. The long heads, on elegant necks, are wedge-shaped and the ears large and wide at the base. Many of the earlier Siamese had squints in the eyes and kinks in the tail and there were even legends to account for what are now regarded as bad faults, although for some years many cat lovers thought they were essential in a typical Siamese. The short fine fur should be glossy and close lying, with the points, ie the mask, ears, feet and tail being in a colour clearly distinct from the body fur.

Through various breeding programmes there are now a number of recognised varieties, but the original Sealpoint remains the most popular, with the cream body colour shading to pale fawn on the back and the points a dense seal brown. The oriental-shaped eyes should slant slightly towards the nose and be a clear, brilliant, deep blue in colour. Bluepoints should have a glacial white body colour, shading into blue on the back, with light blue points and bright, vivid-blue eyes. Chocolate points have ivory body colour and milk-chocolate points and, again, bright, vivid-blue eyes. The body colour of the Lilacpoint is off-white (magnolia), the points pinkish grey, and there are the same vivid-blue eyes. Redpoints have a white body colour, shading to apricot, with bright reddish-gold points, whilst the Creampoint has a white body coat, shading to pale cream and points of a paler cream; both have the usual intense blue eyes. Tabbypoints are recognised in a number of different colours. The body colour should be pale, with contrasting points, and well-defined stripes, and the tail should be ringed. Eyes should be clear blue.

The Balinese are very attractive cats with the same coat pattern as Siamese, from which they have been produced, but with fur of medium length. The characteristics are the same as for the Siamese but the fur is longer, the ears may be tufted and the tail plume-like. The body colouring should be pale, with the clearly defined points in keeping with the various colour-point varieties recognised for the Siamese.

90

There are many cat clubs in existence, including breed clubs for most varieties such as the Siamese, Blue Persian and so on, and many of these clubs run shows for their own particular breed. There are also all-breed clubs, such as the National, the Midland and the Southern, along with others for members who are interested in a number of varieties, or just one or two. These clubs' shows are open to all. The GCCF issue an annual list of clubs (price £1) and anyone interested in joining a club should write to them for a copy. All hold annual meetings and many run shows, whilst some hold teach-ins, and most will help and advise members on any catty problems.

Aga Khan the Siamese is demonstrating the renowned vocal equipment of his breed

THE PADDINGTON CAT

One frosty morning in 1970, an orphaned six-week-old kitten wandered into Paddington station. Unlike Paddington Bear, he didn't have a label attached to him saying 'Please look after me'; nevertheless, he was destined to be famous.

June Watson, the manager of the ladies' loo, found him and took him to work with her – and there he lived for the rest of his life. It didn't take long for the kitten to win the hearts of all the toilet attendants. 'It certainly wouldn't be the same here without him', they said.

Right from the beginning, the tom – named Tiddles – made it quite clear that his diet was not that of a common street cat. He was provided with his own fridge, well stocked with steak, liver, rabbit and chicken, and shortly before his death he won a prize for being the biggest feline in London.

He became an important feature on Paddington station, and received visitors and fan mail from all over the world, as well as appearing frequently in the papers. His luxurious basket was decorated in state for special occasions such as royal weddings and his own birthday. Tiddles was hardly a working cat. A British Rail spokesman said, 'I don't think he could catch a mouse if he tried'. Yet he did go for a stroll down the platform each morning, and loved wandering among the pipes in the station cellar. In spite of his enormous girth, he never got stuck, but he could not measure the size of the gaps he wanted to pass through with his whiskers the way other cats can.

He died in 1983 at the age of thirteen, a fabulous 32lb in weight, and a nose-to-tail length of almost 30in. Going to the toilet at Paddington will never be the same again.

The famous Paddington cat

8
CATS OF CHARACTER

Every passionate cat lover has been privileged to know, at some time in their life, at least one characterful cat. A cat whose personality and behaviour bore the unique stamp of personal individuality, a cat who can never be forgotten. This chapter looks at just a few of these cats, with their stories told by the owners themselves.

Jane on Top
I called her Jane because her mother's name was Emma and I am a great admirer of Jane Austen. My Jane is a Siamese cat who, at just over a year old, climbed – one way or another – thirteen Scottish peaks (eleven Munros) and three Welsh ones. It started by accident.

My previous Siamese, Kismet, was not a great walker and we once took five hours to meander to and from Beinn na Seilg in Ardnamurchan, investigating every blade of grass and every sprig of heather. He also climbed one peak of Sgurr a'Chaorachain in Applecross – but we started from the summit of Bealach na Ba and it was only twenty minutes or so to the cairn at 2,539 ft. We once had a wet afternoon on the marble ridge of An Teallach. So, when Jane came into my life, after Kismet's death at fourteen plus, I was not expecting to have her company often on the hills. Kismet toured Scotland dozens of times but, when I was off walking, he spent a lazy day in the hotel. I expected the same with Jane.

When she was six months old I had a day alone on the Strathfarrar hills and decided to follow it with an off-day with Jane. I wanted a place where I could safely let her off the lead but where she could not easily get hidden in undergrowth. We drove to Torridon and took her along the stalker's path up Beinn Eighe, the one that leads to the Coire an Laoigh with its red spur, starting at a small forestry clump where there used to be the remains of a cottage. I thought I should be able to keep an eye on her on this bare hillside and yet give her a good free run. Till we got well away from the road I kept her on the lead. When I decided to let her off she was thrilled. She is a compulsive purrer and she never stopped purring all that day. She went on and on, following me up the zigzags of the track and, before I was conscious of any great passing of time, there we were in the corrie at the end of the path. The peak of Spidean Coire nan Clach was not so far away so on we went. There is a rather

93

This red and white tabby is game for anything. It is instinctive to keep claws sharp just in case, but there seems little warlike intent here

messy bit, very steep, loose earth mixed with gravel and scree, up which you crawl in order to reach the final quartz slope. On this amorphous section Jane went in front and was always just ahead, waiting for me and purring. She did not like the final scree path to the trig point – it was rough and loose and we came into the wind. We paused for the briefest of moments at the trig point and then began the descent.

I decided to look at the route over the ridge of the red spur itself, rocky and narrow. It was meant only to be a look but we went on and on, the apparent difficulties melting away. Jane was much better on the rocks than I was and when in doubt she simply walked onto my shoulder and I had her loud purr in my ear. It took us three hours to get up and two to descend to the car on the Torridon road and we had both thoroughly enjoyed every bit of it.

Strangely enough, she has never walked so much on a mountain since! She is very particular about the weather; she dislikes cold, wind and rain. If we come into conditions she dislikes, she burrows into my rucksack where, wrapped in a warm pullover, she sleeps her way over the summits. She covers many miles on my shoulder or lying on top of my rucksack. Hot weather does not appeal either – she lies on the track and pants. Whenever we stop she climbs immediately into my lap and curls up, purring. I used to take fresh meat or cat food for her, in a polythene container, but she spurned this on the hills. Instead, I found that a quantity of dried cat-food, which she eats only sparingly in

Opposite Poised for take-off

94

Jessica, another strong personality with definite ideas of her own and a great sense of fun

normal life, was just what she wanted when in the open air.

I realised very quickly that I had taken great risks with her on Beinn Eighe. She was off the lead and I was close to her all the time but I felt that a bird of prey could easily have carried her off if she had been any distance from me. I then acquired a harness for her; to the harness is attached a strong lead and, to the lead, two very long bootlaces. Thus, she is on a 12ft lead, which gives her freedom but allows me control.

I think the Beinn Eighe expedition was the success it was for three reasons: first, it was a novelty for her; second, the weather was to her taste and third, she was free, unattached to lead or harness.

So far her summits were these: in Wales, Moel Siabod, Y Garn and Glyder-fawr. We came down by the Gribin ridge and there is one short, sharp wall where both hands and feet are necessary. Jane insisted in getting on my knee – if anyone has tried to climb down a little rock pitch with a Siamese kitten on his knee he will realise my difficulties! The harness was very useful here; I descended to a safe position and swung her ladyship down to a safe ledge, climbed down to her and she climbed onto me. In Scotland, her first and finest expedition – Spidean Coire nan Clach, one of the 3,000ft peaks on the gigantic Beinn Eighe ridge – was the only one she did on her own little paws. Since then she has insisted on riding on my shoulder or in my ruck-sack, and the insistence of a Siamese means complete despotism. I was the serf. We saw many interesting things: an eagle rising from the carcase of a fawn whose liver it was pecking, several rivers forded and she sat like an image on my shoulder showing no fear; thunder and lightning and rain on Beinn Attow, when she was the only member of the party who arrived back dry, the rest of us were soaked to the skin and mired from head to foot.

She has now been up – on my shoulder or in my rucksack – over forty Munros plus at least six other peaks. We are both getting older – I cannot carry her extra weight of seven pounds, solid ones at that – and Jane is fifteen years old and spends most of her time asleep. But I still remember, as I'm sure she does, the days when an expedition was afoot and she was greatly excited. I think she preferred to be taken along because she is extremely affectionate and enjoyed my companionship, as I did – and do – hers. She was intensely interested by birds, sheep and deer, and seemed to prefer difficult ground, particularly rocks that offered small caves for exploration and temporary settlement. She was always good at crags: what she could not climb she simply jumped up. She has spent several pleasant days at Gruinard Bay where strange and exciting smells on the shore and leapable cliffs provide endless activity.

Jane is always a great personal responsibility on the hills. She requires attention and watchfulness; she is vulnerable; she is very precious in her likes and dislikes of weather and terrain. I take her very rarely now, particularly if I think the weather

96

*Two totally unique individuals,
Toby (top) and Rubik*

conditions or the length of the expedition (for me) are unsuitable. But, I am sure, when the rucksack next comes out, that there will be a small, purring, furry body pushing against it and insisting that she, too, goes to explore the heights.

My Cat Richard

Richard is a character, there are no two ways about that. His appearance is impressive and his size and dense glossy black coat are frequently remarked upon by visitors. His round black face, broad white shirtfront and large white gloves suggest that he has just stepped out of the Black and White Minstrels. It is his eyes, however, which are the most remarkable feature of his appearance, sea-green and round as pennies. An intense interest in life keeps the pupils wide and black so that he usually looks startled and scandalised.

Richard is a coward, a glutton and a thief. He is also quite the most intelligent cat I have ever known and among the most lovable. His sense of humour is marked and verges on the boisterous; he loves to lurk behind doors so as to pounce on any cat coming through. As a result, my elderly Nollie has, more often than not, to be carried into and out of the house. He lies on his back under the divan and walks upside down, his eyes rolling comically. 'Doing an Arthur' appeals to him and he will abandon his dinner plate in order to scoop what's left in the tin. Milk, too, is often investigated and when it is poured into a pan for heating I have to keep it covered with one hand or the lightning paw will flash into it! Milk bottles, also, must be guarded against the

A red tabby shorthair befriending a duckling. Again, introduce your cat early to other household and garden pets, and they will almost certainly be respected – even the goldfish

investigating tongue. Until I put the ash bucket into a cupboard the kitchen floor was continually strewn with fragments of fish bone, looking like filigree, so exquisitely had they been divested of flesh; Richard, of course.

His intelligence is demonstrated by his ingenuity, his capacity for getting his own way and for learning by experience. It took no teaching for him to understand the cat door, only a little observation. Other doors, he knows, open with handles and he does his best to turn them. The front door is a different proposition; Richard knows that even he cannot manipulate that so he rattles the doorchain and knocks on the door to attract atten-

In spite of the myths, many cats and dogs get along remarkably well – provided the cat is on top. The cat usually is on top

99

tion. He knows what the command 'Get back!' means, and he will – quite frequently – obey it, but not stay back, oh dear, no.

His gift for leadership shows itself in the way he has demoralised my formerly well-behaved cats. They know they will be fed, each in his own appointed corner, but Richard, who knows from what sad experience, is never sure. He accompanies me on every visit to the kitchen and climbs all over the dresser, the draining board and even the cooker when food is being served. Alas, the other cats now try to do the same.

Sad experience may also account for his very brief bursts of temper and for his hostile reaction to a sharp tone or a finger shaken in his face. He is suddenly insecure. There is only one way to deal with this – to enfold him in a big hug, saying 'Oh Richard Boy, I didn't mean it'.

I have another splendid black and white boy, Tiki, and the two keep up a rivalry which is only half serious. They can sleep peaceably for hours in the same room, but sometimes their eyes meet and battle is at once imminent. Richard growls and Tiki yowls. Both cats assume immensely dramatic, even balletic attitudes, and occasionally go from abuse to attack. Scratches and minor wounds are inflicted but honour is satisfied.

Richard, as I said, is lovable; he is also loving. He follows me about the garden, conversing freely by means of a waving tail. Friends have his escort along the road when they leave. He loves to sit on the high back of a chair to be petted, and the petting must be rough. Rubbing the 'wrong' way and gentle slapping appeal to him and he braces himself against them. His massive head stoops and bumps against a friendly cheek. If the petting session is too short he simply reaches out and catches the sleeve of the person turning away – a very odd sensation when unexpected, I can assure you. But the best of his loving is done with his eyes. The black pupil closed to a slit, the lids blink slowly from a face sentimentally inclined to one side. He gives me a long eloquent and affectionate gaze. In the words of the song '. . . he looks on me with a loving eye'.

How, you may ask, did this vivid and many-sided character come to live in my home? I will tell you. Two young American cat lovers came here on a year's exchange. They felt that to live for a year without a cat was unthinkable so they went to the Cat and Dog Home and asked to be given whichever cat was most likely to be put to sleep. Bright-eyed with anticipation they surveyed the cages in which attractive cats, with pretty gestures, sought to attract their attention. But no, they were led past these to what seemed to be an empty pen. Stooping down they saw at the back a shapeless dark thundercloud, lit by smouldering miserable green eyes. 'This one we have no hope of a home for,' said the attendant, 'he makes no effort and he's been here ten days and nobody has looked at him twice.' Forgetting all the pretty cats, the young Americans took him to their home and their hearts and set about awakening in him the will to live. How well they succeeded! His veterinary needs (and they were many)

Opposite A cat of great intelligence and the ability to learn from experience . . .

101

attended to, Richard's personality unfolded like those Japanese flowers made of wood shavings that one used to float in water. Being a shockingly bad traveller he could not, as intended, be taken to Indiana, and so he came to live with me. It is a source of gratification that he has so readily accepted my home as his own.

Benson . . . A Live Wire

Little did we realise when we chose this tiny grey tabby from a litter at a farm in Gloucestershire that he would soon lose nearly all of his nine lives at once. We already had three cats at home but Benson soon made friends with them whilst my husband, two daughters and I were soon completely capitvated by his loving and mischievous ways.

This story really begins late one evening when Benson was three months old. My husband and I were downstairs enjoying a late supper when we were joined by our two daughters who had been in bed for some time and should have been fast asleep. Rachel, the younger, said that she had been awakened by '. . . a funny crackling noise', which seemed to be coming from under her bed. She had awoken Katherine, my elder daughter, who had also heard the strange noises. Grumbling a little, Mike, my husband, climbed the stairs to investigate. Seconds later I was summoned by an urgent shout. Benson had chewed his way through the flex of Rachel's bedside light and was now lying motionless and apparently lifeless on the bedroom floor. Mike had found Benson with the flex still in his mouth and the 'crackly noise' heard by the girls was the noise of sparks issuing from Benson's poor little mouth. By the time I arrived on the scene, Mike had pulled Benson away from the wire and he was just lying there with his poor eyes glazed and protruding and his tongue hanging from his mouth. In desperation my husband lifted him onto the bed and began to rub his chest gently and then gave him the kiss of life as well as he could. Miraculously, after about thirty seconds, we were rewarded by a little heave of Benson's chest and the sounds of some very laboured breathing.

I rushed to phone the vet and at 11.30 at night the whole family were at the surgery with Benson lying in my arms, wrapped in Rachel's dressing gown. He seemed very poorly and we were told by a sympathetic vet that there was little he could do but sedate him and place him in the hospital for the remainder of the night. The following morning, fearing the worst, we rang the surgery as soon as they were open and were overjoyed to learn that he had not only survived the crisis but was, in fact, quite perky and taking great interest in his strange surroundings. We were warned, however, that his little mouth was so badly burned that it would be quite a while before he would be able to take any food and that he would have to remain hospitalised in the meantime. Two days later, having rung the surgery regularly, I was asked to collect him as soon as possible as he was eating them out of house and surgery!

102

Mischief asleep . . . Suzuki

Now a year old and as mischievous as ever, Benson is fully recovered and holds a special place in all our hearts, not least my husband's, whose first-aid training stood him in such good stead. I'm sure, though, that he never imagined that he would need to use the kiss of life on a little grey kitten.

Requiem for Coleby

He was, perhaps, seven months old – a shorthaired tabby ex-tom, with big intelligent eyes ringed with dark chocolate and three dark chocolate bands across his chest and forelegs in perfect symmetry. He had reddish ears, alert and foxy, and his white parts – a perfect boiled shirt, belly and all four paws – were biologically clean as in those incredible advertisements. His little pads, by contrast, were black. He was feline perfection and he was just out of kittenhood.

The day we met he was in an outdoor cat pen. His people had gone away and he had been fending for himself in the garden. Winter was coming. 'This is Boris', they said, but he knew, and I knew, that that was not his name. I said 'Hello' to him and he smiled politely, sizing me up. I had no thought of having another cat, not yet, not so soon after my beautiful Wesley had gone. But this little cat had his destiny to follow and that destiny was me. A couple of hours later, when I returned to the cat pen, he came to me as though we had always belonged together. Putting a paw

103

on either side of my neck he looked straight out of his green eyes into my green eyes and said 'Where have you been?'

We did the paperwork which made him mine and I signed for him, promising to look after him according to his proper requirements. When this was done he settled across my chest and shoulder like a Garter ribbon, purred with approval and whispered in my ear, 'Let's go home!'

They put him in a stout cardboard box with holes in and secured it firmly, though he and I agreed that he would be perfectly all right in the car. It would take us a good hour to reach home and darkness was falling. We drove away, he in the unwanted confinement of his box, and I gently talking to him in case he should be afraid. He was not afraid; by the first set of traffic-lights he was through the sticky tape and, by the second set, he was out of the box and on my shoulder. There he stayed, all the way home, rocking slightly when we changed speed or direction, watching the lights of cars advancing and retreating and answering me with little purring sounds whenever I spoke to him.

By the end of that hour we were deeply in love, he and I. We reached home and I carried him inside. I would have expected

Pepsi

an exploratory sniff around the house, an establishing of territory, a location of the food-producing parts of the place. Not this cat. He walked in as though he had lived there always, selected a convenient sheepskin and, with scant kneading and purring and settling, slept.

He was a saint among cats. Not only was he beautiful, he was gentle, too, and playful; obedient and house-trained; clean and tidy in person and he loved to be groomed hard with a bristly hairbrush. He scratched neither flesh nor furniture, he stole no food, he slept on no forbidden beds and tripped no unwary feet. He declined the offer of a collar. Collars are for cats and he knew himself to be people. When it came to a name we were undecided. Perhaps a racing driver – he loved to ride in cars. Fangio? Moss? Piquet? Prrrrost? And then it came to us – COLEBY. Coleby is a very special place to us, a holiday place where we were happy and welcome, where the children were safe and where we were private and made love under the stars. There was a waterfall there, and trees, and the people were our kind of people. So the little cat was offered the name and, graciously, he accepted, his foxy ears responding from the first day. He liked being Coleby.

When we left him in the house we could trust him. When we were in he delighted in batting a walnut about on the carpet or wrestling the sheepskin. He loved to lie with his head on my shoulder, but only when I gave him leave, his paws extended, his body reverberating as he purred. He never demanded attention but was always glad to be invited.

He never had the prodigious appetite of an adolescent but ate daintily, either cat-food or people-food, and washed meticulously afterwards. Gradually he began to eat less. One day he ate nothing. He was a patient little cat and he purred still when we stroked him but he was plainly not well. The inner eyelids were partly across his eyes and he got up only to use his tray. We murmured endearments: 'What is it, Coleby?' we would ask. He smiled and purred and accepted a pilchard. The following day he was much better but slept a lot. For a week he ate and drank little but seemed to be recovering. He watched cars from the window, watched birds in the garden, sat on the central heating boiler and played sometimes with one of his toys. 'Poor Coleby-cat,' we murmured, 'What's the matter?'

The vet didn't know either. Coleby still played with a walnut, but his back legs wouldn't keep up with his front legs and he would fall over, looking perplexed, and rest for a moment before trying again. He behaved more and more like an old cat, less and less like a young one. Taking his pills became more of an effort for us all. Sometimes he would forget he was ill and race across the room before falling over.

The vet, unable to diagnose, became increasingly concerned and finally suggested two possibilities. The likelier of the two was leukaemia and the prognosis in either case was grim. We stood communing; the vet, Coleby and I. And then I shook my

head, said goodbye, and signed for him for the second and final time. The alternative, testing for this and that to explain his constant high temperature, his loss of appetite, his partial paralysis, was unthinkable. Like a little consumptive Victorian heroine he was fading gently away and we all knew.

He lived for only months. He lived with us for only weeks. The joy he brought us, and the awful gap he left in our lives, were the true measure of his loving little feline nature. We hope there was a sheepskin and a walnut waiting for him on the other side.

A Publisher's Cat

Having managed others in the office during the day I go home at night to be managed by my cat. I know that if she jumps on my lap or licks my nose in affection or comes for a short walk, it will be because she wants to – that if it is too cold to walk to a neighbouring house her insistence on going by car will be hard to resist.

My family were all against my having a Siamese. 'Siamese are fierce,' they chorused. 'Siamese do untold damage.' 'Siamese have horrible voices.' But I had seen the advertisement in the local paper, and that was that.

I soon discovered about the voice. On the way home from the breeder, Sara, eight inches in length, was silent only as long as I was holding her paw. The moment I took my hand out of the basket to change gear a fearful cacophony echoed around the car. We discovered other things too. They included her readiness to hiss at the largest of dogs, and, if I accidentally frightened her, to 'take me on' – jumping into the air from my lap, hissing into my face, fur on end, tail as wide as her slender body.

The household was organised around Sara. This did not only mean persistently opening and closing doors to enable her to be on the right side. It involved removing all kinds of creatures, living and dead! Baby rabbits under the bed; a squirrel in the sink; a stoat in the children's brick box – the news of which sent two burly Devon farmers down the drive for fear they would be asked to help remove it. Not to mention endless mice and, regrettably, birds.

The arrival of one baby rabbit meant we were in for a litter within the next few days. One pigeon's egg – brought in Sara's mouth and batted around the kitchen floor – heralded the arrival of a nestful of newly born pigeons.

She did not catch dogs; she merely tormented them. She would run up a post, wait until a large black dog passed underneath, then jump on its back and swing from its tail. She did the same to a stray sheep we were trying to drive out of the grounds.

There is also Sara's life in the family: her companionship; her habit of lying upside down on my lap; her confusion when, having been scolded for trying, while the piano was being played, to climb the chimney above a fire burning in the grate, she assumed, ever after, that the sound of the piano was a signal to do just this!

Above all, she takes it for granted that what is ours is hers and what is hers is ours. Telephone calls are as much for her as for the rest of us – as many a caller has been astonished to learn.

Talk of the ferocity of Siamese cats goes on . . . We have heard mothers warning their offspring against fraternisation. Sara used to jump into neighbours' cars and as a result had all kinds of adventures. In maturity she prefers the back ledge of one particular car, where she crouches, making faces at drivers who are following. At home she is increasingly content just to watch. Yet even in old age she occasionally dashes from under the stairs to trip one of us up – and, when she succeeds, actually laughs aloud!

We have shared a lot. And it has been a richer relationship than would have been possible with a dog, whose anxiety to please would have been greater. With Sara, each day brings something new: pleasure; pride; a desire to be together – this combined with female cussedness; broken crockery; being wakened, if we want to sleep late on a Sunday morning, by her patrolling up and down the terrace; her pretending, too, when we are looking for her, that she is not there – not to mention her howling at 3am when shut in a spare bedroom!

ERIC DELDERFIELD'S TRUE STORIES OF CATS

The following are selected from the two volumes of *Eric Delderfield's True Animal Stories*.

A Touching Friendship
Quite remarkable is the story of the beginning, duration and ending of the strange and unusual friendship between a hen and a cat, at the home of Mrs Collier in the village of North Cadbury in Somerset.

There were two cats on the establishment. One had been a permanent member of the household for a long time. The other was a stray that just turned up. He was not accepted by the other cat and at first they quarrelled continually; but then, as animals so often do, they arrived at a compromise acceptable to both. The household pet reigned indoors, and the stray took up his vantage point on a window sill and slept in the conservatory, so that they rarely met.

This was the situation when one fine summer afternoon a hen arrived, and settled down on the window sill that the stray had claimed as his domain, helping herself to a drink of milk from his bowl. She was a fine glossy Rhode Island Red, well fed and in good condition. Later in the afternoon the tom cat returned and jumped up to his window sill. Strange to say, even at this first meeting the cat evinced no surprise, nor indeed did he seem in the least bit curious, unusual at any time for a cat.

Enquiries were made in the district, but no one seemed to have lost a hen, so she just stayed on with the cat. The pair became inseparable companions, sharing the window sill during the day and sleeping quarters in the conservatory at night. The cat slept on a bed of hay; the hen perched on a shelf above: and they ate together from the same bowl, each giving way to the other in turn. Three weeks later the hen showed her appreciation by laying a large brown egg. This became a daily event and she always laid the egg in the same place.

So this strange pair settled into a pattern which never changed. Every day when the cat was groomed, the hen would fuss around until she too was brushed. That also became a daily routine. Meanwhile the other cat ignored them both. Two years passed in this tranquil fashion, until one day the cat was hit by a passing car, a fact that was only discovered when Mrs Collier went to give the pair their breakfast. Only the hen was there and eventually the cat was found lying on his bed of hay badly hurt. He was conscious and managed to lap up some cream, but he could not stand and his head was injured. The vet arrived but could do nothing except put him out of his misery. The hen stood by, watching every move intently, though she was taken out when the cat was put down. That evening the hen was in her usual place for a meal,

(*continued overleaf*)

which she had before going off into the conservatory for the night as usual. It was the last that anybody saw of her!

Naturally, the strange association of the two was known to the people in the village, and with their help a thorough search was made in fields, woods and gardens over a wide area, but the hen was never seen again and no report of anyone having seen her ever came to hand.

Who knows, as Mrs Collier says, whether the hen is wandering, searching for the cat who shared her life so closely.

Jinx Takes a Spin

During the fierce and bitter winter of 1963 a black cat strayed into the garden of a house overlooking the cove at the North Devon resort of Combe Martin. Mrs N. Laramy noticed the poor cat's terribly emaciated condition. Covered in sores, its ribs showed through its coat almost like a skeleton and it was alive with ticks.

She took the animal in, and weeks of kindness brought him back to some semblance of health, though it took much longer to make him the fine, sleek cat he is today. Thus one life of the proverbial nine, said to be the quota of every cat, had been accounted for by the time Jinx, as he came to be called, settled down with the family and became friends with Lindy, the resident spaniel.

Several years were to pass before Jinx's second life came near to forfeiture by as remarkable an experience as can fall to any cat. Perhaps because he had once been so cold, Jinx was adept at finding extra warm places in which to sit and snooze. He had several favourite hideouts, including a cubby-hole next to a solid-fuel fire, but he was never so happy as when, wash days finished, he could crawl into the front-loading electric washing machine, fluff out his fur and sit dreaming perhaps of that hated white winter of long ago.

It was this habit which nearly cost him his second life. Wash day was almost over, and whilst preparing a batch of woollies for the final rinse, Mrs Laramy left the front of the machine open. Unknown to her, Jinx jumped in. The woollies followed, the machine was shut and the water spin commenced. For the next four minutes the lady of the house heard a continuous strange knocking but could not trace the sound. Eventually the machine was switched off and the woollies removed. But something remained, and an exploring hand brought forth the bedraggled body of Jinx, all but lifeless. Mrs Laramy acted quickly. First she pumped the water from his stomach and then for good measure shook him upside down. Finally, as there was no sign of life, she gave him the kiss of

life . . . and he twitched. Then came a gurgled meeow and finally a teaspoonful of whisky brought Jinx round. Within two hours he was eating his favourite dish, haddock, and it was not long before, sleek as ever, he was his normal self.

He still has his favourite warm spots, but now nothing will induce him to look in the direction of the whirligig. Nowadays, quite an elderly gentleman, he nestles up to the spaniel for warmth, and if the latter isn't available, the cubby-hole next to the fire will do.

Fluffy the Fisherman

Cats are said to hate water, and to go to any lengths to avoid it. An example of the other extreme was Fluffy, a Persian cat owned by Miss L. Dickenson, who lives on St Mary's in the Isles of Scilly.

Fluffy was a cat who loved fishing, and to reach her favourite vantage point she would wade into the water and then strike out quite strongly for the rocks. Once there, she would take up her position and, with typically cat-like patience and inscrutability, would watch and wait. Suddenly – whoosh – her paw would lash out, hooking her prey.

Like all good fishermen, Fluffy liked to bring home her spoils. So, grasping the fish firmly in her mouth, she would slip off the rocks into the sea, and swim back to the beach, all the while keeping a tight hold on her catch. Then she would make her way home, proudly deposit the fish upon the kitchen table, and wait to receive her due quota of praise. The suggestion that she should 'go and catch another one' always pleased her and she would be off like a flash to repeat her performance. Fluffy created several records. In one night she caught seven fish and her largest prize ever was a beautiful 1½lb plaice.

Sometimes she would deign to allow herself to be brought home in state, wrapped in a headscarf and cradled in the arms of some visitor, who had recognised Fluffy even in her soaking wet condition.

On the days when fishing did not appeal, Fluffy would swim to one of the boat anchorages, climb up onto the mooring, clean herself in leisurely fashion and then settle down comfortably to survey her kingdom. Satisfied that everything was in order, she would, in her own good time, make the return journey.

When Miss Dickenson took her dogs along the cliffs for a walk, the cat would always join the party.

Alas, one night this inveterate fisherman arrived home with a broken leg and, in spite of all the vet could do, it was considered kinder to put her to sleep.

9
BREEDING, SHOW PREPARATION AND CARE

There is no reason to think that, because of their exotic appearance, pedigree cats are delicate, requiring special feeding and attention. They live just as long as mongrels, anything up to twenty years being possible, and with an average age of fifteen to seventeen years in most cases. Training is exactly the same, for how a kitten's character develops depends a great deal on the love and care given when very young.

If hoping to go in for breeding and showing, it is advisable to visit a show or two and look at the exhibits, talk to the breeders, and, maybe, eventually order a specific kitten. It is advisable, too, to go to the breeder's house, see the conditions there, look at the kitten's mother, and possibly the father, and, if given a choice of litter, to pick out the kitten with bright eyes, clean ears, a well-groomed coat, with no sign of fleas, and whose little tail is held erect. It should be lively and full of life.

All cats need companionship, and, if the would-be owner is out all day, it is not fair to leave a kitten alone. It will need four small meals a day, and also litter-tray training, and if it is not possible to get home once or twice during the day yourself, the services of a kind neighbour should be sought, who will look in occasionally to see that all is well. In these circumstances it is better to have two kittens to keep each other company.

The shorthairs do need some grooming to remove the old hairs and to ensure that the fur is flea-free, but the longhairs need daily grooming, or even twice daily in the spring and autumn when the coat is changing. If neglected, the coat will knot and mat up very quickly, causing the animal discomfort. If not intending to go in for breeding, it does not matter if the kitten is male or female, but, whatever the sex, it is advisable to have the animal neutered or spayed to prevent unwanted kittens being produced. If allowed complete freedom, an unneutered male will travel for miles looking for likely females, often returning home battered and injured, while a female may well become pregnant before the owner is even aware that she is old enough to have kittens.

Not only show kittens, but all kittens should be inoculated against feline infectious enteritis, a killer disease, and also against cat flu. A would-be buyer of a pedigree cat should check that the strain is free from feline leukaemia virus. It is inadvisable to buy a male and female kitten from the same litter, or even from different litters at the same time. Invariably males and

The moment she puts her nose out of the door, you have no control over what partner she selects. The average cat on heat will have no difficulty in attracting all the local toms

females mature at different ages. Usually the female will come into season for the first time between six and nine months, but it could be twelve months or even later. This depends a great deal on the variety, Siamese females tending to come into season very early while some longhairs may be much later. Males mature at very different ages, some being interested in females when only a few months old, while others may be as much as two years old before being ready. Each kitten is an individual, and it is almost impossible to predict the actual age of maturity.

As a novice breeder, it is far better to buy a female and to make arrangements to send her to stud. Much experience in the handling of cats is needed before keeping a stud. A keen watch must be kept on a young female; she should not be mated at her first call, and should certainly be well guarded against a chance meeting with the local Romeo. Sometimes it is difficult to know whether a female is calling, but usually she will become more loving than before, will roll around the floor, maybe making soft, muttering noises, and sometimes yelling at the top of her voice and making every endeavour to get out of the house. Well before she is old enough to be mated, arrangements should be made for her to visit a suitable stud. It is advisable to visit the stud's owner before booking, to see how the male is kept and to look at general conditions. Try to see the actual house which the female will probably have to share with the male. There should be a separate compartment from where she can see the male, but cannot meet him, until the stud owner thinks she is ready.

When she comes into season for the second time at least, is well grown and is at least ten to eleven months old, the stud

The moment we've all been waiting for

The pleasures of motherhood . . .

A tabby mother shepherds an errant kitten back to the nest box

owner should be telephoned and arrangements made for her to be taken on the second day. She will have to be left for two or three days, probably having two matings. The stud fee must be paid when she is collected, when the owner will be given a copy of the stud's pedigree and the date of the actual mating. If no kittens result, she may be received for a further mating, but this is not obligatory.

It is important to keep her under guard for at least a week when she returns home, until she shows no more signs of calling, as it is quite possible that she could be mated by a stray tom, and, even if already in kitten, could have a dual mating, producing kittens by both males. The first sign that she is in kitten may be about three weeks later, when the nipples may turn pink. An average time for pregnancy is approximately sixty-five days, but may be two or three days longer. She should not be treated as an invalid and should be fed as usual. After about a month her stomach may look a little swollen, showing that she is pregnant, and food may be increased slightly. She should be allowed to play and run around as usual, as the exercise is good for her. It is better to give an extra meal a day, rather than to give larger meals.

A week or two before the kittens are due, provide a cardboard box, in a draught-free quiet corner, that will give ample room to stretch out, but that is not so big that the kittens can roll into a corner and get cold. Put plenty of newspaper in the bottom and introduce the cat to the box. She will probably tear the newspaper into shreds, almost making a nest. Cut a hole in the

112

side so that she can see into the box from outside, and get in and out without treading on her family. Once she feels the kittens are about to be born, she will probably get into the box, even purring happily during the contractions. For a first litter, it is as well to advise your veterinary surgeon of the likely date, but it is rarely necessary to call him unless she seems to be straining unduly and no kittens arrive. Usually the female manages to do everything herself, breaking the cord and cleaning the kittens as they arrive, eating the placenta or afterbirth for each one. It is quite natural and indeed, important that she be allowed to do this as the afterbirth contains essential nutrients. If the day is very cold, it is advisable to have a warm (not hot) hot-water bottle ready, covered with a piece of blanket, in her box and to put the newly born kittens on it as she attends to the next arrival. Avoid handling the kittens too much, as the mother may get upset. It is possible, if she does not object to their being handled, to sex the kittens at an early stage. Under the tail of the male is the anus and, about three-eighths to half an inch nearer the stomach, the rudimentary testicles, giving a bunch effect. Under the tail of the female is also the anus, but, close to it, is a small slit, the vagina. If there are both sexes in the litter, it is much easier to see the difference.

Once all the kittens seem to have arrived, leave her for a little while, having checked that all the kittens appear to be sucking at her side. A little later, remove the soiled paper, and replace this with a thick blanket that cannot ruck up and hide a kitten. Give the mother a warm milk drink if she likes milk, and leave her to settle down quietly with her little family. The number of kittens in a litter varies considerably, the Longhairs having four or five,

Brown Burmese mother working hard to keep her litter clean

as may the British Shorthairs, whilst the Siamese, and some other Foreign Shorthairs, generally have larger litters.

If the kittens seem to be taking plenty of milk from the mother, and sleep quietly most of the time, they are probably doing well. She will be able to do all that is necessary for them for the next ten to twelve days. She should be given good, nourishing food, milk if she can take it, and clean water should always be available. The kittens' eyes begin to open at about eight to twelve days old, depending on the variety, and until then they should be kept away from strong light. At about three weeks, when the kittens start to get out of the box, a little litter tray should be provided close by. Most people are surprised that such tiny things will even try to use it, but quite often they do. Weaning,

Koshka

too, may start at this age, or a week or two later if there are few kittens and the mother has plenty of milk.

At about three weeks old, the kittens can be given just a drop or two of one of the proprietary baby foods, or canned milk, made up as given on the tin. After a day or two, this can be increased to a teaspoonful, given at blood heat, and after a week a second meal can be offered, gradually introducing a little baby cereal in the milk feed. The kittens should soon start to lap from small saucers. When the baby teeth start to appear, cooked minced rabbit or chicken, white fish, or a little scraped raw beef may be given. A kitten's stomach is very small, so meals should not be large. As the kittens grow, the number of meals should be increased until, at the age of eight to nine weeks, they are having four or five small meals a day and are on a good mixed diet. This will teach the kittens not to be fussy about food when they are older. Two meals could be milky and the others of cooked meat, lamb or veal, cooked or raw beef, cooked white fish, without bones, tinned kitten food, tinned pilchards, or eggs, raw and mixed with a little cereal, or scrambled. A few cornflakes, or a little crumbled brown bread, added to each feed, will help the teeth and give roughage. At six months, three larger solid meals

Charlie No-Nose

A face appeared at the cat door late at night. It was hideous; the ears lop-sided, the head misshapen, the nose grotesque with a lump protruding from the right nostril.

'Hello, old man,' said I. 'What's your name?'

'Charles,' said he; and that's the truth, even though everyone accuses me of exaggerating. The cat said, 'Charles'.

Fascinated, I crept forward and slowly opened the door. He just stood there. He was a large, black and white tom . . . no! He was a large, black and yellow tom, the white parts so dirty he looked as though he had been smoking Woodbines all his life!

After some preamble, he decided to move in. I had no choice in the matter and neither did my husband, David, or our three other cats, Chloé, William and Jasper.

We had to spend a fortune on him to make him even remotely acceptable. We had him neutered, of course, but he used to cough up live worms on the sheepskin rug and sneeze green slime on the window panes! His tail was strangely flat, as though it had been steam-rollered and the end of it was hairless, like a rat's tail.

At first Charles treated David and me as no more than walking larders. He ate like a cat possessed . . . anything from peeled prawns to my mother's iced madeira cake, despite the handicap of having virtually no teeth at all! Gradually, however, he began to realise that there was more to this domestic business than meets the eye, and he began to give us the benefit of his not inconsiderable affection and loyalty.

Around this time, we noticed that the lump on his nose seemed to be getting bigger. We took him to our vet – again! – who said that,
(*continued opposite*)

should be given, plus a milky feed, and at nine months, two large meals, plus milk if it can be taken. A large raw beef bone can be given to chew on, but cooked bones should not be given at all, as they may splinter, causing internal problems.

Grooming can start at three weeks for longhaired kittens. Gently brushing the fur with a baby's soft brush will encourage it to grow the way it should, and will also get the kitten used to being handled and prepared for the intensive grooming needed later.

Cats need some grooming, whether long- or shorthaired and whether pedigree or pet. Grooming does not mean just a few quick strokes with a brush and comb, but also looking into the ears and wiping them very gently with a small piece of cotton wool, slightly dampened, or with an orange stick covered with cotton wool, as recommended for babies. Never poke right down into the ear, as this may cause damage. If there appears to be a discharge, or if there is a smell, these may be signs of ear mites, frequently referred to as canker, and it is as well to consult a vet as there are several forms of ear mites and the correct treatment is necessary. Again, a cat may pick up a flea, particularly in hot weather. Small black specks in the fur, like tiny pieces of coal dust, are the faeces of the flea. A spray that is safe to use on cats may be obtained from a vet, but never use this on a very young kitten. Instead use a very fine-tooth steel comb. Any dirt in the corner of the eyes should be wiped away with a little cotton wool.

Daily grooming is essential for a longhair, and this will remove the loose hairs which would soon mat up if left unattended, and which can cause fur balls if the cat should lick them down when washing. The coat should be combed through with a wide-toothed steel comb, teasing out any knot in the fur with the fingers, and being careful not to pull unduly. Talcum powder may be sprinkled right down into the roots of the paler-coated longhairs to help to remove grease, but must be brushed and combed right out. Powder should not be used on the darker coats as, if any is left in the coat, it will look like scurf. A little surgical spirit, or eau-de-cologne, on cotton wool will remove the grease from dark coats, but care should be taken to keep it away from the eyes. The fur around the head, known as the frill or ruff, should be brushed up to form a frame for the face. The tail needs careful brushing out too.

Several weeks before the show, the grooming should be intensified, but care must be taken not to pull out the fur, particularly around the neck. The day before the show it is essential that all traces of powder are removed, otherwise the cat may be disqualified. Blow the fur up to make sure that all the powder has gone.

Grooming a shorthair is much simpler. Hard hand stroking will remove the old hairs, and combing with a narrow-toothed steel comb will take any dust and dirt out of the fur and also catch the occasional flea. Polishing the coat with a piece of velvet, or chamois leather, will give the fur a beautiful sheen. Never use a very wide-toothed comb on the shorthair coat, as it tends to leave unsightly ruts.

Condition is important in presenting a cat on the show bench; indeed, it is important for all cats for whom a correct balanced diet is essential. A cat that is overfed will be too fat, and, if underfed, too thin, and, in either case, will lose points. By the show day the cat should look as perfect as possible, with every hair and whisker in place, and, we hope, be a really worthy prize winner.

Pedigree shows are organised by the cat clubs under the auspices of the Governing Council of the Cat Fancy. A list of the shows held each year is published by the GCCF and can be obtained by sending £1 to them at the address given on page 206. Pedigree cats and kittens must be registered with the GCCF before they can be exhibited at their shows, and any transfer to a new owner must take place at least three weeks before a show.

It is not necessary to belong to the cat club that is organising a show, but members are usually allowed to enter at reduced prices, and there are often special prizes for members' entries. The classification is numerous, and, if intending to go in for breeding, winning at the championship shows ensures that stock will become more valuable and possibly more in demand.

There are three types of shows. Exemption is the first show which a club is allowed to run. These are comparatively small shows where the rules are not so strict. They are ideal for novices, as they serve as introductions to the show world, giving them a chance to see how their animals behave and how they fare in competition. Usually the judges officiating have time to talk to owners, to give an opinion on their cats, and maybe to advise about breeding.

Sanction shows follow the Exemption, and a club may be

unfortunately, it was cancer. He recommended drastic surgery – the amputation of the whole nose-hood. We agreed and went home to wait; we knew he was oldish and that oldish cats can often succumb under the surgeon's knife, particularly if they have not had the care which they should have had in the past. We convinced ourselves that he would die.

We need not have worried! Charlie returned, looking even more ugly than before, and proceeded to get well with alacrity. He now weighs 13lb, is the possessor of a beautiful coat and is not averse to chasing a piece of string around when the mood takes him. He also beats up our other cats fairly regularly – and the cat next door, who is terrified of him. I think Charles thinks it is a bit of a lark!

Recently, we found out something about his background. He was born on a farm, apparently, and eventually moved in with an old man who was taken into hospital a few weeks before Charles came to us.

Taking everything into account, Charles must be at least 17 years old and the vet says he'll see us all out! – *The Cat.*

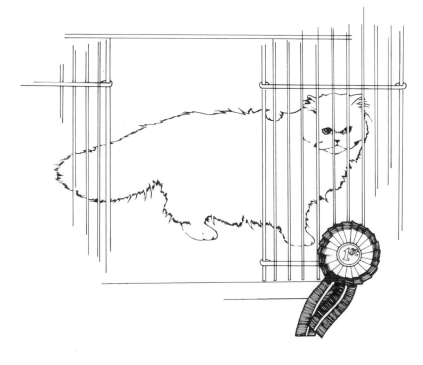

First prize: both cat and owner will be delighted by all the attention

given permission to run a Sanction show if it has run three very good Exemptions. A Sanction is a rehearsal for the Championship show, as it is run on similar lines, but no challenge certificates are given. The rules are very strict, the classes much more numerous, and well-known judges officiate. Ably run Sanction shows are usually followed by the Championship shows. These are important in that challenge certificates are awarded to the winners of the Open or Breed adult classes. Three challenge certificates, won at three such shows, under three different judges, means a cat may become a Champion. There are also classes for the Champion winners, known as the Champion of Champion classes, and it is possible for a cat to become a Grand Champion by winning this class at three shows on the same terms.

Neuters, too, can win Premier certificates for winning their Open classes, and can progress to become a Premier under the same rules. Ultimately, it is possible for them to become a Grand Premier, by winning the Premier of Premier class, again under the same rules, and by winning under three different judges.

Many shows have a section for pet cats which need not be registered with the GCCF, but must not be pedigree, and there are also classes for half-pedigree cats, with one registered parent and one unknown.

Kittens cannot be shown until they are at least three months old, and, for some varieties, such as the Siamese, four months. Once they are nine months old, they have to enter the adult classes.

To enter it is necessary to apply for a schedule and entry form at least three months before the date of the show. The schedule contains details of the various classes, both open and miscellaneous, and also club classes put on by the various clubs. It is

Opposite
The judging that will please or disappoint one anxiously waiting owner. Cat shows, like any get together of cat enthusiasts, are pleasurable occasions and stretch the individual owner's experience. But don't be in a hurry!

Arthur featured in television advertisements for eighteen weeks each year, and starred in thirty-five films

also necessary to be a member of the specific club to enter the club classes.

Once having received the schedule, the entry form enclosed should be filled in with the exact details given on the cat's registration form; any error in these may mean disqualification. It is usual to enter at least four classes, but not more than eight. If a first-time exhibitor, it is better to enter the cat in four only, to see how he behaves when being handled by the judge and steward. Some cats are quite happy about it all, but others are very nervous, and may bite and scratch the judge. It is as well not to attempt to show a nervous animal again, as biting and scratching are frowned upon, and may mean a report being sent to the GCCF. If this happens several times, the cat will be banned from any further shows.

Correct show equipment is essential. A clean warm white blanket, without any markings, and not cellular, must be provided. A plain white litter tray of adequate size is also needed. A white water container must be put in the pen, possibly one that hangs on the side of the pen and which cannot easily be spilled. White feeding bowls, with the cat's favourite food, may be placed in the pen about lunchtime. Some exhibitors do not feed their animals on the morning of the show in case they suffer from car sickness when travelling. Here again, this depends a great deal on the cat's own temperament.

As well as being registered with the GCCF, every exhibit must have a current vaccination certificate against infectious feline enteritis, issued at least seven days before the show.

On receiving the schedule and entry form from the show manager, it should be completed and returned as soon as possible, together with the correct moneys, as most shows receive so many entries that the hall soon reaches its capacity,

Even the best fed puss enjoys exercising its hunting prowess

and some entries have to be returned. A stamped, self-addressed envelope should also be included if this is asked for. This is usually sent back about a week before the show, enclosing the numbered tally and a vetting-in card. Some shows prefer to give these out on the morning of the show, but details will be given in the schedule. The numbered tally corresponds with the pen which the cat will occupy in the hall. It is also a good idea to enclose, with the entry, a stamped self-addressed postcard bearing the words 'Entries received' which the show manager can return as proof of receipt of the entry.

The exhibit must be taken to the hall by the owner, or his representative, in an adequate carrying container, such as a basket. The exhibit must not be carried in the arms or taken on a lead. There may be queues for the vetting-in, but no animal is allowed into the hall until it has been examined thoroughly by the veterinary surgeon. He will ensure that there are no fleas or flea dirt in the fur, that the ears are clean, with no signs of ear mite, that there is no skin complaint, that the eyes are not running, and, generally, that there is no sign of illness. So it is up to the owner to present an exhibit that really is in beautiful condition.

Once through the vetting-in, the exhibitor should go to the pen displaying the cat's tally number. The pen may be wiped down with a little cotton wool, dampened with a non-toxic disinfectant, before the cat is put in. A hot-water bottle, concealed under the blanket, is allowed if the weather is very cold. The cat may be given a final grooming, but, even in the case of a longhair, must not be powdered in the hall, as any powder found in the fur by a judge may lead to disqualification. Most shows clear the hall until about midday, when the public are admitted, and when cats may be fed. It is possible that some classes still have to be judged in the afternoon, and the owner should never be near the pen while the judging is going on, nor should any attempt be made to speak to the judge. One or two of the larger shows allow the public in all day.

When the catalogues are on sale, the owner should check that the cat's entries are correct, and, if not, should go quickly to the Award table and point out any error. Most shows present rosettes and some give prize money, and both should be collected on the day. The award slips are displayed on special boards, so that owners may see how their exhibits are doing.

Most shows close about 5.30pm. On returning home it is as well to isolate the cat exhibited from others in the household, just for a few days, in case any infection has been picked up at the show. Some exhibitors wipe the cat's fur over with a very mild non-toxic disinfectant and also give the cat half a teaspoonful of whisky or brandy with a little milk. As the cat will have been shut up all day in the pen he may be very lively on his return, rushing around madly and not nearly as exhausted as his owner who might also like a little brandy or whisky and who will be looking forward to retiring to bed!

Lost mouse

'Min caught a mouse, and was playing with it in the yard. It had got away from her once or twice and she had caught it again, and now it was stealing off again, as she was complacently watching it with her paws tucked under her, when her friend, Riorden, a stout cock, stepped up inquisitively, looked down at the mouse with one eye, turning its head, then picked it up by the tail, gave it two or three whacks on the ground, and giving it a dexterous toss in the air, caught the mouse in its open mouth. It went, head foremost and alive, down Riorden's capacious throat in the twinkling of an eye, never again to be seen in this world; Min all the while, with paws comfortably tucked under her, looking on unconcerned. What did one mouse matter, more or less, to her? The cock walked off amid the currant-bushes, stretched his neck up and gulped once or twice, and the deed was accomplished. Then he crowed lustily in celebration of the exploit. It might be set down among the *Gesta gallorum*. There were several human witnesses. It is a question whether Min ever understood where that mouse went to. She sits composedly sentinel, with paws tucked under her, a good part of her days at present, by some ridiculous little hole, the possible entry of a mouse. –' *Henry David Thoreau.*

121

WORKING CATS

There are many theories to account for the development of the relationship between cat and man over the centuries, but it is very likely that it all began when puss cottoned onto the fact that association with the human way of life brought with it a readily available supply of food. In spite of modern developments in pest control and storage facilities, there are still, today, many thousands of cats filling the role of rodent-control operatives, as they would no doubt be called if they were organised, unionised, or even recognised.

Farm cats, an all-embracing term to cover not only those working on farms, but also in stables, dairies, grain stores, market gardens and elsewhere, are not, with notable exceptions, the best cared-for animals in the country. There is still a widespread belief that hungry cats make better mousers, whereas, in fact, the reverse is the case, as the well-fed and cared-for cat will hunt much more actively, and have the stamina and vitality to do the job well. It is commonplace to see numbers of unwanted kittens in evidence in such situations, all competing for a limited food supply and often showing signs of the detrimental effects of continuous inbreeding. Of all places where veterinary services are readily available, farms and stables must top the list, and it would be a very simple matter to arrange a regular neutering and inspection programme if the will and the willingness to pay the vet's fees were there. This, together with the realisation that cats respond to food and a dry and comfortable place to sleep, would not only provide a better life for the cats but would inevitably improve their business efficiency.

Cats in factories, hospitals, shops, warehouses and so on seem, on the whole, to have a rather better life, but the problems arising from lack of neutering are still very much in evidence. The difficulties of neutering are often purely practical, such as how to set about things, and who is to pay, and, if this is the case, one caring person should contact a local animal welfare group to see if they can help. The Cats Protection League, and other organisations, have assisted in many such cases by trapping cats, arranging and paying for neutering (and usually a medical examination, too) and then returning the cats to the site. By this means the number of cats is kept at a reasonable level, and what might have been an unacceptable situation is changed to one where the cats are welcome, not only for their pest-control activities, but also for their leavening effect on what are often stark surroundings.

Whilst cats in industry are not in the same position as domestic pets, they are, nevertheless, dependent on the human presence, and this should be borne in mind at weekends, holiday times and on other occasions when the workforce is absent. Arrangements must be made for the daily provision of food and water (not three dishes left out for three days, please), and whilst there are sometimes problems over security arrangements, these can always be overcome with a little commonsense.

The British Post Office has a tradition of cats on

its payroll dating back to 1868, when complaints of letters being chewed up by rats and mice led to their official establishment as employees at one shilling (5p) per week, to cover food and milk. This Royal Mail feline brigade has continued to be regarded as essential to the efficient operation of the Post Office and at the present time there are more than thirty on the official payroll, and, no doubt, many moonlighters. Pay has risen, too, and is now £1 per week or, in the case of the Headquarters cat, who is presumably regarded as a sort of brigade major, £2 per week. There have been some real characters on the payroll including the truly enormous Tibs, who weighed-in at 10.4kg (23lb) and was the official mouser at Post Office Headquarters in St Martins-le-Grand, in the City of London, for fourteen years up to 1964. A later incumbent of the same office was Blackie, whose picture appeared many times in the press and who even featured on BBC television.

In the Southern Highlands of Scotland, at Crieff in Perthshire, there is a notable cat named Towser, who is the official mouser of the Glenturret Distillery. She is remarkable for two things; she is reckoned to have accounted for well over 25,000 mice in the course of her official duties and she reached the truly splendid age of twenty-four years in April, 1987. Her hunting prowess and her longevity are attributed to the fumes in the still house, where she spends much of her time, and to the fact that she takes the occasional dram of the house product.

Perhaps the most unusual working cats are those on the staff of the Anderson House Hotel in Wabasha, in the Hiawatha Valley area of Minnesota, where it is possible for guests to hire a cat for company for an hour or two, for the evening, or to stay the night. The cats come complete with food and litter tray which is removed by the maid when the room is cleaned next day. John Hall, the owner of the Anderson House and a feline afficionado, began the service when a cat-lorn guest inquired if he could borrow the hotel cat for a while, for company, and now Morris, Sydney, Tiger, Aloysius and the rest of the ten-strong feline staff are in great demand, so much so that regular visitors book room, bath and cat of their choice in advance!

The aristocats of the working population are presumably those who work in advertising and films. They, at least, are cared for (even if the motivation is profit rather than affection), and, apart from appearances in such obvious areas as cat-food advertisements, they also pop up very frequently elsewhere, usually promoting the image of cosy domesticity, as in advertisements for central-heating installations, gas and electric fires, carpets and so on.

Cats are far too sensible and independent in their nature to lend themselves to training, but they can be persuaded to do certain things in return for food, which explains why, in the advertisements, the cat eats from dish A rather than from dish B (just what is in dish B?) and why they will make off in a particular direction – towards a source of food, off-camera, of course. Perhaps only a cat lover wonders what appetising smell is on the shoes in that scene in the film, *The Third Man*, where the presence of the supposedly dead Harry Lime is revealed when the cat makes its way to the doorway where Harry is concealed, and rubs itself round his legs.

Finally, a thought for the poor unfortunate and totally involuntary animals held in laboratories for experimentation. It is open to question whether the mutilation and sacrifice of even one animal can be justified.

10
THE BOARDING CATTERY

Earning a living at home has an instant and enormous appeal for many. There was, at one time, a publication which gave details of how to do this and listed suggested occupations, from antique dealer to zoo keeper. Unfortunately, but understandably, much of the information given was incorrect and incompletely researched, but it was, of course, seized on eagerly by a number of people. Those with the good fortune to be the proud possessor of a large shed on their land, or in their garden, were given to understand that they could embark on running a cattery, and expect to earn good money. Nothing is further from the truth. In the present political and economic climate, an increasing number of people are dissatisfied with their lot, have been made redundant, are unemployed, have taken early retirement, or are merely anxious to opt out of either the rat race or a dreary day-to-day existence bounded by seemingly endless industrial disputes. Thus, many seek an independent means of livelihood which will mean being one's own boss, and, to some, or so they hope, prove an easy way to quick money. Make no mistake, running a boarding cattery is no money-spinner.

Regrettably there are, throughout the country, a great number of so-called boarding catteries, among which are some adequate ones and a few really good and reliable ones. Before people commit themselves irrevocably to such an undertaking, they should examine their motives very thoroughly and face up to, and accept, a number of facts, some of which are unpalatable.

1) Capital expenditure is unavoidable. The cost of building a correctly laid-out cattery of some twenty chalets, with the obligatory isolation unit, and ancillary buildings for reception, kitchen, storage, etc, is considerable. Because of inflation it is futile to quote figures, but, at the time of writing it would probably work out at something like £500 to £600 per unit.

2) Boarding catteries are best sited in rural areas, and planning permission must be obtained. This can prove protracted, tiresome and fairly costly.

3) Given that planning consent is granted and the cattery built, a licence must be obtained from the Environmental Health Officer of the local district council, in accordance with the Animal Boarding Establishments Act, 1963. Under the Local Government Act, 1974, individual councils may levy their own licence fee. This is an annual fee and varies from £10 to £40.

Reasons to keep your cats in at night

They may be stolen by night prowlers on the look-out for anything to steal, and meet with dreadful deaths for the sake of their skins.

They may contract diseases from contacts with strays.

They may be attacked and injured by cats stronger than themselves.

They may be run over and injured or killed.

They may stray away altogether and become permanently homeless.

They cannot keep down the mice properly if turned out: these hide during the day but come out at night.

The law considers 'negligence leading to suffering' as 'cruelty' and punishes it. Turning out your cats at night is a form of negligence and should they suffer in health or be injured, you may be punished.

There is no excuse for turning cats out at night – they can all be house-trained. – *The Cat*, 1935.

124

A grave cat at Kensal Green Cemetery

4) It is one thing to build a cattery, but the day-to-day running of it is a horse of an entirely different colour. No matter what weather conditions obtain, what social attractions beckon, or what malaise strikes, the unvaried routine must go on seven days a week and fifty-two weeks a year. Freedom is curtailed to the extent that to leave the premises, even for a few hours, can be a major problem. The telephone will ring constantly, and at the most inconvenient moments. The one decent television programme of the week, to which one has looked forward, can be entirely wrecked unless, of course, it has been videoed. Thereafter it is often difficult to find the time to watch even this.

5) Proprietors of good boarding catteries, once they become known, will find that they have to turn away a number of cats. This, in fact, does no harm at all to their reputation, but to many it offers the temptation to expand, and this must be firmly resisted. The over-large cattery cannot be as well run, efficient and caring as the reasonably sized one, ie a maximum of forty to fifty cats. This, of course, does not mean fifty chalets, as many people have two, three or four cats, who can share accommodation because they come from the same household. Thus twenty-five or twenty-six chalets, of which two or three are larger family units, will suffice.

6) It is often thought that several acres of land are required, but, actually, a third to half an acre is quite sufficient. The maintenance of excessive land is costly in time, energy and money.

125

The CPL's shelter at Bredhurst, Kent, a model of its kind

Assuming it is finally decided to build and run a cattery, the choice must be made between an outdoor or indoor one. Of the two, the former is preferable.

There are two main hazards with boarding cats. These are cross-infection and escape. The first must be prevented by constant vigilance, meticulous hygiene and scrupulous management. It is impossible to avoid infection coming in, as cats can incubate infection for anything up to about twenty-one days, and the stress of boarding may trigger off a lurking condition. The second must *never* happen; it would be inexcusable and could never be justified.

An outdoor cattery, built to the correct specifications and dimensions, gives a free flow of air around each unit and the space between each run (at least 60cm, 2ft) reduces the risk of cross-infection to a minimum. It also ensures that the cats can see each other and communicate, but that direct contact is impossible. Cats are great spectators, and every effort must be made to combat boredom. Over the years it has been found that a correctly structured, and correctly run, outdoor cattery is readily and happily accepted by cats. For geriatric and convalescent cats, it is akin to paradise.

An indoor cattery, properly structured and, of course, correctly run, can be very good, but has certain insuperable snags. There must be outside runs, and, inevitably, if the cats are housed in a building, these will adjoin the building and will each have a full-height, impermeable barrier between each run. If the barrier is completely transparent, it will allow the cats clear vision of their neighbours, but the only flow of fresh air will come from the front. Inside, it is inevitable that the minute a door is opened from the centre corridor, the air supply and its accompanying bacteria are shared by all.

The prospective boarding-cattery proprietor must decide his or her priorities. It is a straight choice between the needs and welfare of the cats and the imagined comfort and convenience of those who will run the place and care for the cats. Admittedly, in the winter, conditions in an outdoor cattery can be harsh for those who care for the cats. Agonisingly frozen fingers and toes

An outdoor run that gives the cat a good vantage point is absolutely ideal

The tragedy of cats

Cats are in many ways outside the laws governing other domestic creatures, being possessed of great independence of character and, therefore, never having been reduced to complete slavery. Man has been unable to adapt them to serve any purpose of his own. They have really no definite place in his scheme of things, they do not provide his food, nor share in his wars, his sports or his work. The life-history of the ordinary cat contains possibilities of tragedy greater than that of any other animal, such as drowning or more brutal destruction as kittens – subjection to cruel operations by unqualified persons – and being turned out every night in all weathers, and also during owners' absences. When homeless, they face the risk of being picked up by evilly-disposed people. If no rescuer comes they may join the huge army of semi-wild, half-starved back-alley scavengers, diseased and disseminators of disease.

Consideration of these tragic possibilities which are, only too often, actual happenings, should be enough to convince all humane persons that something must be done to stop so much unnecessary and unmerited suffering.

And all these things, as we stated three years ago, are still happening and need special attention. – From the first issue of the CPL's magazine *The Cat* in 1934.

are the norm. However, the cats, in their heated chalets, are warm, comfortable and at little risk from infection. Running an indoor cattery probably means warmer working conditions for the people, but presents a number of possible health problems for the cats.

To set up a cattery from scratch involves much forethought and planning. Whether it be the construction, administration, accounting system, cleaning or disinfecting routines, all these things must be kept as simple and straightforward as possible. It must be accepted from the outset that the cats' needs are paramount. Broadly speaking these can be summarised as follows: security, simple comfort, strict hygiene, individual diet, and, above all, *care*. How then is this achieved?

Construction

Many firms advertise cat accommodation, but purchasing these off-the-peg buildings can prove an expensive mistake. The firms concerned are interested only in selling their products and may have no knowledge of, or interest in, cats' needs. In the main, the buildings are flimsy, insufficiently insulated for winter or summer conditions, and too small for one cat, let alone two from the same household.

Chalets and runs should be mounted on a concrete pad which has been hand-trowelled to a really smooth finish, and there should be a 1.25m (4ft) wide safety passage. The concrete should have a 7.5cm (3in) fall to the rear, to facilitate hosing away dirt and debris. Let it be clearly stated that grass runs are not admissible. Disinfecting grass is virtually impossible, and the inevitable vomit and excreta are splendid sources of infection. The runs and safety passage should be roofed with corrugated PVC. There is a make on the market which filters the sunlight, and thus the cats will be cooler in summer, warmer in winter and able to sit or play in their runs whatever the weather. The other consideration is that those who do the cleaning and feeding can do so in dry conditions.

Administration

Thought must be given to this whilst the cattery is under construction, and all the necessary printing done in plenty of time. There should be a brochure which states clearly and simply what accommodation is provided, the details of feeding, inoculations required (owners should be asked to bring the relevant certificate), terms, hours of business, and shows a clear map indicating the position of the cattery. It is always a help if cat owners can find the place without an extensive tour of country lanes. Each cat should have a record card; it is a condition of the licence that strict records are maintained and are open to inspection. The card, which is filed under the owner's name, should give complete details about the cat, ie its name, age, description, whether long- or shorthaired, sex before neutering, dietary preferences, dates of boarding and inoculation. Some catteries use a booking form which is completed by the owner. As most bookings are taken by telephone, as the postal service is no longer renowned for prompt delivery, and as owners' handwriting and interpretation of the questions varies, it is far better that the boarding-cattery proprietor maintains a clearly written card-index system. Each card provides a permanent record, as it gives complete information about the cat's requirements and its medical history.

Accounts, simple and clear, must be maintained and, difficult though it is, kept up to date and audited annually. There should be a book which records the actual boarding fees, the name of the owner, with the cat's name in brackets, and whether the payment was made by cash or cheque, a day book showing receipts and payments, and a petty cash book. A good accountant who understands a small business is a priceless asset.

All bookings must be carefully and accurately recorded and entered on a booking sheet which shows a month at a glance, and on the cat's record card. Unless this procedure is strictly observed, nightmare situations can arise, and no sane boarding-cattery proprietor wishes to be confronted by three cats from different households and only one vacant chalet.

Each cat has an individual diet and each day a menu must be compiled showing clearly what each cat will be given to eat. It is useless to serve a general diet, as cats will only eat what they like, and are reduced to near starvation level before they will eat something to which they are unaccustomed. The function of the boarding-cattery proprietor is to *care* for the cats individually. The diet is shown on the record card. On the grounds that what goes in must come out, when the morning cleaning is done, a record must be kept showing that the cats have urinated or defecated. This is not in the least complicated, as a tick or cross in the appropriate place tells all. These things must be prepared whilst the cattery is being constructed. The secret of administration and accounting is simplicity and clarity.

During the construction period, it is essential that contact is made with a veterinary surgeon. In most areas there are generally two or three veterinary practices, and it should be ascertained which one specialises in small animals, with particular reference to cats. A close liaison must be maintained between the veterinary surgeon and the boarding-cattery proprietor. The veterinary surgeon must know that he will not be called out unnecessarily, and the proprietor must have confidence that the veterinary surgeon will always respond to a cry for help, and dispense advice over the telephone.

As soon as the die is cast, and there is to be a cattery, every effort must be made to acquire as much knowledge and understanding as possible about feline disorders. The moment will undoubtedly arise when the decision has to be made, 'Do we or do we not send for the vet? Dare we wait until the morning or does that cat need veterinary attention now?' This knowledge is something one either has or has not got. With some it is instinc-

Daffodils bloomed sixteen times while this kitten grew up, lived a secure life and died. Sixteen years of happiness for owner and cat alike

129

Thoughts from a foster mum
I have 14 cats.

This number was not intentional – they just crept up on me gradually. The trouble is I get too fond of them. I tell the CPL, but good intentions waver as the time passes. There are many excuses: they have settled too well; or the others will miss them (which means I will miss them); they will be lonely on their own in a new home with no others to play with. So, in the end, I decide 'just this one' . . . and so it goes on. Lulu, Twiggy and Peachy are my original cats, mother and daughters. Tiddly-Pom neighbours literally kicked out when she was found to be pregnant; she had five kittens and I kept one, Sweep, and found homes for the other four locally. Timmy was one that was left behind when his owners moved. Napoleon and Josephine, mother and baby, came when they had a bad time in kennels; Napoleon was so nervous, he would not be separated from his mum and nobody wanted either of them. Ladybird was bought on a street market at three weeks old by a woman who had her a week and then decided she couldn't cope with her. Lizzie was found late one night in the middle of a large car park.

Baby was brought by someone who did not really want a black and white kitten; she has never grown much bigger than a six months old kitten but has an appetite of a much larger cat. Henry was going to be put down by his owner who had kept him shut in a cupboard as she could not bear to look at his slightly deformed back feet. Little Man was found and never claimed but it is the most affectionate and friendly of cats. Pooky is the latest arrival, or should I say the *last* arrival . . . how could I have turned him away?
(*continued opposite*)

tive, and it can be acquired through experience. Boarding-cattery proprietors must never play at being veterinary surgeons and think they know the answer. They cannot, they are in no way qualified, and, no matter how experienced, they cannot afford to endanger the life of someone else's cat. Nevertheless, it is their decision whether or not to call the veterinary surgeon. If in real doubt, and if they have the right relationship with their veterinary surgeon, they can always seek advice by telephone, but they must know how to describe the cat's condition. So one returns again to continuity of *care*, the fact that the same person every day notes the condition of each individual cat, and can therefore describe over the phone, to a veterinary surgeon, any deviation from the norm, and thus come to a decision.

Ancillary Buildings

Having decided what accommodation the cats require, thought must be given to other buildings which are vital to the cats, the boarding-cattery proprietor and the smooth running of the business. The following are essential: reception, store, kitchen and isolation unit.

It is a crashing mistake to have the reception in the house. Boarding-cattery proprietors are well advised to keep their business separate from their home. Sometimes people who think of boarding cats tend to overlook the fact that they still have to perform the thousand and one daily tasks which fall to everyone's lot. Reasonably regular meals are important.

Litter, litter trays, beds, whether cardboard cartons or plastic, wood wool for bedding, etc, all have to be housed and, to save leg work, which is considerable day after day, the store should be sited as near to the cattery as possible.

The kitchen must be separate from the family's, and, again, sited as near to the cattery as possible. A sink, with hot and cold water, deep freeze, refrigerator, small cooker and shelf space are essential. If the house is fairly close to the cattery and has a utility room, it is possible to convert this to a cat kitchen. If the boarding-cattery proprietor has a family cat or cats, or other animals, on no account must it or they be allowed access to this kitchen. Transference of any infection must be avoided at all costs. Prospective boarding-cattery proprietors are well advised to lay in a stock of disposable feeding dishes which can be burned after use, and all drinking dishes must be numbered so that the same cat retains the same dish throughout its stay.

The isolation unit is obligatory and must be positioned at least 30m (100ft) away from the main complex, preferably downwind. Its construction should be identical and there should be an escape-proof entrance.

Equipment

The furnishings of a chalet must be reduced to a bare minimum. Many catteries stress 'luxury'. Cats do not need this, and fussy furnishings are unnecessary. For example, shelves for beds and pretty curtains, although adding interest to the human eye, and appealing to some cat owners, present an infection hazard to the cat and increase the work load. Again, simplicity is the answer. The best form of heating is undoubtedly infra-red dull emitters. Not for nothing are they used in treatment for arthritis, and in mink farms for the benefit of the animals' coats. Each chalet should have one suspended about 1m (3ft) above the cat's bed and each heater must be *individually* thermostatically controlled. An elderly Siamese is obviously going to require more warmth than a young and active tabby. It is, however, a fact that in the United Kingdom there are many nights when at least a touch of heat is necessary.

Standpipe
Runs have to be hosed down and scrubbed every time a chalet is disinfected after a cat's departure. From time to time, the whole complex has to be hosed and scrubbed. Therefore, a hose which runs the entire length, and is fitted with a pressure nozzle (brass is preferable to plastic) is essential. It is possible to obtain double standpipes so that the hose can remain permanently fitted to one while the other tap is used for washing litter trays. This task must always be done outside. If a porcelain sink can be found in a builder's yard, this is very useful.

Regrettably, throughout the country, there are a great number of so-called boarding catteries, many of which are truly appalling, some adequate and a relative few really good and reliable. This chapter has dealt only with the setting-up of a cattery, but really this is only half the story. The best buildings in the world, with all the sophisticated equipment that one can think of, are utterly useless unless the management and hygiene are meticulous. Nevertheless, there must be no compromise or cutting corners in construction and prospective boarding-cattery owners must learn and understand the reasons for correct construction, and ask themselves if they can undertake the unremitting daily responsibility, the continual vigilance and checking to see that all is well. There can be no let-up.

It does no harm to ponder for a moment on what the boarding of cats really means. It is this. The proprietor of a boarding cattery shoulders an immense responsibility in undertaking the care of other people's much-loved, irreplaceable animals. Owners must be able to go on holiday, go to hospital, move house, or rescue an ailing relative, sure in the knowledge that their cat will be returned to them in as good, if not better, condition than when it was admitted. This is not always very easily achieved, but, for the boarding-cattery proprietor, the reward is the contentment of the cats and the gratitude of the owner. Only those who care and are prepared to stomach the snags, and there are snags, should undertake this work. In short, if you don't care, don't do it.

It is the financial side that makes one say, *no more*; that is, unless I win the pools! People are always surprised when they come to my home for the first time. 'But it doesn't smell of cats!', they say. Readers will agree that if you have healthy cats with free access to the garden, there is no reason why there should be any smell. They all get on well, the younger ones playing together. It can get a little chaotic on a wet day when they stay in but race around the house using the bath as a ski run and the shower curtain as a climbing frame but all the hairs and muddy feet marks are a small price to pay for the pleasure they give me.

I wouldn't part with one of them! – *The Cat.*

Note
Full details of specifications, management routines, working drawings, publications and training courses relating to boarding catteries can be obtained from
The Boarding Cattery Officer, Feline Advisory Bureau, 1 Church Close, Orcheston, near Salisbury, Wiltshire SP3 4RP.

IN MEMORIAM

Offering a Velvet Paw in Comfort

Though it is exactly a year since I said the agonising last farewell, it seems as though it were only last week and the hurt is still there.

We had been together for 21 years, from my mid 30s to my mid 50s, the years in which we are supposed to achieve it all. She spelt continuity through dramatic personal and career changes, stability in a topsy-turvy world.

She mellowed all who came to know her, undoubtedly played an important role in the development of my children's characters, and provided us with much of our amusement.

She ruled with a velvet paw, and even now as I type this 'column' I feel her presence beside me on the desk, watching the keys go to and fro and occasionally adding her own touch.

She was a Siamese. Among her peculiarities was the fact that she grew to believe that cat was an especial form of endearment and purred louder when it was shouted at her than when her name was called and gentler things were said.

I would shout 'Cat, cat' into the night to bring her back to the fireside. She always came, though it might take 15 or 20 minutes while she completed the piece of hunting in which she was engaged and romped home across the fields, hedgerows and lanes.

I chose her from the rest of the litter because she came up and bit me.

All cat lovers claim that theirs was the most outstanding character of catdom. I certainly do. She commanded every member of the family, got into everything, was reported by neighbours wandering miles from home and often followed me on walks.

Like most Siamese, she was primarily a people cat, in need of close human companionship. If we delayed getting up on a Sunday morning she would go out of her cat-flap and into the garden to yowl and wake not just us but the whole neighbourhood.

Naturally she especially liked the laps of supposed cat haters and of course made her converts (with the exception of the vet who regarded her as his worst patient and was afraid of her evil spirit even in her 21st year). And of course she hated farewells, her very stature declining as she dejectedly walked away when she saw the luggage out.

She would purr when I spoke to her on the telephone, perhaps from Australia. But would try to punish me when I returned, by pretending to ignore me – though a minute later her emotion would overcome her and she would dash into my lap, where she always insisted in being held in exactly the same upside-down position.

For many years I wondered if I would find her when I returned from long trips – through her early, mid and late teens until she all but became of age, a truly venerable cat who no longer left the garden but was still very aware of every movement in the house, and until the end added to her remarkable repertoire of sounds, including a deep yodel in her last year.

There is nothing specially remarkable in this tale; many families have their own pet story to tell. But it does no harm to admit what are the important things in our lives. And through the years when my cat gave me so much comfort, especially at times of crisis, it often crossed my mind how cruel was the rule that pets could not be accommodated in much council and institutional housing. There is a cat at an old people's home near me, and you have only to see what attention it receives to realise it must do considerably more good than most medicine.

Indeed, we are told that human hearts beat softer when we pay attention to a dog or cat.

11
HOW FERAL IS FERAL?

A feral animal is one which was once domesticated, but has now gone wild, or which was born in the wild although its ancestors were domestic-living, so a feral cat is a 'gone-wild' cat. Nonetheless, there is a lot of truth in the belief that even the most pampered and domestic-living cat essentially still has a wild nature under that veneer of good living! The cat was one of the last animals to enter into a domestic alliance with man and the more independent-minded stray easily, reverting to a wilder life.

The line of distinction between a feral cat and a domestic-living house cat is much easier to draw in Britain than in many other countries, due to the very domestic way *we* now live. In many parts of the world even house cats tend to live alongside man in a wilder state, rather than as lap animals. From small Spanish Pyrenean villages to Nepalese Terrai homesteads, house cats have the free range of the house, but live more in the manner of a farm cat when compared with the cat in present-day Britain. Certainly some food is given, but the cats are expected to catch part of their diet for themselves.

What has caused the difference in Britain and countries like Britain? Well, *we* have become suburbanised, and, as our homes have changed, so have our house cats. Today, wall-to-wall carpet, polished floors, neat lawns and flower beds have banished dirt-floors and yards with chickens which spilled into the house almost to the realms of folk memory in Britain, and yet such apparently rural dwellings were still to be seen in our towns of the 1930s. Many farm cats today in Britain live a life part way between feral and domestic.

However, even in Britain's suburban landscape, distinctions are blurred by the existence of strays. They are feral inasmuch as they have 'reverted to the wild', but most do not lead the more colonial life of the feral cat that is born in the wild state. Instead, they lead a grace and favour existence, ghosting around the home ranges or areas of domestic cats. Many will later be reabsorbed back into a domestic household, for at least one in five of our house cats were adopted as strays into our houses.

A study of feral cats now for a number of years in Britain (particularly London) and abroad, reveals a direct relationship between the availability of food and the number of feral and semi-feral cats about. More food means more cats! However, despite their superb anatomical design as hunters, most of the food of the urban feral is scavenged, or handouts. London, cer-

Will there be enough to go round?
No question here as to whether
the food is well balanced. Just, is
there enough?

Hunting may be fun, but it is also a
matter of survival. Did this cat go
to sleep hungry?

tainly, has its vast unco-ordinated army of cat-feeders, but it is not unique in this. Wander around the streets and classical ruins of Rome, ancient Athens, or the thoroughfares of Turkey's Istanbul, and you will come across devoted cat-feeders. But you will also find groups of cats whose feeding activities centre on a group of bins, rubbish skips, or just piles of rubbish that regularly mount up in a particular location. These are not just random cats that wander at will throughout our cities, for the same cats usually collect at the same bins, and theirs is a well-ordered society.

Although they hunt alone and are self-sufficient, cats like company. For cats that live with people, we make tolerable companions, but, within a feral group, other members are recognised as being of that group and non-members are often not appreciated. Within the group, close family ties often mean that, when the group is not together to feed, small groups of two or three cats will move to their own exclusive resting area, while others rest alone.

The group has an identifiable core area where they all come to feed. The timing may be connected to the time a feeder regularly visits, or to the time scavengeable material is usually dumped, but, left to their own devices, the cats prefer to assemble towards dusk when the city streets quieten and they can feed undisturbed.

135

The good old days

Do you remember the Cats' Meat Man of before the war? As a child living in London during the twenties and thirties, I remember that, for sixpence a week, the Cats' Meat Man would push through your letter box every day, a small wooden skewer with about six slices of cooked horsemeat on it. In the days when we also had a dog, it was a race with Fido to see who could reach the doormat first.

By today's standards we were poor, my father being 'on the dole', such as it was, in the Depression Years. My mother had to work, too, to help feed the three children, so there were hardly any scraps to spare for animals. Although our cats – only one at a time, though – were pets, in those days, many were kept because of the prevalence of house mice in those old houses. And there were always kittens! Kittens which we children loved and neighbours always wanted one – for free, of course! As for veterinary care, I remember the shop-surgery in the nearest main road, run, I expect, by the PDSA. You would pay for treatment by putting what you could afford 'in the box'.

Beyond the core area, each cat has its own area in which it normally moves about, its home range, which contains its favoured sleeping and sunning spots. These ranges will often partly overlap another group member's range. Toms generally have a much larger range than queens; roughly ten times the area. This is useful, for it means that toms can act as a buffer between the closer-knit groups of queens. We still see an echo of this pattern in our own house cats where, generally, toms hold bigger ranges than queens. However, neutering toms often reduces their range to varying extents.

Although urban feral cats live at a much greater density than their rural equivalents, nonetheless, in Britain, the urban feral does not reach the very high densities of our inner suburban house cats. Consequently life is quieter for the ferals than it is for those house cats, or for us! Fighting and caterwauling are much more common for the suburban house cat, as cats meet more frequently over their small ranges and territories.

Territories and home ranges are not the same thing, even though the area may be similar. The home range is where the animal normally lives and moves; the territory is the area it normally defends and so is smaller. Figures are often given for different species of animals for their territories, as if there were absolute values, but, as with home ranges, they vary considerably. A home range has to be big enough, primarily, to provide sufficient food to survive on, and so cats living wild in towns, with plentiful scavengeable food, can have much smaller ranges than their rural counterparts. No need to travel further than you have to when you could be sensibly snoozing! Similarly, territories are variable, and certainly smaller when the weather is too cold or wet. Territory size also depends on which cat is being confronted, and the outcome of this is usually affected by previous encounters.

How does a cat know where another cat's range begins, or even what its own should be? The cat family originally evolved in a wooded landscape where it was not possible to see far across one's range. When the domestic cat evolved among Middle Eastern townscapes and alleyways, things were not so very different. Today's cats in British cities now live in an urban jungle in which visibility is just as restricted. In each case the importance of scent marking has remained paramount.

We are all familiar with the all-invasive pungency of the intact tom's spray – it is more a system of passing messages by megaphone rather than by whisper! Nonetheless, 'quieter' systems are at work too. Cats have scent glands in their skin, more on some parts of their body than on others, and they will rub against objects in the area, like railings, and each other, and so transfer scent. At times, when cats come together in their groups or colonies, they will increasingly rub against objects by walking against them. Similarly, on greeting each other, they will often give a 'trill' call and head- or side-rub. So cats develop a group scent, come to appreciate each other's scent and, significantly, leave a greater amount of rubbed scent marks around the core area than elsewhere within the range.

Similarly, cats will 'chin', that is rub their chins on the ground, leaving a scent, but this is usually done as part of an elaborate piece of behaviour where they will check the scent, sniffing carefully and re-chinning. It will often develop into a protracted occasion, with head rolling as well. In these actions the cat is using its curious ability to 'taste-scent' a smell in its Jacobson's organ above the roof of its mouth. We do not have this ability!

The cat will also use the same scent-checking system when it 'chins' against scene-sticks, that is against odd twigs which project into a cat's path at cat height. These obvious points of investigation for a cat are usually overlooked by us, but then some of us even manage occasionally to miss ten-foot-high signs telling us which exit to leave by from a motorway!

Although cats do clawmark semi-peripherally to their range edges, they also often mark in this way near to particular sunning-spots, and also on trees or wood near where they will meet in core areas. The rough bark of most mature trees is useless for this activity, but trees up to 15cm (6in) diameter, which still have smooth bark into which claws can sink, are preferred – ideally fruit trees! The cats of my Fitzroy Square study area in Central London use two such young trees for clawing within their core area. Alternatively, soft old wood in manmade structures is liked for the same reasons. An overlapping key area of the cats in my Amsterdam study area has one of these, used by a number of cats.

Cats will often stretch and claw on greeting, and certainly sharpen their claws, but they also leave both a visible and scented mark by this means. Those sharpened claws are not so much used to catch mice or birds as to open the modern plastic waste sack. However, more often than not the sacks do not need opening as the waste spills out anyway. In Britain our climate can mean that we have to resort to heating for a large part of the year to keep our buildings warm. That once meant hot ashes, before the advent of the Clean Air Act. The disappearance of hot ashes has meant a massive decline in metal bins and the take-over by the paper and plastic sack, accessible to urban scavengers, fox, cat and man alike. However, it is not just Britain which has reeled before the sea of plastic sacks. All across Europe, and throughout the Mediterranean, the march of the black plastic sack has been unstoppable. Consequently urban feral cats, from Tottenham to Turkey, now have easier pickings.

Although a country like Turkey may, at first sight, seem very different, many of the cat activities in London or Istanbul are in many ways similar. One identical piece of city architecture is the car. Cats in both cities will rub against front number plates, spray against hub-caps and use lines of parked cars at street sides as safe tunnels and shelters. However, I am pleased to be able to confirm that cats in both cities are even more inventive than that. Whilst watching a young family in the Hippodrome,

Naming cats

Shakespeare, with his rather sweeping assertions about the rose, is usually regarded as the authority on names but even the Bard would have needed to tread rather carefully on the subject of naming cats or, more accurately perhaps, kittens. It is a matter of supreme indifference to the cat itself for it is unlikely to respond to the name unless it just happens to suit its immediate plans to do so. Perhaps this is just as well for otherwise calling for Blackie, Stripey, Tiger, Tibby, Tiddles, Thomas or the ubiquitous Puss might produce a positive stream of arrivals from near and far.

Some cats have very grand names but even the most aristocratic of pedigree cats is likely to be known *en famille* as Tom or Binkie; quite apart from alarming the neighbours the strain of opening the door and shouting for Champion Newbridge Bulkington Croix Rouge several times a day could well prove fatal.

It is interesting to see how the professional users of words approach the problem. T. S. Eliot, in his *Old Possum's Book of Practical Cats*, has some advice on the subject, avowing that a cat needs no less than three names; a family name, a more formal name and one known only to the cat itself. He was, in fact, a master namer himself with his *Macavity: The Mystery Cat, Bustopher Jones: The Cat About Town* and the rest. Beverly Nichols, as readers of his books will know, has a rather different approach and christens his cats with numbers, although he has not taken it to extremes and his cat, Oscar, is a familiar denizen of his books along with Four and Five.

So, what shall we call the cat? Willow is a very nice name. Willow? Yes, Pussy Willow!

Feral kittens, about six weeks old, playing outside their hollow log nursery. What does the future hold for them?

Istanbul, I saw that the four young kittens were deep in a game of batting a piece of paper about under the wheels of a parked car, while mum watched them benignly. Then, suddenly, there were only two, then one, then none, then two again, then four, then two and so on. They were not being whisked away by magic carpet, they were just employing the same trick as cats in London and elsewhere, diving up inside the car to sit on axles and the cool parts of the engine compartment!

In London many people are often surprised that the feral cat population is so high for, as they walk or drive about, they do not see that many cats. But daytime snoozing spots, empty basements and the cover of parked cars can make any cat a Macavity! However, go at dusk and look in the right places, and it is a different matter. In contrast, holiday makers around the Mediterranean shore often return home with stories of large numbers of cats only too visible. But these feral cats are often just a reflection of the tourist numbers and tourist food and so

138

surface when they are about. The quayside tavernas on Greek islands often *do* have numerous cats but they have access to food when tourist boats land. Go into the village beyond, and the number of cats drops to normal levels. Go further into the arid hills and numbers are at the relatively low levels of arid farmland. Mediterranean cities have high levels of cats, reflecting city food availability rather than tourists.

A typical group of taverna-living cats is in many ways like a community of farm cats, for, though most remain wild, they have to allow the close proximity of man. Their range feeding focus often depends on our geography. If there is only one taverna for a stretch there will probably be a semi-resident group which stays predominantly in and around that restaurant. In one such, which I studied in Turkey, I found that a lactating tortoiseshell cat had given birth to, and was feeding, her kittens in the false rattan ceiling above the restaurant tables. As in many such focal sites, this state of affairs was tolerated by the staff and management, and the cats recognised as 'semi-resident'. However, where a group of small restaurants sit in a small area, then the cats will rotate around their range very much in the manner of Bustopher Jones!

In a country like India a reverse situation can be found, with very few feral cats about. This is due not so much to the initial lack of scavengeable food, but rather to the huge numbers of competing scavengers, like dogs and holy cattle.

In Britain the impact of feral cats on our wildlife is not too marked, for the rural ones are at a much lower density than the urban ones, ten to one hundred times less. The higher numbers

. . . What intenseness of desire
In her upward eye of fire!
With a tiger-leap half way
Now she meets the coming
prey . . .

> William Wordsworth,
> 'The Kitten and Falling Leaves'

of urban cats generally have less access to small mammal prey than their country cousins, and small mammals are more frequently caught than birds. Indeed, in many ways our domestic cats are more significant as predators.

The same cannot be said for feral cats in some specialised habitats around the world, particularly on islands, where the range of species are generally few, but those species may well be peculiar to those islands. Then, the impact of feral cats, particularly on seabird colonies, can be devastating. However, it is a remarkable reflection on the cat that it can survive the harsh extremes of island life, from the equator down to the sub-Antarctic islands. The latter may present problems of freezing conditions and lashing gales, but in such hot and arid conditions as are found on the Galapagos Islands, with their lack of fresh water, the survival of the feral cats is truly staggering.

One advantage for a feral cat living in our more northern European climes, is that conditions are more balanced. We do have frosts and snow, but here the city counterpart of the rural feral has a decided advantage. The buildings of cities hold onto their heat during the day, and slowly let it out at night, cocooning the feral cats from the worst of the cold. The centre of London is indeed fortunate in suffering very few frosty nights a year. To add to that, the trick of leaping up under the bonnet of a car adds a snug place to snooze. The essential trick is to avoid putting your paws on the hot engine itself! At least, in a town or city, there is always a choice of recently warmed cars from which to choose!

Our building structures provide additional sites. Hospitals and factory sites are common places to find feral cats in Britain, and both normally have numerous buildings on open sites, with ducting and steam pipe conduits providing warmth and shelter. The very high density of domestic suburban house cats, with their own tight patterns of home ranges and territories, means there is little room for feral colonies to exist. However, wherever there is a gap with available food and shelter, and hospitals and factory sites provide these, then colonies become established. Consequently, in London, in general, feral colonies and suburban house cats tend to remain fairly separate.

Nevertheless, our constructed landscape can change that. For example, in suburban London the houses may reflect the road grid system, giving a group of back gardens, surrounded by houses, which is in turn contained by a square of roads, but there will normally be alleyways linking the squares of gardens and the outside. Not so in most of Amsterdam's big suburban nineteenth-century belt of housing. Here flats, built in continuous blocks, fully enclose a central yard or group of gardens, with no access to the outside world, except through the flats. Whilst in Britain such an area would contain a grid of house cats and a few semi-nomadic strays, in Amsterdam these suburban enclosures contain both trapped feral and house cats. Densities can be very high, but, as elsewhere, are a reflection of the avail-

140

able food. Tenants, on different floor levels, tend to have house cats, as well as those on the ground floor, and the cats gain access to the garden areas by climbing on occasional ramps. The house cats are well fed and, normally, at two or three places around the garden area, different people feed the ferals. Even at this enforced proximity, there is a tendency to keep to distinct group areas for the feral groupings, but, of necessity, with considerable overlap. Significantly at such high densities, key crossing points, as between sheds, can spark a ranking aggression more often than that seen in lower-density feral colonies, and cats are more noticeably aware of personal space. I have noticed there that feral feeding queens will dash in, with speed and displays of aggression, to obtain a tossed piece of food ahead of all other cats. However, even at these overlapping high densities, most meetings are not aggressive. Being enclosed, numbers are also more controllable and the Dutch Feral Cat Foundation (*Stichting de Zwerfkat*) is following a neutering campaign.

That our housing landscape and food availability can modify the shape and density of the general cat land-use pattern should come as no surprise, for such differences have been discerned over the last ten years, even to the extent of the difference between house and feral cats. Further, the very origins of the so-called domestication of the cat seem to have been the appearance in Egypt, or nearby, of a free-living cat that evolved in some of man's earlier townscapes, scavenging for food. It is highly likely that, rather than some magic 'act of domestication', some of these wild-living street cats (so similar to today's ferals), scavenged around the food stalls and street vendors, in the temples and into yards and open houses, as many feral taverna and semi-house cats do in the Mediterranean and Middle East today.

For most of the period since the believed point of domestication of the cat, most cats have lived a wilder life than the British suburban house-tabby.

It is so easy to forget that the acceptance of the house cat, as we understand it today, came with the advent of the British suburban villa. Today's picture of one in four homes in Britain having a household pet cat is largely due to one man, Harrison Weir, who decided to popularise the cat by holding cat shows. From the splendid idea of a Victorian suburban man, the suburban house cat was born.

Cat-in-the Snow

Mystery all around.
She sits primly upon the doorstep
Sheltered: meditating
Upon the complete loss of the
    world.
Yesterday, there it was:
Grass, trees, soft brown earth:
    little paths
And tunnels through hedges.
Green, brown and blue. Now –
    white nothing,
Bright and asparkle and
    frightening.
Tentatively she raises one paw
And holds it, consulting
With herself. Mysteries must be
    solved.
The paw is placed lightly
Upon the soft snow and slowly
    sinks
Two inches to firm ground.
Encouraged, she tries a second
    paw.
Two more and she stands firm.

She scoops a fist of foam and
    drops it.
Soft, melting magic.
She sends flying the frothy white
    flakes
She darts and springs and makes
Deep tracks showing the familiar
    green.
Birds fling snowflakes at her
Their feet kicking little branches
    bare.
Cold and wet penetrate
And Cat returns through her own
    rough tracks
To the fireside, leaving
Little flurries of snow on carpets
And paw-printed patterns
And dreams of solving white
    mysteries.
    Diana Berlow, *The Cat*, 1984.

Ode to the Common Cat

Oh frisk my whiskers, catch a rat!
There's no such thing as a common cat.
Don't common people realise
That scientists now rhapsodise
About our great intelligence?
Doctors are placing prominence
Upon our skills to help the ill.
Our purrs prove better than a pill
And we can save the very old
With body heat to stay the cold.
(Unlike the opposition dog
You needn't exercise a mog!)

Unique with monkeys and with you
We too use insight to undo
Many a teasing circumstance
With all of that's significance!

We're not aloof. We can respond.
You only get the vagabond
When you neglect to care for us.
Stroke us for purrs. Be sensuous!

In your world of conformation
Concrete piles and regulation,
Praise the tabbies, ginger tom cats
And city slicks in black and spats.
You need our singularities,
Our torn-eared eccentricities.

Nature's links are being broken.
Love your feline jungle token.
Ring out the purrs. MagnifiCAT!
There's no such thing as a common cat!

Barbara Joyce, *The Cat*, 1985

The Cat's Prayer

O my Master,
Do not expect me to be your slave, I have
 a thirst for freedom.
Do not probe my secret thoughts, I have a
 love of mystery.
Do not smother me with caresses, I have
 a preference for reserve.
Do not humiliate me, I have a sense of
 pride.
Do not, I beg, abandon me, I have a sure
 fidelity.
I'll return your love for me, I have a sense
 of true devotion.

Belgian traditional

To a Cat

Stately, kindly, lordly friend
        Condescend
Here to sit by me, and turn
Glorious eyes that smile and burn,
Golden eyes, love's lustrous meed,
On the golden page I read.

All your wondrous wealth of hair
        Dark and fair,
Silken-shaggy, soft and bright
As the clouds and beams of night,
Pays my reverent hand's caress
Back with friendlier gentleness.

Dogs may fawn on all and some
        As they come;
You, a friend of loftier mind,
Answer friends alone in kind.
Just your foot upon my hand
Softly bids it understand.

A. C. Swinburne.

Night Cat

When evening shadows smudge and blur
And blackbirds chack to rest,
Then Cat uncurls his supple self
To yawn and sniff and stretch.

Some vestige of the jungle clings
As eyes all tiger bright
With whiskers pricked and tail aloft
He melts into the night.

A noiseless Nemesis he prowls
Along his secret trail
Until he hears the pantry click
Ah! that's another tale.

In seconds flat, he's at the door
All innocence sublime,
Pretending he had *no* idea
That it was supper time.

All thoughts of mouse safaris
And tiger hunts have fled,
Pampered puss is home again
Asleep upon the bed.

W. Girt, *The Cat*, 1985

12
PHOTOGRAPHING CATS

I began photographing cats at a very early age. My father, who was a very keen amateur photographer, was always out and about taking pictures. I seemed to have inherited his keen desire, and, at the early age of eight, was given my first camera, a Box Brownie. He gave me basic instructions on how to load and unload, to wind on, following the numbers until eight was reached, and then winding-off, never to shoot into the sun, to try to get as much of the subject into the photograph as possible, and not to have just a small dot on the horizon which was, in fact, grandma! 'Get in as close as you can,' was his motto.

Film in those days was only orthochromatic, which means that it was not sensitive to red light, hence the very black and white pictures which it produced. Nowadays panchromatic film is sensitive to all colours. Another early problem was that the film speed was very slow.

I have always loved animals ever since I can remember. Usually we had a cat and a dog, but there were times when only the cat reigned supreme. Fascination with the feline form meant spending hours in the garden keeping a beady eye on a ginger and white tom called Twango. How he came by his name was uncertain, unless it was because he seemed to bound and leap like a taut bowstring. Twango would climb up into a high tree and leap from branch to branch, getting higher and higher. To a small boy of eight the tree seemed hundreds of miles high, but, on revisiting the old house many years later, there was the tree, still there, all fifteen or twenty feet of it!

Good props don't necessarily come expensive. A good habit is to use up rolls of holiday film on your cat. That way you get your holiday snaps quicker, too

Capturing character as well as beauty: black and white film is ideal

Part of the joy of owning a cat should be to record its various stages of development for posterity, and share them with distant friends. Who could not be proud of this cat, and the photo of Boots on the prowl, taken with a Nikon (F2 with FP4 film)?

One hot and sultry July afternoon, sitting beneath Old Suzanna, as I called my tree, trying in vain to draw Twango who was asleep under a bush, a hand on my shoulder announced my father with a glass of cold lemonade and chocolate cake to soften my frustration. 'Why not try photography?' was his suggestion. Now, that was a thought, but was it possible to get close enough? The cat being in a deep slumber, father said that there was a good chance, and so I went indoors to collect my precious camera, checking that it was loaded with film, as does every good photographer.

That day in July will always be regarded as marking the beginning of my career in cat photography and the memory of Twango is still treasured. Lying on my tummy and slithering forward, there was my cat stretched out in the shady part of the bush in all his glory. I sat up, raised the camera and, to my horror, he opened one eye and then the other and stared at me, but then, as all superb felines do, he posed and posed and the shutter clicked until all the film was gone. My father developed and printed the film that evening. 'Not bad,' he said, 'not bad at all,' and my chest swelled with pride.

The picturing of cats continued; all sorts of cats, sleek black cats, skinny grey cats, fat beady-eyed cats and snooty Siamese cats. There was demand for my pictures, from the little old ladies in the two-up and two-downs to Mrs Mary Chambers who lived in the big house. As time went by more sophisticated cameras were acquired and photographs were sold to the London newspapers and even to *Country Life* magazine.

Later, on entering the film industry, the photographing of cats continued, but these were now owned by stars. These cats were loved and adored by their famous owners: James Mason, Doris Day, Edward G. Robinson, Anna Neagle, Gary Cooper, Gregory Peck, Vincent Price, and the late Marilyn Monroe's Twinkle.

Cats really do get under your skin, a delight to have and a joy to be with, but, as everyone must know, they own you and you will never own them! On leaving the film industry, I took a job with a man who photographed horses, which was not as silly as it sounds, because his son was a notable cat and dog photographer in the Westcountry. Two years later came the parting of the ways and the beginning of my present association with the world of felines and their owners.

Capturing Character

The photography of cats is a little more difficult than might be imagined, especially when producing a superb picture which portrays character, as seen by the owner, as well as beauty. It is doubly difficult with pedigree cats, as each breed has physical attributes which need special treatment to show all the relevant points and positions demanded by the shape of the cat, although the golden rules apply to all photography of cats, whether pedigree or non-pedigree. I will, however, try to tell you how it may be done in the least complicated way, to enable you to

obtain the very best possible results with the equipment you have at your disposal, no matter how simple.

Choosing a Camera

There is a very large selection of cameras on the market, from the simple 'point and fire' instant type to the sophisticated, computerised 35mm models.

For the absolute beginner, the instant camera, a simple automatic with a fixed lens, is the best answer. All the well-known manufacturers make these models. The price range is very competitive, and they are all very cleverly designed. It is only necessary to set the film speed, point the camera and press the shutter release. The camera lens is always in focus, whether the subject is close up or far away, although some have a special close-up mechanism which enables very close-to-subject photography to be undertaken. The exposure is also taken care of by the camera. All have a built-in flash which is operated by pencil batteries.

For the more adventurous, there are more advanced cameras which have refinements such as the ability to fit different lenses to the same camera body (interchangeable lenses), which enable taking of wide-angle shots or zooming into close-up without moving the camera position either forwards or backwards. The very latest combine telephoto with a wide-angle lens. These cameras can also have a motor-drive which enables the film to advance to the next frame automatically without the photographer using the lever. Some of the simpler cameras also have this refinement now, which cuts out the terrible shake and chance of out-of-focus shots which previously occurred when winding on by hand too quickly.

Go to a good store, camera shop or second-hand dealer to purchase your camera. It can be risky to respond to seemingly exciting advertisements in magazines and newspapers, unless they refer to well-known stores. Always go through the workings of the camera with the sales assistant who will be only too happy to help you with this, and to answer your queries.

Some may wish to purchase a second-hand camera, and again, provided a good store is used, the end product should be quite satisfactory. Many professional photographers purchase cameras in this way, and there is no reason to suppose that the final results will not be good.

With a new camera the usual term of guarantee is one year, but with a second-hand camera, three months only is generally the rule. This is a factor to consider when making your choice. It is advisable to buy a case for the camera, or a gadget bag which will hold the camera, lenses, films and accessories safely, so that they will always be at hand when needed.

Choice of Lenses

This is only applicable to those cameras for which interchangeable lenses are available.

Felix indoors with bounced flash. There is an inevitable shadow, but you can almost feel the fur

146

Perfect timing!

The standard lens for reasonable close-up shots is 50mm, provided that the cat does not mind close encounters, as cat and camera will come fairly close together. To avoid this, a long-focus lens should be used to enable close-up shots to be taken from a distance. If only one long-focus lens is to be purchased, a zoom lens would be the most practical, and the 75–200mm is suggested as being the most useful. This also has a fine-focusing ring which enables a position close up to the subject to be taken, thus ruling out the need for a standard lens, although the longer the lens, the poorer the quality of the result.

There is no need to obtain a lens made by the manufacturer of the camera, as there are firms which make lenses only, usually at considerably more reasonable prices, and which are excellent value. Amongst the possibilities are Vivitar and Tamaron.

Film Types and Uses

There are two types of colour film; negative and positive transparency. From negative films prints can be made, whilst the other type produces colour slides which can be projected, although it is possible to have prints made from these also.

Films come in various speeds, each with an ASA number which is marked on the pack – 50, 64, 100, 160, 200, 400 and 1000.

147

Camouflage cat, in shadowless, cloudy, bright conditions. Your cat will always find the perfect setting to set itself off to best advantage: all you have to do is be there with your camera

Whenever your cat does something special, think photographically. Oliver may have been on the roof, but he could still be captured with the zoom lens

Most people will want prints of their cats, and, for this, negative film is required. For general use in summer, and for bright conditions, ASA 100 is recommended, and for winter ASA 200 or ASA 400. Faster film will make it easier to capture movement, but it must be remembered that the faster the film, the more it loses quality when enlargements are made. However, to capture fast-moving felines, ASA 400 is best, although the simpler cameras are not always able to cope with this speed of film. Certainly, if flash is not to be used, ASA 400 is superb indoors, and it also corrects different lighting conditions, ie mixed daylight and tungsten or fluorescent lights.

How to Photograph your Cat

Now that the camera is fully loaded and you are ready to meet the challenge, remember that this is no ordinary foe which you are about to encounter. Swift, cunning and very agile, the feline can disappear into the woodwork, so to speak, crawl under the settee or hide in a cardboard box. To counteract this, you must begin to think like a cat, to anticipate its movements and desires so that, wherever possible, you can be one jump ahead. But, you may think, I feed this creature, it jumps on my lap and purrs, climbs onto my bed on a cold winter's night, surely it will do what I ask it without question. Do not be fooled. As soon as the camera is produced the situation changes and your faithful feline is quite likely to disappear without trace.

Felines come in three categories. The 'I'm a star' variety will pose anywhere. Just produce a camera and it will freeze into a classic position, lean against a cushion, having first chosen exactly the right colour to set off its coat, or stare you straight in the eye. The second category is 'Catch me if you can'. This cat saunters up to you with a nonchalant air. You think 'This is going to be so easy', but not so. With one bound it is off like greased lightning, and so the game goes on. The third type is 'For food I'm anyone's'. This character can be tempted with titbits of its favourite food. In return it will allow itself to be photographed indefinitely. Sadly, many keen photographers end up with very fat cats! The real answer to these problems is thought, planning and patience.

How to Photograph your Cat Outdoors

There is no doubt at all that photographs of cats taken outdoors are the most exciting and attractive. Here they seem to be in their natural habitat, however relaxed they may be in the house, and are certainly at home in the branches of a tree, or in a special hideaway.

It is most important that a note is kept of your feline's activities; where it spends most of its time and its secret places. Have a notebook handy and, after a while, a full picture of events will have been built up.

The best weather for outdoor photography is cloudy-bright. Bright, strong sunlight causes heavy shadows, and only very experienced amateurs can cope with reflectors. However, if there is someone to help, they could hold large sheets of kitchen foil near the star of the show to soften the heavy shadows.

Having loaded the camera and noted the place where the cat is located, move carefully forward, pretending not to be at all interested in Tiddles, Maisie, Louise or Biggles. When the whole frame is filled with the subject, go down on one knee, or even on your tummy, get ready to fire, and hold your breath for one second whilst releasing the shutter. Take two or three shots, but do not waste film. Make the most of the moment.

The viewfinders on instant cameras are a little above the film to be exposed, so that very often the subject is not as it is seen. It is worth while experimenting, and it may be found that it is necessary to point the camera a little up or down to centralise the subject. With single lens reflex cameras this is already accounted for in parallax correction. If the camera has interchangeable lenses, then the cat can be captured from afar, which opens up all sorts of interesting possibilities.

Rain should not be allowed to stop photography, especially on a spring or summer's day. Have a faster film always at hand, and the results will be found to be soft and appealing. Many cats take no notice at all of the rain, except when torrential, and can often be found sitting out on wet days. Some even enjoy the snow. The main thing is to avoid harsh sunlight and heavy shadows. Harsh sunlight destroys texture and detail, and should only be used for special effects.

Always look for lovely poses, at which cats are past masters; Tomkins on the water butt, asleep with a soulful expression on his face, Betty-Lou with one paw under her chin. Photograph

Ambrose. Proud, substantial, lovable, always interested. The surroundings may be untidy, but the four paws aren't. Nikon F2, 35mm, FP4 film, indoor flash

149

your cat walking in leisurely fashion; follow it in the direction in which it is going with a slow panning action and you will capture its movement. Do not worry about a little loss of sharpness in this case, as it will add to the effect of the picture.

Another interesting aspect is to include a person in the photograph. Small children make wonderful additions to any animal study. Provided that the cat is used to children, and safe with them, many natural situations can be captured. Try to think out some poses before taking the photograph. Apart from capturing the natural situation when it presents itself, many a so-called 'natural' study has been posed with great care. Perhaps a little boy could be sitting in the shade of a tree, with a leafy back-

Cats in the tack room: a superb photograph in its own right

Tommy on the move

ground, with your cat or kitten nestling in his arms. Your wife, husband, boy- or girlfriend could be looking over a wall or log with the cat beside them. If you are worried about the cat running off, a thin lead attached to a harness (not to its collar) could solve the problem.

Photographing your Cat Indoors

Of course, as we spend a great deal of our time indoors, particularly during the winter months, and most of our cats do likewise, indoor photography is a must. Our felines have so many places which they treat as their own, in which they can look decorative, interesting or even amusing, that the possibilities are unlimited. There are two ways of taking pictures indoors, either with flash or by natural, that is available, light.

For the flash-user, the main problem which people seem to encounter is red-eye. This can be avoided by making certain that the flash is not directed straight into the cat's eyes, but rather from an angle from one side or the other, or by bouncing the flash off the ceiling, wall or a reflective surface. With the more expensive cameras, the flash is placed on an attachment known as a hot shoe, and automatically fires the shutter. The flash has to be set to correspond with the speed of the film being used and can also be set for varying distances so that both near and far subjects can be covered successfully.

*Smokey in 'Look Back in Anger'
The art of successful cat
photography is capturing the
expressive moment or gesture that
says everything about its unique
personality*

With instant cameras the flash pops up at the touch of a button, but the subject should not be approached too closely or the light will be too much and 'burn out' the photograph, causing it to be too light with very little, or no, detail. Too great a distance from the subject for the strength of the flash, on the other hand, will lead to the photograph being too dark. Experimentation is the order of the day.

Available light photography requires the use of fast film and Kodacolor 400 or Fujicolor 400 is recommended. It offers so much scope for exciting effects that it should be used whenever possible. Sunlight streaming in through the window, falling onto the cat's fur, makes a silhouette against the light, set off by a golden halo. Cats can be captured looking round a door, or peering from beneath the sofa, and with no flash to startle, or cause burn-out, using long-focus lenses, you can be like the invisible man. The shutter speed must not be below 1/15th of a second or the film will show only a blur. With the instant camera, when the light is below a certain level, a light will automatically come on to show that flash should be used. In every case, look for the natural picture and capture that magnificent moment to treasure forever.

If two, or even three, cats will pose together, make certain that the situation is attractive. Avoid chair legs (unless a cat is wrapping itself around one, or it is especially relevant to the picture) and fussy backgrounds with masses of ornaments. It is the cat that counts.

Backgrounds and Settings

Always remember that all colours reflect light, and, although this is not apparent to the naked eye, give a cast of their own colour to any object which is near them. For example, wearing a green blouse or shirt will result in green being reflected onto the skin, altering the skin tones. With felines, a white cat sitting on a red cushion would come out with a red cast, whilst a blue cat in the same setting would appear brownish fawn. Backgrounds must be chosen with great care to see that they compliment the cat's colour. A white cat on a blue background, for example, would be perfect. Experiment with your cat and find out which colours suit it best.

You could place your cat in attractive settings (sometimes they will surprise you and stay put for a while), with flowers, shaped vases, books – whatever takes your fancy and you have to hand at the time. Perhaps go to the cat's own special place and then wait for the most appealing moment. Many a good photograph is spoilt by pressing the shutter just a little too soon; knowing when to take the shot, neither too soon nor too late, is one of the secrets of the winning photograph.

Black and White Photography

If it is at all possible, try some black and white photography, known officially as monochrome. Sadly, there are not so many

*Opposite Twitch is a picture of
contentment*

processing stations as there used to be, as it seems to be out of fashion at the moment. However, some excellent and dramatic effects can be obtained, both indoors and outside, even under very dull conditions, which would be very boring and flat in colour. Texture and coat patterns, especially of tabby cats, are most effective in monochrome. For the summer months the film to use is FP3, or the all-rounder HP5 or TRI-X. These are fast films, and, with interchangeable lenses, will give a range of possibilities.

A book on black and white photography might be a help; it might be possible to find one in a second-hand shop. This will give an idea of the range of tones which can be obtained. Although colour is eternally flattering to both human and animal subjects, nothing is nicer, to my mind, than a black and white enlargement of my favourite cat, every hair bristling with life, highlights reflecting from a flickering eye. An important fact to remember is that monochrome's high contrast can show up badly if not handled carefully, unlike colour, which, by its very nature, copes better.

Caught in the act!

Points to Remember

I could go on, for hundreds of pages, to give a detailed description of feline photography, but, since space does not allow this, I have tried to be concise and explicit without being too technical. Important points to remember are:

Choice of camera – within your means and use.
Choice of film – negative for prints, positive for transparencies.
Watch your cat – be familiar with its habits.
Backgrounds – consider colour, complicated surroundings, interesting, or complimentary settings.
Harsh sunlight – beware – except for special effects.
Best conditions – cloudy/bright.
Dark conditions – do not shoot at below 1/15th second.
Available light – use indoors wherever possible.
Flash – do not use too close to subject.
Flash – do not shoot straight into the cat's eyes.
Flash – bounce wherever possible.
Do make every shot count.
Do not waste film.
Do experiment and make notes of your results.
Try to learn from your mistakes and aim to improve.
Progress to a more advanced camera as you become more proficient.

Follow the golden rules and the joys of feline photography can be yours.

154

13
CATS AND THE LAW

The first Act of Parliament for the protection of domestic animals was passed in 1822, since when there have been many enactments dealing with the welfare of domestic pets, and it is interesting to note that, since the Dog Licences Act, 1867, Parliament has passed some nine Dogs Acts or Dogs (Amendments) Acts, or similar legislation relating solely to dogs, whilst it has, at no time, ever passed a Cats Act nor any act solely devoted to the welfare and protection of cats.

It does seem that the law recognises the essential difference between a cat, which roams independently and at will, and a dog which has complete dependence on man who must keep it effectively controlled. Among all domestic animals, the cat is the only one not subject to the laws of trespass.

Although there is no Cat Act as such, there is a wealth of legislation which covers the protection, from cruelty, of domestic animals, including cats. One early act, which remained on the Statute Book for over a century until its repeal in 1986, was the Cruelty to Animals Act, 1876, which prohibited painful experiments on animals without adequate anaesthesia and made places where experiments on animals were carried out registerable and subject to licensing by the Home Office.

Perhaps one of the most important acts passed for the protection of cats, and, indeed, all animals, was the Protection of Animals Act, 1911, which endeavoured to define offences of cruelty and gave the courts power, when the owner of an animal had been found guilty of an offence of cruelty, to order the destruction of the animal if the court was satisfied that it would be cruel to keep the animal alive. It also gave the courts power to deprive the owner, guilty of an offence of cruelty to an animal, of ownership of that animal. The Act similarly gave a police constable power to order the destruction of an animal, if it was in such a diseased or injured condition that there was no possibility of removing it for treatment without further cruelty.

So far as cats are concerned, an act of cruelty under the Act of 1911 would be:

(a) for any person to cruelly beat, kick, illtreat, torture, infuriate or terrify the animal or to permit any animal to be so treated or by wantonly or unreasonably doing or omitting to do any act or causing or procuring the commission or omission of any act so as to cause any unnecessary suffering to a cat.

Cats' eyes
A familiar feature of travelling by
night is the recurring sight of cats'
eyes, both the ingenious markers
of the centre line of the road and
the genuine articles. Normally
green, although the colour can
vary, cats' eyes reflect light by
virtue of the tapetum lucidum, a
mirror-like lining to the back of
the retina, which is common to
many nocturnal animals.
Incidentally, cats cannot see in
total darkness but they can most
certainly see in very poor lighting
conditions where the human eye
has no vision at all.

(b) for any person to carry or permit to be carried a cat in such a manner or position as to cause a cat unnecessary suffering.

(c) for any person wilfully and without reasonable cause to administer or cause to be administered any poison or injurious drug or substance to a cat.

(d) for any person to subject or permit to be subjected a cat to any operation which is performed without due care and humanity.

(e) for any person to sell or offer or expose for sale or to give away any grain or seed which has been rendered poisonous (except for bona fide use in agriculture).

(f) for any person to put on any land or building any poison or any fluid or edible matter which has been rendered poisonous (not being seed or grain).

By the Animals (Anaesthetics) Act, 1919, it was made unlawful for the carrying out of certain operations on cats unless, during the whole operation, the cat is under the influence of a general anaesthetic of sufficient power to prevent the feeling of pain. Such operations included the neutering of a cat and certain amputations. The Act permitted the use of local anaesthetics for certain operations of a lesser nature, provided that such local anaesthetic was of sufficient power to prevent the cat feeling pain.

The Pet Animals Act, 1951, first made pet shops subject to licensing by the local authority in whose area the shops were situated and, in determining whether a pet shop should be licensed, the local authority had to have regard to:

a) the suitability of the premises in respect of size, temperature, lighting, ventilation and cleanliness;

b) the means of supply of food and drink;

c) that pet animals were not to be sold at too early an age;

d) that reasonable precautions be taken to prevent the spread of infectious disease among the animals;

e) that appropriate steps be taken to prevent the spread of fire.

The Act gave the local authority power to inspect pet shops from time to time and also banned the sale of cats in the streets or other public places, other than from a stall or barrow in a market place. It also banned the sale of cats to any person believed to be under the age of twelve years.

Very considerable suffering by cats was alleviated in 1954 when the Pests Act of that year prohibited the use of certain types of spring traps for the trapping of rabbits and vermin, other than traps of an approved kind, and the sale and owner- ship of spring traps not of an approved kind was made illegal.

Another act which reduced distress among cats was a very short one, the Abandonment of Animals Act, 1960. In effect it made any person, being the owner or having charge of a cat, who, without reasonable cause or excuse, abandoned it whether

permanently or not, in circumstances likely to cause the cat unnecessary suffering, guilty of an offence of cruelty within the meaning of the Protection of Animals Act, 1911.

The Animal Boarding Establishments Act, 1963, made all animal boarding establishments subject to licensing by the local authority in whose area they were situated. In deciding whether such an establishment should be licensed, the local authority must have regard to the suitability of the premises, the need for the security of the animals boarded, the provision for feeding and watering, the prevention of the spread of infectious diseases and the spread of fire, and the cleanliness of the premises.

A boarding cattery is also compelled to keep a register of all cats admitted, with dates of arrival and departure, and the owners' names and addresses. The licence is renewable annually and the establishment is subject to inspection from time to time by officers of the local authority.

Cruelty or causing unnecessary suffering to cats is forbidden by law

157

Tree climbing and claw sharpening in someone else's apple tree at dusk? The cat is the only domestic animal not subject to the laws of trespass

The most recent legislation affecting cats is the Animals (Scientific Procedures) Act, 1986, the provisions of which came into force on 1 January 1987. The Act is intended to tighten up the control of experiments on living animals and provides for a wide-ranging system of licensing for the individuals involved and for the appointment of inspectors and an advisory committee. One of the most important features of the Act, so far as cats are concerned, is the provision, in Clause 10, that no cat shall be used in an experiment unless it has been bred at, or obtained from, a designated breeding establishment holding a certificate issued by the Secretary of State. This firmly establishes the illegality of obtaining cats for experimentation from any other source and should go a long way towards stamping out the illicit trade in animals stolen for this purpose.

Apart from the above enactments for the protection and welfare of cats, many other Acts of Parliament affect cats, including:

The Theft Act, 1968

Under this Act a domestic cat is deemed to be a chattel, just like a piece of furniture, and is capable of being stolen. Even though the cat is lost or strays, it remains the property of the owner. It is only when a cat reverts to its wild state that it can no longer be owned and therefore cannot be stolen. Feral cats cannot be owned.

Sale of Goods Act, 1893

Again, under this Act, a domestic cat is treated as a chattel for sale purposes and the general law relating to the sale of goods applies to cats. In the purchase of a cat the legal maxim *caveat emptor* applies, in other words, let the buyer beware. A buyer must accept the cat in the condition that he finds it, and has no

The law recognises that the cat roams independently at will

158

Famous cats
One of the best known cats of all time is Puss in Boots. There are many versions of this legend in many countries, but the theme of them all is the same: Puss brings fame and fortune to his master, including a beautiful bride. Even more well known is Tom of *Tom and Jerry*, who never survives an episode without being flattened, stretched or otherwise assaulted, yet who always emerges triumphant over his adversaries.

The affinity between writers and cats has often been noted, especially as, if a cat is to be recorded for posterity, he needs his Boswell to make him famous. Dr Johnson's famous cat, Hodge, was regaled with the occasional feast of oysters, which the good Doctor purchased himself '. . . lest the servants, having that trouble, should take a dislike to the poor creature'. Edward Lear, of *The Owl and the Pussycat* fame, is said to have had his new house in San Remo built to exactly the same specifications as his previous residence, so that his much-loved tabby, Foss, would immediately feel at home. Sir Winston Churchill's marmalade tom contributed to the war effort by sleeping on the foot of his master's bed and keeping him warm.

Ernest Hemingway had thirty cats in his house on the top of a hill in Havana. The reason he had so many was his great appreciation of their 'absolute emotional honesty'. Human beings can be devious or dishonest about their feelings for all kinds of reasons, but a cat is not; he will not pretend to be something other than he is merely for approval. While living in Paris, Hemingway also used to leave their baby son in the care of an affectionate and reliable puss called F. Puss. The neighbours were greatly concerned at this, (*continued opposite*)

legal redress later against the seller. However, a buyer can gain some measure of protection by requiring an express warranty and making it a condition of the purchase that the animal is reasonably suitable for the particular purpose for which it is required. A purchaser of a pedigree cat required for breeding purposes would be wise to obtain from the seller a warranty, in writing, that the cat is suitable for this purpose and an undertaking that, in the event of the cat proving unsuitable, the seller will take the cat back and refund the purchase price.

The Road Traffic Act, 1972

Under this Act, if an accident occurs and an animal is struck and injured by a motor vehicle, the driver of the vehicle must stop and give his name and address, the name and address of the vehicle's owner, and the registration number of the vehicle to any person having reasonable grounds for requiring such information. If there is no person around requiring such information, the driver must report the accident to the police within twenty-four hours of the occurrence. However, under the Act the term 'animal' means any horse, cattle, ass, mule, sheep, pig, goat or dog. A cat is not included in the definition, and there is no obligation on a driver to stop or report an accident involving injury to a cat.

Firearms Act, 1968

This Act is mentioned because of the appalling incidence of cruelty to cats and other animals by the indiscriminate use of airguns and, latterly, crossbows. The definition of a firearm under the Act is 'a lethal barrelled weapon of any description from which any shot, bullet or missile can be discharged'. The definition includes airguns but not, sadly, crossbows because they have no barrels. As a result, a crossbow may be purchased over the counter in a sports shop without any form of licence. Because of the frequent and serious injuries caused to people and animals by these weapons there is, at the present time, a great deal of agitation and pressure to bring crossbows within the scope of the Firearms Act.

There are some questions which are frequently asked regarding cats and the law, of which the following are typical.

Q) Recently I bought a lovely kitten from a pet shop. The following day I discovered that it was completely deaf and blind in one eye. Can I recover the price I paid from the pet shop?
A) No. By examination of the kitten you could have discovered these defects before you bought it and there is no redress. *Caveat emptor* applies.

Q) I recently purchased a young cat from a pet shop. It seemed fit and lively, but by the following morning it had severe flu and I paid out considerable amounts in vet's fees to get it well. Can I recover the vet's bills from the pet shop?

A) No. The cat appeared well when you bought it and there is no reason to think that the pet shop owner knew that it had been infected with cat flu. Pet shops purchase their stock from all sorts of sources and could not possibly guarantee that all their animals were free of infection. Under the Sale of Goods Act you purchased the cat in the condition that you found it and there is no redress.

Q) I have lost my pedigree cat and believe it to have been stolen by a person in a nearby street. Can I advertise for its return, offering a reward and stating that if it is returned no questions will be asked?

A) No. To use words indicating that no questions will be asked, or implying that a person stealing a cat would be safe from prosecution, is in itself an offence for which the advertiser could be prosecuted.

Q) Some weeks ago my cat strayed and I have discovered that a nearby resident has taken it into her home and has been feeding it. She refuses to return the cat unless I pay her for the cat's keep while she has been looking after it. Can she do this?

A) No. Although the cat has strayed, the property in the cat remained at all times vested in you. The finder cannot demand payment from you. However, as a matter of commonsense, and to prevent illfeeling between neighbours, it might be prudent to pay a reasonable demand.

Q) My cat returned home with airgun pellets embedded in its side. I know that a boy living locally has an airgun. What action can I take? Can I claim damages?

A) Without the strictest proof, no action can be taken. It would be necessary for you to have conclusive proof that the boy fired the gun and hit the cat. Unfortunately, boys rarely fire at animals while people are watching. Even though you had such proof, a claim for damages would be likely to be uneconomic. After all, what value would a court put on an ordinary crossbred cat?

Q) My cat wandered into my neighbour's garden, ate some slug pellets which had been put down and became very ill. My vet's bills for treatment of the cat were considerable. Can I claim the cost from my neighbour?

A) Sadly, not if the pellets were put down for genuine horticultural purposes. A cat cannot trespass and, for that privilege, must bear the penalties of its actions.

Q) My cat wandered into a nearby house which was being treated for woodworm infestation, and, as a result of inhaling fluid used in the treatment, became very ill and subsequently died. Can I sue either the owner of the building or the wood-treatment firm?

A) No. For the reasons given in the last answer, no action would lie against either the owner of the building or the firm carrying out the treatment.

but F. Puss sat there erect, keeping guard, and if he slept he lay at a safe distance from the child's face.

Real cats apart, many writers have created cats that have come alive for their readers, from T. S. Eliot's characters in *Old Possum's Book of Practical Cats* (featured in the musical *Cats*) to Beatrix Potter's mischievous Tom Kitten who climbs up the chimney where he shouldn't go and gets himself made into a kitten roly poly pudding by a pair of rats. Is it possible to imagine a world – real or fictional – that would not be infinitely the poorer without cats?

What do you do when your sixteen-week-old kitten alleges it's stuck right at the top of the tree? Many more cats claim to be stuck than actually can't come down, but rescuing the few that are genuinely stuck can be embarrassing and expensive

Scrumping. At nine weeks old, it's still a little young to have them thinking about calling the fire brigade out . . . but not too young to start learning . . .

THE NATURAL HISTORY OF CATS

We have remarked in a former letter how much incongruous animals, in a lonely state, may be attached to each other from a spirit of sociality; in this it may not be amiss to recount a different motive which has been known to create as strange a fondness.

My friend had a little helpless leveret brought to him, which the servants fed with milk in a spoon, and about the same time his cat kittened and the young were dispatched and buried. The hare was soon lost, and supposed to be gone the way of most foundlings, to be killed by some dog or cat. However, in about a fortnight, as the master was sitting in his garden in the dusk of the evening, he observed his cat, with tail erect, trotting towards him, and calling with little short inward notes of complacency, such as they use towards their kittens, and something gamboling after, which proved to be the leveret that the cat had supported with her milk, and continued to support with great affection.

Thus was a gramnivorous animal nurtured by a carnivorous and predaceous one!

Why so cruel and sanguinary a beast as a cat, of the ferocious genus of *Feles*, the *murium leo*, as Linnacus calls it, should be affected with any tenderness towards an animal which is its natural prey, is not so easy to determine.

This strange affection probably was occasioned by that *desiderium*, those tender maternal feelings, which the loss of her kittens had awakened in her breast; and by the complacency and ease she derived to herself from the procuring her teats to be drawn, which were too much distended with milk, till, from habit, she became as much delighted with this foundling, as if it had been her real offspring. – Gilbert White, *The Natural History of Selborne*, (1776).

The 'deceitful domestic'

This animal is so well known as to make a description of it unnecessary. It is a useful, but deceitful domestic; active, neat, sedate, intent on its prey. When pleased purres and moves its tail; when angry spits, hisses, and strikes with its foot; when walking, it draws in its claws. It drinks little; is fond of fish; washes its face with its fore-foot, (*Linnaeus* says at the approach of a storm). The female is remarkably salacious; a piteous, squalling, jarring lover. Its eyes shine in the night; its hair when rubbed in the dark emits fire; it is even proverbially tenacious of life; always lights on its feet; is fond of perfumes; *Marum, Catmint, Valerian,* &c. – Thomas Pennant (1776).

The Libidinous Cat

The maner of their copulation is this, the Female layeth downe and the Male standeth, and their females are aboue measure desirous of procreation, for which cause they prouoke the male, and if he yeeld not to their lust they beate and claw him, but it is onely for loue of young and not for lust: the male is most libidinous, and therefore seeing the female will neuer more engender with him, during the time hir young ones sucke, hee killeth and eateth them if he meet with them, (to prouoke the female to copulation with him againe, for when she is depriued of her young, she seeketh out the male of her own accord,) for which the female most warily keepeth them from his sight. During the time of copulation, the female continually cryeth, whereof the Writers giue a double cause; one, because she is pinched with the talants or clawes of the male in the time of his lustfull rage, and thother, because his seed is so fiery hot, that it almost burneth the females place of conception. When they haue litered or as we commonly say kittened, they rage against Dogges, and will suffer none to come neere their young ones. The best to keep are such as are littered in March, they go with young fifty daies, and the females liue not aboue sixe or seuen yeares, and males liue longer especially if they be gelt or libbed: the reason of their short life is their rauening of meate which corrupteth within them

Cleanliness

It is a neate and cleanly creature, oftentimes licking hir own body to keep it smooth and faire, hauing naturally a flexible backe for this purpose, and washing hir face with her fore feet: . . . And her nature is to hide her own dung or excrements, for she knoweth that the sauour and presence thereof, will driue away her sport, the little Mouse being able by that stoole to smelle the presence of hir mortall foe. – Edward Topsell, *The Historie of Foure-Footed Beasts* (17th Century).

14
FELINE PHYSIOLOGY

The cat is the near perfect animal. Evolution over thousands of years has produced an animal with a sleek hunter's body and a body function that allows it to live with or close to the human population. Body function in the cat is very adaptable to a variety of climates, it allows the cat to thrive on a great number of diverse foodstuffs, and to be successful in combating most parasites and other infections.

In comparison with other domesticated animals, the cat has suffered little from man's interference in artificial breeding. In other animals selection for show points, extremes of body shape, speed and stamina, milk production (as in cows and goats), to name a few, have produced grotesque shapes. The dog, more than other domestic pets, suffers from selective breeding which has brought about many disease conditions resulting from inborn defects.

The cat's physiology is beautifully organised, allowing a comfortable and satisfactory existence, but with one extreme, an apparent necessity to breed remorselessly. It is fortunate that there are surgical and medical means of controlling breeding in the feline population.

A brief description of the functioning of the various organs of the cat will illustrate how each part contributes to the harmonious existence of the whole animal.

The inner structure of your cat, showing the basis of its exceptional grace, strength and flexibility

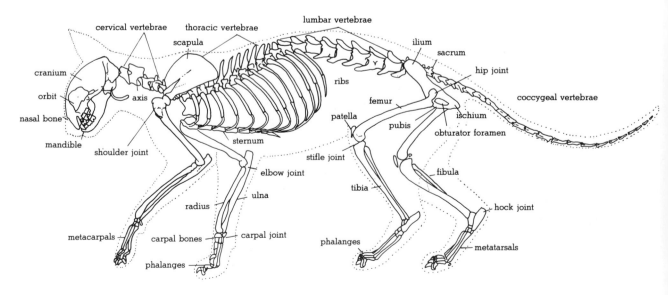

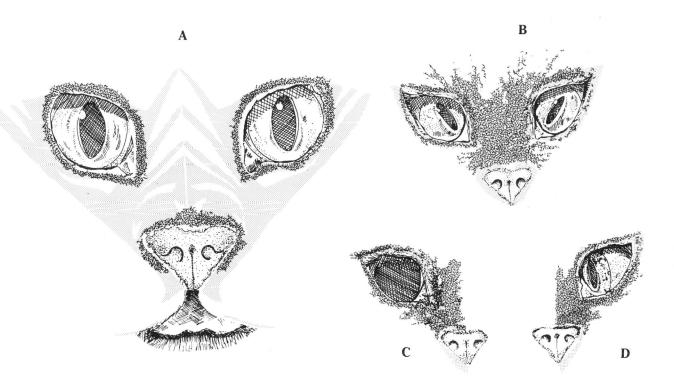

The Eyes

As a hunting animal, the cat has eyesight specially sensitive for night vision. The eyes are adapted for gathering all available light, and receiving this on sensitive nerve receptors that lie in the retina at the back of the eye. The shape of the pupil is unlike that of any other domestic animal. In dim light, or when the cat is frightened, the pupil appears as a very wide aperture and the iris forms only a narrow ring inside the white of the eye (the sclera). At other times the iris is very visible, with delightful gradations of colour that make for interest in the cat's face. Colour of the eyes and shape of the eyelids contribute much to the appeal of looking at cats. In the brightest sunshine, the pupil is reduced to a narrow vertical slit, and the amount of light reaching the retina is reduced.

The retina is backed by the reflective tapetum which is responsible for the greenish-coloured glow seen when a light is shone into the eye. This reflective layer acts like a mirror, doubling the amount of light that the nerves in the retina can receive. It is necessary that the pupil can constrict rapidly to protect the sensory layers of the retina from overbright light. A scissor-like action of the muscles in the iris produces this quick response, which allows a cat to stalk a garden bird in the bright sun, then hunt a mouse equally well indoors or at dusk. The retina is rich in rods and has a large number of cones concentrated at the centre for high visual receptivity. It seems probable that the cat has colour vision.

The third eyelid lies in the corner of the eye and is a structure that protects the eye from injury. The cat has the ability to

Eye Disorders
A The normal position of the cat's eyes
B An inward squint of the eye pupils caused by paralysis of the abducent nerve
C A dilated pupil in one eye can be caused by a detached retina or nerve blindness
D An eye with the pupil out of position caused by trochlear nerve paralysis

165

retract the eyeball, so that the third eyelid comes across the front of the eye to cover part or all of the cornea. This response is also seen when there is an injury, such as a cat scratch or when a cat is suffering from dehydration or any debilitating illness. The eyelids also protect the eye, and they may suffer injury during fighting between cats.

The Ears
The cat's ears are sensitive to touch, and its hearing ability is very acute. The chambers of the middle ear also control a cat's balance and head position; a cat with an ear infection, or other internal nerve damage, may drop its head on the side where the ear is affected.

Taste and Touch
Two other well-developed special senses in cats are taste and touch, the vibrissae, or whiskers, responding to the slightest deviation, and thus aiding movement in the dark. The tongue and the nose are used when a cat explores a new situation, the tongue may often be seen transferring mucus and moisture onto the nose. The distress of an ill cat, with a dry crusty nose and dry mouth, is obvious, while bouts of sneezing and salivation disturb a cat and may contribute to loss of appetite.

The cat is reluctant to breathe through its mouth and it is only at times of extreme stress, as seen in shock or heat exhaustion, that a cat pants with mouth wide open. It is not easy to see inside a cat's mouth, but the tongue should be long and pink with many fine white papillae in the centre near the tip. These rough papillae are used, when the cat laps milk or other fluid, to throw the liquid onto the back of the throat. The rasp-like feel of a cat's licking comes from these papillae; they have a further function in the grooming of the coat. It is a delight to see a cat carefully lick its paw, then introduce its foot into its ear or some other part of the body that its tongue cannot reach. Elsewhere the tongue is applied direct to the coat and the papillae remove loose fur, some of which may then be swallowed during the grooming process.

The Teeth
The teeth of a cat also deserve study as they form an arrangement suitable for a hunting animal. The front teeth are very small, and may be used more for grooming than in feeding. The very long slender canine teeth are deeply rooted in the upper and lower jaws. These are curved, with sharp points, and ideally placed for gripping and holding small rodents. The molar teeth have rounded cusps on their masticatory surfaces, and the bite of the upper on the lower molar produces a scissor cut. The lower jaw can also slide sideways to produce a stronger gnawing or chewing bite. The largest tooth, with three roots, is the third premolar in the upper jaw, whilst, in the lower jaw, the first molar is the biggest tooth.

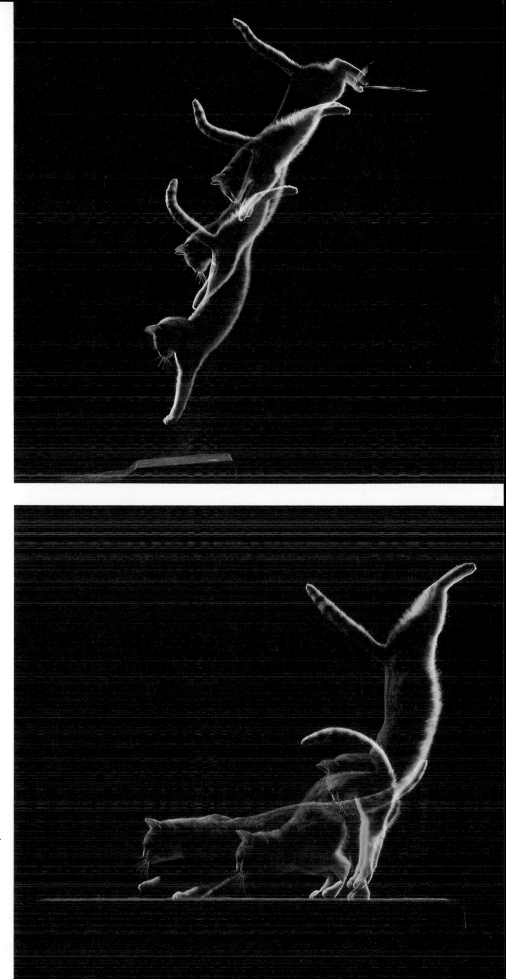

The strongest muscle in cats runs along both sides of the spine, and enables the cat to spring up in the air or leap considerable distances; the arch of the spine straightens out as the muscles contract, and the tail is used for balance

The Digestive System

The digestive tract of a cat is adapted to deal with whole animals, eaten as prey, or with soft canned food. The pharynx at the back of the mouth is easily distended, so that large pieces of food can be swallowed and propelled down the oesophagus to the stomach. Provided there is adequate lubrication from salivary mucus, it is quite rare for anything to get stuck. Once food reaches the stomach, it remains there for one to three hours, being further softened and digested by acidic gastric juices that contain enzymes used to split up fats and proteins. The exit from the stomach is through the strong pyloric sphincter which allows semi-digested food to pass into the small intestine where peristaltic contraction passes the food along while it is subjected to further digestive processes.

Vomiting is not unusual in the cat and may help to protect the animals from food poisoning, especially if the stomach juices cannot penetrate all of the food mass that has been swallowed. Cats will also be sick when anything blocks the exit from the stomach. A *fur ball* may form in the stomach when fine hair is swallowed faster than it can be passed on through the intestine.

The act of vomiting is under nervous control and in some cases commences with a wave of antiperistalsis in the intestine, so that alkaline bile is brought into the stomach and this stimulates a vomiting reflex. The act of ejecting stomach contents, whether this is a fur ball or food, starts with a closed pylorus and relaxation of the cardiac sphincter. Muscle contraction presses the stomach against the fixed diaphragm so that the stomach contents are squeezed into the oesophagus and then out through the mouth. Antiperistaltic waves in the oesophagus also help in the expulsion. It is a normal way for cats to eject one or more hairballs from the stomach; some longhaired cats accumulate a large mass of very fine hair which is difficult to dislodge. Such cats always seem hungry but can eat only a small amount of food at a time, because the stomach is overfull.

Nourishment is obtained when digested food is absorbed through the wall of the small intestine and conveyed by the blood to the liver and elsewhere for storage and reprocessing. The liver is a key organ and susceptible to damage by chemicals and toxins. Fortunately it is not as often subject to disease as the dog's liver. The liver, too, is involved in the digestion of fat; animal fats are beneficial to the cat and may form up to 9 per cent of its diet. The cat requires more protein than the dog and most proprietary cat-foods take this into account and are based on formulas that provide for the maintenance of health. There is a specific requirement in the cat's diet for the amino acid taurine, and cats that are fed mainly on canned dog-foods may develop a form of blindness (FCRD) because of a lack of this amino acid. Milk contains the protein casein but is deficient in taurine, and cannot be used to make good any deficiency.

The large intestine does not absorb nutrients, as it lacks the villi (small protuberances) that provide an extensive area for

168

absorption in the small intestine. The colon stores the waste products of digestion and allows water to be absorbed back into the body, thus making the faeces firmer. The cat can survive by drinking very little water because it has this efficient method of recycling fluid from food eaten and reabsorbing water from the large intestine. However, fresh water should always be available, as the cat may need to drink in warm conditions, or during dehydrating illnesses, such as diarrhoea or kidney disease, where water is quickly lost. Faeces are stored in the rectum and voided once or twice a day. Cats can be very secretive about their elimination of waste and may become voluntarily constipated rather than deposit faeces in an unsuitable place. At other times a cat will expel faeces, and sometimes urine as well, to show its presence or to draw attention to itself.

Persistent diarrhoea may cause dehydration and here the young kitten is especially at risk, having less reserves to maintain its fluids in balance. Enteritis is quite common, and malabsorption may also cause soft faeces since water is drawn from the body into the intestine by the digestive products that remain within the tube of the intestines. Inflammation of the colon is not common in the cat, but, if present, may indicate that one constituent of the diet is causing diarrhoea originating in the large intestine. A cat with an irritable colon may pass faeces six to eight times a day, sometimes with painful straining, and an outpouring of jelly-like mucus from the intestine wall.

A physiological problem of the intestine, seen in the older cat, is *colonic impaction*, where weakness of muscle contraction and a lack of fibre in the diet may result in a swollen colon full of soft, putty-like faeces.

Grass-eating by cats may be an attempt to obtain extra moisture and vegetable fibre, but all that can be said about cats who 'graze' excessively is that this indicates some sort of abdominal disease and compulsive grass-eating should be investigated by a veterinary surgeon. The provision of recently sown grass is a natural treatment.

The elimination of waste has an especial interest to those who study cat behaviour. The acts of urination and defecation are not necessarily performed together, at the same time, or at the same place. Some cats prefer to cover or bury their faeces or urine, although at other times urine may be sprayed onto vertical objects and faeces may be deposited in prominent places, such as the centre of the lawn or, occasionally, indoors. It seems that these highly odoriferous materials are being used here as a form of advertisement. Breakdowns in house-training may often be the result of some stress in a cat's life and can be compared to the writing of graffiti in public places.

The Kidneys

The cat's kidneys are located in the abdomen just behind the ribs and are well protected from injury. Some entire male cats become very thin during the breeding season, and their kidneys

A cat's physiology is beautifully organised; Ted's pupils are reduced to a narrow vertical slit in the bright sunlight; in darkness they open up completely

may become so large as to cause bulging of the emaciated abdomen. Renal failure is not uncommon in the older cat and is shown by weight loss, lethargy and inappetence, the kidneys becoming small and contracted at this stage of illness. The bladder can store urine for twelve hours or more, but there is a greater risk of *cystitis* if cats store urine for long periods, or take insufficient exercise. In *urinary obstruction*, sand-like material (calculi) may form and cause a blockage of the cat's urethra. Calculi are composed of struvite which is rich in magnesium. They seem to lodge in the penis of the neutered male, or, occasionally, deeper in, at the level of the bulbourethral glands. Females may have bladder calculi and blood loss in the urine, but this is not always seen at first until an 'accident' happens indoors.

Sexual Maturity

Female cats mature soon after six months of age, oestrus being first detected by the behaviour known as 'calling'. It is not usual to see any discharge or swelling of the vulva. Ovulation occurs twenty-four to thirty-six hours after mating which, at the very beginning of oestrus, has a high conception rate, although repeated matings may be needed to stimulate necessary

170

hormones in the queen. In unmated queens, a return of calling can be anticipated after one week. Longhaired cats seem to breed less frequently. It is possible to suppress breeding by hormone tablets or by injections, but it is much better to remove the ovaries and uterus of the young kitten (the operation known as spaying) to prevent any breeding. Once a queen has had her kittens, oestrus may show within a week of the birth, and conception is again possible, but it is more usual for a queen to call first about a week after the kittens have been weaned and removed from her.

The male cat matures sexually soon after six months, and the onset of a breeding season may be demonstrated by the spraying of strong-smelling urine, especially in the house. The testicles can first be recognised in the scrotum of a very tiny kitten. As the kitten grows, they increase in size, and are especially prominent in some oriental cats. The penis is normally directed backwards and is not visible. During mating the penis becomes directed forwards, the erectile tissue being supported by bone (cartilage in the younger tom) and this allows for rapid mating with the queen. The tough papillae of the penis stimulate the queen and seem to cause pain in some matings, although there is a fairly quick return to further matings if the queen and tom are left with each other. The sperm released move rapidly and may be found near the ovary within half a minute of being deposited near the cervix in the vagina of a queen.

Other Systems

Other physiological matters can be described more briefly, as they are of less practical application. Breathing in a cat goes almost unnoticed, except when the nose is blocked as in cat flu. Any cause of *nasal obstruction* distresses a cat and repeated bouts of sneezing are necessary to clear the nose. Mouth breathing is unusual except in distress: it may indicate the onset of shock after a road accident or possibly that the cat has become too hot. Panting, as a method of heat control, is far less usual than with the dog. It is very important to avoid a heat build-up, such as might result from shutting a cat in a hot room, a car, or any container left in direct sunlight.

The *endocrine system* is very important in maintaining homeostasis, the hormones produced by the cat all helping to maintain good health. Unfortunately, excess or insufficient hormone secretion may be the first time the cat-owner becomes aware of the important role they play. *Diabetes* can be detected in some cats, and this disease occurs when there is a lack of natural insulin from the pancreatic gland. The importance of the cat's thyroid gland has only been recognised quite recently when hormone-level tests at specialised laboratories became available. An *over-active thyroid* can be a cause of weight loss and may be confused with kidney disease in cats.

Train driver rescues kittens
For no apparent reason, the train stopped on a ridge with the wind whistling round us and nothing to be seen for miles except flat fields. The driver and guard jumped out and, shortly afterwards, returned with a box which they showed to the passengers: five tiny kittens! Fortunately, the driver was observant – and kindly – for he chuckled as he sucked a finger, 'One of the little bs bit me!' he said, beaming. They were handed over to a waiting station official, and everyone hoped they would find a more considerate owner than their first. – *The Cat.*

171

Muscle and Bone

The litheness of the cat's movement is attributed to its finely developed musculo-skeletal system. A healthy cat moves with grace and agility, but all of this is lost in the overweight domestic pet and control of the diet is important in preventing excess fat from being deposited under the skin. The cat's skeleton has the same arrangement of bones as other mammals, but each bone is light in construction. The leg bones are gently curved and this, with the rounded skull and undulating curve of the spine, produces the shape of the cat we know. It should be mentioned that the cat has a collar bone, or clavicle, a bone that is not found in the dog or horse's skeleton. The weakest structures appear to be the pelvis and the lower jaw bones, as these areas seem to suffer most in road-traffic accidents in which cats unfortunately are more and more involved.

The muscles that cover the bones of the skeleton are lean and there is an absence of large fleshy masses. This can make for certain difficulties when a veterinary surgeon has to give an intra-muscular injection for any reason. The strongest muscle is the main muscle that runs along both sides of the spine, which is especially well developed in cats. This allows a cat to spring up into the air, or leap prodigious distances, because the arch of the spine straightens out as the muscles contract. The tail contains mainly tendons which position it, and are important for a cat's balance. The tail is often used to indicate annoyance when it is held low, or pleasure when raised almost vertically.

In this brief account of physiology it is not possible to cover all aspects of body function or their relation to the cat's health. A further reading of more specialised texts will be necessary before some disorders can be understood, but such a study will certainly benefit a cat once its owner is better informed.

Henry slept and slept and ate and ate, and grew and grew

MY NAME'S HENRY

Nobody meant to be unkind, indeed nobody was unkind, just perhaps not very thoughtful or far-seeing.

It all began when my step-daughter-in-law rang up to say she was thinking of getting another cat.

'Oh, yes,' said I, thinking I might be able to home one in need.

'Yes,' she said, 'I thought I'd like to have a Burmese.'

However, she had seen an ad in the local paper for white Persian kittens. I pointed out that Persian cats have to be groomed every day; where was she going to find the time?

'Oh, well, the children could comb him,' came the reply.

Even with five children, I thought this most unlikely and said so.

'Yes, well, I really want a Burmese,' and the conversation turned to other topics.

Time went by and my husband arrived home, to tell me that the family had acquired 'the most beautiful, sweetest little white Persian kitten' and that 'you must go round and see it'. Eventually, I managed to call round only to find a pathetic little runt with a blocked tear duct and almost continuous diarrhoea. Hastily, I gave my step-son, who was holding the fort – and the kitten – some words of advice. They were obviously trying very hard to care for the little one despite two large dogs, five children and, inevitably, a very busy life style.

Four weeks later, on 22 December, we went round to have a Christmas drink and exchange presents. Small cat was nowhere to be seen and we talked for over an hour whilst the children made futile attempts to find him. Suddenly, the most bedraggled little animal I had ever seen shot from under a large armchair and ran across the room, straight up my side to end clinging to my neck. He still had diarrhoea, had that day been up the chimney and had also fallen in some cooking oil that someone had spilt on the floor. With Christmas just a few hours away, the children were naturally very excited, but with every whoop and scream and laugh, little man clung tighter and tighter and I knew that I just had to take him home with me.

After some thoughtful discussion, this was agreed to and little one accompanied me to the car, curled up in the bottom of my sweater and purred all the way home.

He was, by then, six months old and weighed just under two pounds! Our ancient Siamese greeted him with no hostility but seemed to know that he needed help. Little white cat had still not been given a name but, as he sat on the kitchen floor, he looked up at me and said, 'My name's Henry', and, indeed, Henry it was.

Next day, even though it was Sunday and almost Christmas, our vet was holding a small surgery and Henry and I duly went along. The vet was of the opinion that if anyone could pull him round it would be me (very flattering), but pointed out that he was very weak and that he stood quite a chance of *not* making it. Duly armed with all his pills and potions, Henry and I made our way home and prepared for the long journey to Dorset.

We decided to let Oliver travel in his usual basket but to put Henry in the regulation RSPCA carrier as we felt it was better for him to be enclosed. By Stonehenge, my husband could stand it no longer and even I had begun to think that we had a dead kitten on our hands. With much trepidation we opened the box and a little head looked up and said, 'Oh, hello, I was having such a lovely sleep!'

On arrival, we teased my sister-in-law unmercifully that we had brought a 'refugee', but that he had brought his own food. When we brought Henry in, everyone fell in love with him, but he was quickly taken up to a warm, quiet room and left with his litter tray and bowl of water.

Henry slept and slept and ate and ate and grew and grew. He never did return to my daughter-in-law who is now the proud owner of a beautiful, healthy, Burmese, but stayed to take us over completely and to keep Oliver up to scratch. He has the most lovely and loving nature – Henry loves everybody and everybody loves Henry – and he has a new friend, a magnificent Blue Persian, James, who certainly wasn't magnificent when we got him . . .

15
ALTERNATIVE MEDICINE FOR CATS

Alternative medicine in general, and homoeopathy in particular, has been the subject of considerable attention in recent years. This is not to say that it is a recently discovered form of treatment, however, for the homoeopathic principles, on which modern treatment is based, were devised and tested by the German physician, Dr Samuel Hahnemann, almost two hundred years ago and, indeed, the basic concept of 'treating like with like' was known to the Ancient Greeks.

Homoeopathy is based on a law of nature, namely that every stimulus induces a vital reaction, and it is a natural healing process where the remedies act by stimulating the body's own defence mechanisms to assist in regaining normal health. Dr Hahnemann worked with minute doses of substances which, in larger amounts, were capable of producing the symptoms of the disease or condition which he wished to cure. Thus, he induced symptoms resembling those of malaria by taking large doses of an extract of cinchona bark (quinine), and then relieved the symptoms and the fever by taking minute doses of the same substance, cinchona. His process of 'proving' the remedy, as he called it, namely by trying it on himself, would today be regarded as highly dangerous, but, with the help of friends and students from the medical school where he taught, many plants and other materials, some of them toxic in their natural state, were 'proved' and added to the range of homoeopathic remedies.

A word of caution is necessary at this point. Homoeopathic remedies are not magic cure-all potions, nor are they a substitute for the skilled veterinary attention which is required, not just for treatment, but, even more important, for diagnosis. However, the remedies are increasingly regarded as a much more natural and acceptable approach to healing than the use of artificial chemical drugs, and they have the great advantage that they can be used quite safely and effectively in conjunction with any other prescribed medicines or treatment.

It will come as a surprise to many people to learn that homoeopathic remedies are not the exclusive prerogative of the human race, but are equally applicable and effective for use with animals. Because of the minute amounts of the element used in the remedies, the tablets, and other forms of treatment, sold at chemists and health food shops for human use, are perfectly safe for use with any animals from mice to elephants and, of

Opposite *Oddy, a picture of health*

175

course, for cats and kittens. The small size of the tablets and the ease with which they can be dissolved or powdered make them very easy to administer.

There are a number of common cat illnesses and conditions for which homoeopathic remedies are suitable and some of these are listed below.

Abscesses and Bites

Cats as a species often seem to enjoy a good fight, although usually there is more huffing, puffing and noise than damage. However, if injury does result the following are useful.

Local treatment

Apply diluted *Calendula* lotion two or three times daily to the wounds, having first bathed them with weak saline solution (half a teaspoonful of salt to ½ litre (1pt) of warm water).

Remedies for shock

If the cat is distressed use *Aconite* and *Arnica* (see *accidents*).

Abscesses

On the 'like for like' basis, the angry hot swelling of an abscess is not unlike the painful effects of a bee sting and *Apis mel* (the honey bee) works well if an abscess is developing. If the abscess is difficult to clear, even with antibiotic treatment, a five- to seven-day course of *Hepar sulph* will often help to resolve the problem.

Accidents, Shock, Broken Bones

Immediately after any shock or sudden trauma, a few doses of *Aconite* may be given. This is a rapid-acting but short-lasting remedy and, therefore, four to six doses may be given at intervals of five to fifteen, or even thirty, minutes, according to the severity of the incident.

Bruising and swelling

Arnica is obtained from *Arnica montana*, a remarkable little plant which grows on the slopes and mountainsides of Switzerland where it has been used for centuries as a treatment for bruises and injuries incurred in the mountains. Homoeopathically it can be taken by mouth and is excellent for the treatment of any injury where there is bruising, swelling or haemorrhage. It follows Aconite very well because it is also a remedy for shock. It is usual to give four doses daily at four-hourly intervals for a few days.

Broken bones

Where broken bones are diagnosed, *Symphytum officinale* will assist in helping the fractures knit together (hence its common name of Boneset) and will also help to reduce pain at the site of the injury. One tablet may be given three times daily for ten to fourteen days.

176

Birth and Pregnancy

Arnica is again very useful at the time when kittens are born, reducing bruising, pain and swelling during and after the event. *Caulophyllum*, known as 'Squaw Root' because it was (and probably still is) chewed by North American Indian women when the birth of a baby was imminent, is another useful remedy if there is difficulty at the time of kittening, whilst *Pulsatilla* can also be beneficial during labour, easing the process if it is inclined to be prolonged. A tablet should be given every thirty minutes until all the kittens have arrived.

Bleeding and Haemorrhageing

Arnica is again the first choice of remedy. Where bleeding of any sort persists for more than a few minutes, veterinary attention should be sought immediately.

Colds, Coughs, Sneezes, Catarrh, Sinusitis and Cat Flu

Cats are very susceptible to all these conditions, and so, for the sake of simplicity, they are listed together. In the case of suspected cat flu, it is important to seek veterinary advice to prevent the condition becoming chronic, and the symptoms of catarrh, and so on, persisting. If cat flu is developing, the cat will be off its food, very off-colour and almost always running a temperature. *Belladonna* repeated frequently (every two hours during the first two days – six to eight tablets daily) will help to bring the temperature down and allow the cat to feel much better. Other remedies which are useful in these conditions:

Running eyes
Allium cepa, ie onion, on the principle of 'like for like'.

Coughing
Bryonia, if the cough is worse when the cat gets up and moves about. *Belladonna, Drosera* and *Ant tart* are other useful cough remedies, if they suit the symptom picture.

Catarrh and *Sinusitis*
Use *Kali bich*.

Sneezing
Use *Arsenicum album*.

Constipation

Elderly cats often suffer from constipation, and, in addition to liquid paraffin or vegetable oil given from a spoon or in the food, a few doses of *Nux vomica* can be tried. This is an especially good remedy if there is also irritability of the digestive tract or colon.

Diarrhoea and Enteritis

Suspected cases of infectious feline enteritis should, of course,

177

Opposite Jaspar (top), and Minnie, communing with nature

be referred at once to a veterinary surgeon, but the following remedies are also indicated. *Mercury* is the first choice of remedy for this condition, *Merc cor* for the really acute case, particularly if there is blood present, *Merc sol* for less acute diarrhoea, and *Arsenic alb* if there is vomiting and diarrhoea. If the cat has overeaten, perhaps a whole rabbit or something of that sort, *Nux vomica* is the recommended treatment.

Ear Conditions

Cats frequently have trouble with their ears and often small mites, living in the wax, are the cause of the otitis. In addition to veterinary treatment to kill the mites, *Merc sol* is useful if there is eczema of the inside of the ear, or *Hepar sulph* if there is chronic (long-lasting) infection.

Eyes

For conjunctivitis, *Euphrasia*, by mouth, and also as a very dilute solution, in water, to bathe the eyes once or twice daily, is very beneficial.

Key-Gaskell Syndrome (Feline Dysautonomia)

The cause of this newly recognised and very distressing disease of cats is as yet unknown. Homoeopathic treatments based on the various symptoms can be tried, eg *Belladonna* for dilated pupils, or *Arsenic* for vomiting, but it must be accepted that many cats die from this condition.

Kidney Disease (Nephritis and Cystitis)

Nephritis is inflammation of the kidneys, and cystitis is inflammation of the bladder with irritation as the urine is passed. Both are quite common in older cats and the recommendations are *Merc sol* for nephritis, and *Cantharis* for cystitis.

Liver Problems

The cat itself is likely to know what natural treatment it needs

These usually require veterinary treatment, but *Chenopodium* can be given in conjunction with ordinary treatment.

Mouth, Gums and Teeth

Veterinary attention may become necessary as cats get older, but *Merc sol* is a good general remedy for sore and infected gums, whilst *Hepar sulph* can help with more chronic cases.

Operations (including Dental Treatment)

Arnica is unequalled for use before and after any sort of operation or dental work. Three doses daily for three or four days before and after the event will cut down haemorrhage, reduce bruising and promote healing.

Pain

Pain can be difficult to assess in animals, and it is often far from easy to locate the painful area exactly. For general use, *Chamomilla* is indicated for acute pain, whilst *Hypericum* is useful for injuries to limbs, feet and claws.

Abdominal pain

This usually shows itself by a varying degree of restlessness and discomfort, leading, in severe instances, to the spasmodic colic pains similar to those suffered by humans. *Colocynth* given frequently (every five to fifteen minutes, if necessary, up to six to eight doses) can help, but veterinary treatment is essential if the pains do not subside quickly.

Rheumatism, Arthritis, etc

Rhus toxicendron is indicated when the discomfort of the condition is eased, even if only slightly, by movement, whilst *Bryonia* is used if the cat is obviously better when resting.

Sedatives

Sleeping tablets (sold by Nelson under the name of Nocturna) are a mixture of four remedies and are useful as a mild sedative.

Senility

Old age comes to everyone in time, felines and folk alike, and it is naturally hard to treat. However, it is worth trying a short course of *Baryta carb*, say three tablets daily for three to five days, repeated every two to four weeks, as this sometimes helps.

Skin Conditions

In cats, eczema is a quite common condition in the neutered male and female, and it does not always respond very well to homoeopathic treatment. This may be due to the fact that the condition is not really a natural illness, and hence the homoeopathic approach, of encouraging the body's own resources to bring about relief, does not work. However, it is worth trying remedies such as *Arsenic, Apis, Cantharis, Rhus tox, Sulphur* and *Urtica*, but it is important to try to match the signs and symptoms of the skin condition with the properties of the remedy before making a choice, and this is really best left to a veterinary surgeon specialising in homoeopathic treatment.

Tonics

Rescue Remedy is a herbal medicine which is excellent for the treatment of shock, for use as a tonic after illness, or for reviving weakly kittens.

The various remedies mentioned may be obtained from Ainsworth or Nelson, homoeopathic chemists in London, or from Weleda, or other chemists. They may be given as powders, tablets or pillules (very small round pills) which are placed in the cat's mouth. The generally available Potency 6 is recommended as the most suitable strength for use with cats. The dosage and frequency of treatment should be matched to the nature of the condition but, as a guide, the following suggestions are made.

For urgent acute attacks one tablet every fifteen minutes up to four doses, then one tablet every two hours up to another four tablets.

Less urgent condition one tablet three to four times daily for two to three days, until relief.

Long-standing or chronic use one tablet three times daily for four to seven days or longer, or cease treatment for a while and repeat when necessary.

Homoeopathic remedies are best given as little or as often as they are needed and treatment should cease (even after one or two tablets) if there is a good response, or if an aggravation, ie a worsening of the symptoms, (usually transitory) should occur.

Further study of homoeopathic treatment for animals can be undertaken by reading the books recommended on page 206, whilst contact with a veterinary surgeon practising homoeopathy can be made through the British Association of Homoeopathic Veterinary Surgeons, at the address given on page 206.

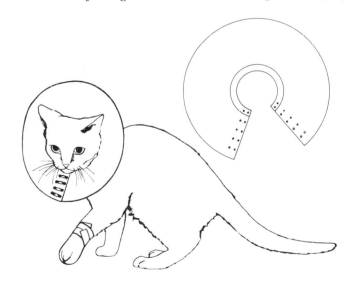

An Elizabethan style collar can stop a cat from scratching or licking a head wound which needs to heal or which has ointment on it, or from rubbing sore eyes or ears. A piece of bandage or tape along the inner edge will stop it chafing – just overlap the holes, and lace together

CHURCH CATS

There were for a long time three black and white cats – a father and two sons – attached to the church of St Mary Abbots, Kensington.

When an organ builder to whom they had belonged left the neighbourhood, they installed themselves outside the church, attracted by the warmth of the paving stones which were heated by boilers below. A kindly verger, Mr Reginald Racher, gave them food and drink.

The saga with which I am concerned began one icy morning when the vicar, the late Prebendary Eley (subsequently Bishop of Gibraltar), arriving to take early service, found one of the cats lying stretched out, stiff with cold, on the pavement. The boilers below had failed, and the cat appeared to be dead. Indeed, he would have died if the vicar had not taken him indoors and fed him with teaspoonfuls of egg whipped up with brandy.

Restored to health, the cat was given the name Thomas Aquinas. His brother, because he was of a somewhat timid disposition, was called Thomas Didymus: it was only after some time that this cat ventured inside the church, but having done so he made himself at home. The father, who was named Thomas à Kempis, never went into the church. The verger built him a house outside and saw that he was fed and cared for.

St Mary Abbots church was infested with mice: they even nibbled the candle-wax in the sanctuary. Thomas Aquinas and Thomas Didymus put this to rights. They smelt the mice and heard them scampering below a grille in the floor, above the furnace. Sometimes they could see a mouse through the bars of the grille, but were unable to get at it. Eventually they contrived to find a way down. The slaughter was on a vast scale. Yet out of all those mice the cats not only spared one, but made a friend of him. This mouse used to be fed on cake and biscuits in the vestry, in the company of the cats, and when the verger was serving in the sanctuary he would see the mouse sitting up, a yard or so away.

Nor was it unusual during service for one cat or both to sit respectfully in the sanctuary. Or they might choose a position from which they could look up at the royal pew – at Princess Alice, Princess Marina, or Princess Margaret.

On Thursdays at 11.30am a Communion service was held in the chapel of St Paul: because there were no steps it was convenient for elderly persons. Among those who attended was a Miss Bell who was particularly fond of the cats. Each Thursday, on their own initiative, the two cats used to take up their positions one at each end of the pew in which Miss Bell sat. While she went to the altar they remained behind with perfect decorum.

When Miss Bell died the cats met the coffin, walked ahead of it up the cloister that leads into the church, and, when it was placed on trestles and covered with a pall, sat underneath, remaining there through the night. Next morning, as the cortège moved down the aisle, the cats were sitting on the radiators to either side of the door.

The cats participated fully in the life of the church. At a baptism they would move among the people, giving particular pleasure to the children. At weddings, Thomas Aquinas had a way of sidling between the bride-to-be and her father as they went up the aisle. Then the two cats would slip away and appear again outside on the pavement among the guests, when the bride and bridegroom were getting into their car.

Over the Christmas period they sat in the crib, in the hay, eyes glinting. A child was heard to exclaim: 'Why! they're *real* animals!' For days the cats' fur smelt of hay. Parishioners brought them Christmas gifts: packets of cat's food – even a small roast chicken!

Inevitably there were those who objected to cats in a church. For a while an effort was made to discourage the Thomas brothers, but it was a half-hearted gesture. Most of the congregation liked them.

Besides, they were not in church all the time. Thomas Aquinas used to take himself off to Peter's Eating House, which was close to the entrance of St Mary Abbots, where he was made much of and fed on steak. Or he would cross Church Street – looking to right and to left – to the 'Prince of Wales', where he enjoyed a sip of beer. The proprietor threatened one day that he would have to send in a bill to cover Thomas's drinks!

One of the verger's tasks was to count the collection. He did this in the vestry, arranging the coins in neat piles: coppers, sixpences, shillings, florins and so on. Thomas Aquinas and Thomas Didymus would sit on the table watching. Then suddenly out would come a paw, scattering the coins like a child overturning a tower of bricks!

The pulpit was a forbidden area. One day the congregation was waiting for the service to begin, the loudspeaker set for a visiting preacher, when a rhythmic sound began to fill the church – growing to a crescendo, then abating, only to increase again. People did not know what to think. Then the verger had his suspicions. Sure enough, Thomas Aquinas had found his way into the pulpit and was purring full strength into the microphone.

16
THE A–Z OF CAT AILMENTS AND DISEASES

There may be several common names for the same conditions, but, where possible, the details have been set out under the most commonly used name, with extensive cross-referencing to other names or symptoms. This has been done so that someone whose cat is, for instance, bleeding, and who, in the general panic of the moment, may not be able to think of the word 'haemorrhageing', will still find himself directed to the correct information.

I am deeply indebted to Dr T. J. Gruffydd-Jones for checking this chapter and for his advice.

Abortion
Abortion is fairly uncommon in the cat, although it seems to occur more frequently in the very young (five to eight months old) and in Persian queens. Any infection which causes a high temperature, eg *cat flu*, or *abscess*, can cause abortion to occur and this may account for a one-off abortion. Abortions may also be found in catteries where *FeLV* is present.

Often a cat will seem quite well, even though she is aborting, and one may simply find odd bits of tissue or blood stains as the only evidence. Occasionally the womb will be infected, and there might be pus at the vulva; in this case the cat may be ill. If abortion is suspected, the cat should be checked by a veterinary surgeon as soon as possible.

To prevent unwanted litters, spaying can safely be performed by a skilled veterinary surgeon right up to the last week of pregnancy. Whilst to some people this may not seem ethical, it is, in my opinion, preferable to the fate of the large numbers of cats left to fend for themselves as strays. I have performed a large number of these operations and the cats all recovered within twenty-four hours, ate a hearty meal, and were quite unaware of losing the pregnancy. It is much kinder than removing the kittens after birth, when maternal bonding has taken place.

Abscess
Abscesses usually result from cat bites although they may appear after other wounds. Often one is unaware of the initial wound as it is hidden by fur. Signs begin anything from twenty-four hours to a week after the fight, the cat goes off its food, sleeps more than usual, and it may be possible to find a painful swelling. Often, before the abscess bursts, the cat feels very ill and runs a high temperature. When the abscess bursts, smelly, red-grey or yellow blood-tinged pus will emerge. The cat should be taken to a veterinary surgeon at the *very first* sign of illness because complications may arise. Some abscesses, especially on the back, can track along under the skin and large areas can become necrotic (dead) and slough off. Also, the cat may develop a septicaemia and die. The veterinary surgeon will usually provide antibiotic treatment.

When an abscess bursts, use a salt solution (two teaspoons of salt in ½ litre (1 pint) of boiling water), allowed to cool to hand-heat, and gently clean up the area with cotton-wool swabs. Repeat the bathings, keeping the wound open as long as possible to drain out the poison. Do not use household disinfectants such as TCP or Dettol as these are toxic to cats. If it is known that the cat has been bitten, application of surgical spirit to the bite immediately after it has happened, although it stings, often prevents an abscess forming.

Acne
Feline acne and *stud tail* are conditions which have the same cause but which are found in different places, ie under the chin and on the top side of the tail respectively (stud tail is a misleading name as castrates and queens are also affected). These places have a heavy concentration of the sebaceous glands used to mark the cat's territory. These glands can become blocked, when the secretion turns blackish. A mild form can simply look like a little flea dirt in the fur, but the overlying fur will look greasy, and the area may become bald. In more severe cases bacterial infection results and pustules are formed. Antibiotic treatment from the veterinary surgeon may be needed, and the owner will have to clean the area regularly with a skin cleanser provided by the veterinary surgeon.

Alopecia

Alopecia means baldness. Alopecia between the eye and the ear is normal and so, to some extent, is baldness on the tummy between the hind legs, extending down the hind legs when the twice-yearly moult is taking place. After the moult, the hair should regrow after four to eight weeks. Sometimes there is also a considerable loss of hair after giving birth, but this grows back after weaning. In these cases there is no itch, and no red spots appear on the skin.

Cats are also prone to an alopecia which affects the lower abdomen and back legs, like the moult mentioned above, but the hair does not regrow. It is not usually itchy although the cat may lick it. The cause of this is not known but it often responds well to thyroid hormone or Ovarid.

Nervous, highly strung cats may pull out their hair if under stress, say in moving home or on the arrival of a new pet or baby. This is uncommon, however, and a cat with alopecia should always be thoroughly examined for parasites.

Alopecia starting at the base of the tail, and extending up the back in a line, is associated with *miliary dermatitis*, whilst alopecia in one or more circular patches is probably *ringworm*; reference should be made to the entries under these headings. See also *eczema* and *eosinophilic granuloma*.

Anaemia

It is easier to notice any change in the cat's colour if it has white fur around the head; here the nose and inside the ears will usually be pink. In a dark-coloured cat one must look at the mucous membranes (the gums, the tongue and inside the lower eyelid) to assess the cat's normal membrane colour. It is good to become familiar with the normal colour of one's cat, so that any change can be detected.

Unfortunately, it is often difficult, even for a vet, to detect that the cat is anaemic until there is quite considerable blood loss, so a blood test might have to be taken where anaemia is suspected.

Anaemia makes a cat excessively tired, off its food, sometimes thirsty, and, if it is really bad, it will make the cat very weak. Some cats develop a craving for unusual foods or lick at the wall or the soil.

Sometimes the cat is brought to the vet because it has actually collapsed through severe anaemia. It may cry out in a horribly distressed way and its gums and conjunctivae look white. Depending on the reason for the anaemia, a cat in as poor a state as this might have to be put to sleep.

The main causes of anaemia are:

Feline Infectious Anaemia (FIA)   As its name sug-gests, this form of anaemia is caused by an infectious parasite (called *Haemobartonella felis*) which gets into the bloodstream, and causes the destruction of the red blood cells. The initial symptoms may easily go unnoticed by an owner; they are a high temperature, sometimes as high as 105°F, general malaise and being off food. The cat will have symptoms off and on and seem to get over them himself. At this stage it is difficult to distinguish FIA from the early stages of other diseases, eg cat-bite *abscess* or *FeLV*. As more and more red blood cells are destroyed, the frequency of the bouts of illness will increase, as will its severity. When there is a sudden massive breakdown of red blood cells, *jaundice* may appear, the cat may collapse, deteriorate over a period of twenty-four to forty-eight hours, and die.

The veterinary surgeon can do a simple test, using a tiny drop of blood smeared on a slide, and stained to reveal the parasite which appears as small dots on the red blood cells. However, the organism is not always visible, and the vet may have to take a drop of blood every day for a week before it can be found; a single negative result is therefore not conclusive.

The organism can usually be killed by an antibiotic, called oxytetracycline, which must be given for three or four weeks. Some cats remain carriers for life, even after treatment, and it is a good idea to test again after treatment to assess their progress.

Unfortunately, quite a lot of cats which contract FIA also have FeLV so this should also be tested for, particularly when there is a poor response to treatment.

Feline Leukaemia Virus (FeLV)   FeLV causes suppression of the bone marrow where red blood cells are produced, so that, as they die off, they are not replaced and the cat gradually becomes more and more anaemic. FeLV lowers the cat's resistance to other infections and therefore it becomes more likely to get *FIA*.

There is also an acute variant called *FeLV–C* which attacks the blood so vigorously that the cat may die in as little as twenty-four hours after showing the initial signs. See under *FeLV* for further details.

Haemorrhage   This is loss of blood because of a wound. If there is an external wound bleeding is obvious, but, if internal, it may be possible to surmise that the cat has had a road accident, or some other trauma, by examining the claws which are usually frayed. The membranes of the gums and the inside of the eyelid will appear white. This is obviously a dire emergency and veterinary help should be sought at once. Keep the cat warm, using a covered hot-water bottle, and wrapping the cat in a blanket to take it to the vet. If a road accident is suspected, open the mouth and check that the airway is clear.

Internal haemorrhage can occur because a fragile tumour has burst, or because of rat poison, such as Warfarin, which prevents the blood clotting and causes the least knock to set off a bruise which will not stop bleeding. See also under *bleeding*.

Poisoning Rodent poisons (eg Warfarin, Dicoumarol), see above, under *haemorrhage*.

Phenol (In most disinfectants and wood preservative.) Depresses the bone marrow.

Chloramphenicol An antibiotic, safe in moderation, but if used for too long will depress the bone marrow.

Phenylbutazone (Also called Butazolidin and Buvetsone.) An anti-inflammatory drug sometimes used to treat arthritis, but will also depress the bone marrow if used for too long or in too high a dose.

Paracetamol

Chronic kidney disease This will also cause anaemia. The kidneys produce a substance called erythropoietin which is necessary for the production of blood.

Heart disease This will often produce pale mucous membranes due to shock, but does not cause what would strictly be termed *anaemia*.

Treatment will depend on the cause and the veterinary surgeon is the best person to advise on this. Anabolic steroids often help, as do iron supplements, either as tablets or as red meat. It has been found that adding folic acid to the diet helps considerably (Haliborange Vita Plus tablets, available at any chemist). Unfortunately, anaemia is often very severe and will not always respond to treatment.

Anal Glands

These are two little glands on either side of the anus which secrete the cat's own particular smell. The secretion is usually greyish in colour and smells fishy. The glands normally empty during the passage of faeces, but, if the faeces are loose, or if the cat is overweight, they may fill up and become irritated. The cat will then spend more time than usual trying to lick this area or will scoot its bottom along the ground. If left unemptied the secretion will fester and an abscess will develop.

Anorexia

This word has become synonymous with a slimming disease in humans, but it started life as a technical term for simply not eating.

Cats, much more than dogs, are notorious for being fussy little blighters when it comes to food!

Usually this is not a problem in a multi-cat household, where if one cat will not eat what is offered, another cat will. It tends to be the single cat who goes on hunger strike just to see how ingenious its desperate owner can become in the gourmet cat-food line – salmon, liver, steak, cod roe – everything is tried! It is a good idea to get a kitten used to tinned food right from the beginning, give this at room temperature at a fixed time and take it up fifteen minutes later, eaten or not. Once puss is spoiled it is nigh impossible to go back.

Most owners can tell when their cat is just being finicky, and when there really is something wrong. Many of the diseases listed in this chapter have anorexia as one of the symptoms; it is usually one of the first signs that something is wrong, and, if the cat is also a bit miserable, or lethargic, veterinary advice should be sought.

Cats may also become anorexic when they are pining. The cat, more than any other animal, needs a lot of love and fuss to keep its will to live.

Vitamin B_{12} stimulates the appetite and can be given by injection, or by using Marmite which can be mixed with water and given to the cat. Brand's Essence, obtainable from chemists, contains all the nutrients a cat needs and is good for a convalescing cat.

Arthritis (See also *lameness*)

Arthritis is not very common in the cat and usually results from an old injury, or from a bite into the joint. The lameness thus produced appears sometimes months or years after the initial injury and gradually gets worse. Treatment is difficult because so many of the arthritis drugs for humans and dogs (eg aspirin and phenylbutazone) are poisonous to cats. The vet will advise if corticosteroid treatment is necessary and will prescribe a regime of gradually decreasing doses. The minimum of this substance should be used because it tends to increase the appetite, which is counterproductive. Arthritic cats should be kept as lightweight as possible to reduce the stress on the affected joints to a minimum.

Feeding raw liver can result in the cat getting too much Vitamin A (Vitamin A toxicosis or hypervitaminosis A). This causes new bone to be laid down on the vertebrae of the neck, which pinches the nerves leaving the spinal column; this, and new bone laid in the joints, causes lameness and pain. As the condition worsens, the cat becomes unable to raise or lower its neck comfortably, eating becomes difficult and painful. In the early stages it may be enough to discontinue liver in the diet to effect a cure.

185

Asthma, see under *cough.*

Balance, Lost, see *ear, feline infectious peritonitis* and *stroke.*

Baldness, see *alopecia.*

Bite, see *abscess.*

Bleeding

Obviously, if there is bleeding, the sooner the cat is seen by the vet the better. Keep the cat warm, wrap it in a blanket and put a covered hot-water bottle beside it to transport it to the veterinary surgery.

If a cat has a cut and is bleeding, pressure is usually the best way to stop the flow, by applying a clean pad of cotton, linen or paper hanky to the area and pressing lightly. Do not keep wiping the blood away as this prevents it from clotting and causes further bleeding. If the blood seeps through, more padding should be applied. If it is a leg which is bleeding, it may be possible to secure a bandage with Elastoplast, Sellotape or insulating tape. Take the cat to a veterinary surgery as soon as possible. A tourniquet should only be used as an absolutely last resort. Tie a piece of bandage around the top of the leg above the place where the blood is pumping out. The tourniquet *must* be loosened and then replaced every ten minutes until the veterinary surgery is reached.

Rat poisons, such as Warfarin, prevent the blood from clotting and cause many haemorrhages; blood may appear in the faeces and urine, and in the mouth there may be small red patches on the gums. This poison is reversible by daily injections of Vitamin K for three to five days. There are also other conditions which stop the blood clotting and cause haemorrhage, and it is important to see a vet as soon as possible if haemorrhage is suspected.

See *anaemia* for signs of internal haemorrhage and blood deficiency for other reasons.

The veterinary surgeon should be provided with as detailed a history as possible.

Blockage, see *constipation* and *feline urological syndrome.*

Breathing Difficulty

A gasping cat may be a very serious problem, unless it is simply too warm. Although heat stroke is very serious, it is uncommon in cats in the United Kingdom except when they have been left in a car on a very hot day.

Cats sometimes smell the air through an open mouth, but it should be obvious that a cat doing this is not in any distress. A cat which is having difficulty in breathing will sit up; if it has fluid in the chest it will be unable to lie down, eat or drink, because it cannot stop the breathing effort long enough to do so.

Breathing is necessary to supply the blood with oxygen, and a difficulty in breathing will result from a problem either in the lungs or in the supply of blood to the lungs (*anaemia, haemorrhage* and *heart failure* can cause gasping). In these cases the mucous membranes of the gums and inside the eyelids will look pale or blueish.

Fluid in the chest will cause a physical obstruction which will make breathing difficult. This may be blood (eg from a trauma such as a road accident); watery fluid (eg from a tumour, usually a thymic lymphosarcoma, see *FeLV*); heart or kidney failure; *FIP*; *ANTU poisoning*; or pus (eg from a penetrating bite wound).

A road accident can rupture the diaphragm, allowing the contents of the abdomen (liver, intestines, etc) into the thorax, which then obstruct the lungs. While this has a sudden onset, it can remain like this for ages if not diagnosed and treated. *Asthma, bronchitis* and *lungworm* usually cause coughing, and, if *pneumonia* ensues, they could also cause difficulty in breathing. Obviously these develop over a few days or longer.

Gasping is a very serious symptom and should always receive veterinary attention.

Broken Leg, see *lameness.*

Bronchitis, see *cough.*

Burns

Fortunately cats do not often suffer from burns and scalds, probably because they move so quickly. However, if one should occur, cold water should be run over the area immediately. If cortisone cream (eg Betsolan, Vetsovate or Betnovate) is available, apply it immediately, but no other kind of cream should be used. The cat should be taken to the vet as quickly as possible.

Initially the area may look all right, especially if it has been scalded by boiling water, tea, etc, and the fur is still intact. It may not be possible to see the damage but the cat *must* be treated for shock and to try to prevent the sloughing off of the skin, which will inevitably follow a few days later. If a very large area of skin is lost, the cat may need to be put to sleep unless skin grafting can be done.

In burns caused by fire the smoke can damage the lungs. Just as burnt skin exudes fluid, so does the lung, and the cat may drown. It is essential that the head be kept upright, and the tongue pulled forward to ensure the airway is clear.

Calling

Female cats begin calling (coming into heat) at any time from four months old, and usually at six months. Longhaired and British shorthaired cats, however, may not come into call before one year of age.

Their behaviour can be quite extraordinary, rolling around on the ground, crying out as if in pain, holding the rear end up and twisting the tail round to the side. They are usually much more affectionate at this time and they may try to escape.

Calling can last from two or three days up to ten days. If no pregnancy occurs, the cat may come back into heat within a few days or weeks. Spaying is the best way to stop this and should be done at around six months of age.

Canker, see *ear mites*.

Cat Flu

Cat flu is mainly caused by two viruses, *feline viral rhinotracheitis* virus (FVR) and *feline calicivirus* (FCV). Cats become infected by breathing in droplets sneezed or coughed out by another cat, or through contact with contaminated dishes, cages, hands etc.

Initially the cat may show nothing more than listlessness and a high temperature (up to 105°F), but soon its eyes will start to run and sneezing begins. If left untreated, the conjunctivae (the inside of the eyelids) become swollen and red, and a green-yellow discharge will be produced. The nose will also have a thick discharge.

In calicivirus infections the tongue and inside of the mouth may be ulcerated, and the cat may drool if it becomes too painful for it to swallow the saliva. Obviously it will not want to eat. Sometimes the virus progresses to the lungs, and a severe *pneumonia* can ensue, causing death.

Treatment from the vet usually consists of antibiotics and eye ointment, but the most important part, I feel, is the nursing. Cats easily give up the will to live, and one must often persevere with force feeding for days or even weeks; some cats die of dehydration. Cats are often happier in their own home with their owners, so, where possible, this is best, although the vet may have to hospitalise the most severe cases.

The eyes and nose should be gently cleaned with warm salt water (two teaspoons of salt in ¼ litre (½ pint) of water). Vick should be put under the chin to help to clear the nose, and the cat placed in a steamy bathroom to help clear its airways. A cat will not eat if it cannot smell the food, so very strong-smelling food, such as sardines, pilchards and liver, should be offered to overcome this. If the anorexia becomes too bad, food may have to be syringed into the cat. Many people use milk for this feeding, which can cause diarrhoea, so it is better to use Brand's Essence (available from any good chemist) which has all the nutrients necessary for convalescing animals. Alternatively, make a beef broth, or boil a piece of fish or chicken, and use the enriched water from that.

You may have to help the cat to keep clean, as it will not be able to wash itself; sponging its chest and legs gently every day.

Some of the worst cases end up with chronic *rhinitis*, that is they sneeze, either continually or in recurring episodes, and these cats may have to be on antibiotics, on and off, all their lives. Sometimes an intra-nasal vaccine helps to reduce this.

Prevention, of course, is better than cure and vaccination should be done from nine weeks old, initially two shots, three or four weeks apart, with a booster every year.

Claws

It is very uncommon for a cat to need its claws cut except as it gets older (over about ten years), and does not exercise as much. It can then happen that the claws grow right round and into the pad.

If a claw gets broken off, it can bleed profusely. The claw should be unsheathed, by pressing the pad underneath, and a wad of clean cotton or linen pressed onto the area for five minutes. If there is a fragment still hanging on, it is best to pull it off in a quick, sharp movement.

Frayed claws are often a sign of a road accident, or some other trauma, and it would be wise to have a vet check the cat over if this is suspected.

When cats use a scratching post they are actually cleaning, not sharpening, their claws. A good scratching post is made from a piece of wood covered in carpet, or a piece of carpet fixed to a wall up to a height of about 1m (3ft).

Declawing is an unethical procedure and will only ever be done by a vet for medical reasons.

Conjunctivitis

Conjunctivitis is when the inside of the eyelids appears red and inflamed, and the eyes have a watery, or green pus-like, discharge. This can cause sneezing as the discharge runs down the inside of the nose.

It is usually the beginning of *cat flu*, but can be an odd bacterial infection (cold in the eye) just from sitting in a draught or too close to a heater.

It may result from a scratch in a fight and in this case only one eye will be affected. On close inspection it may be possible to see a scratch or ulcer on the surface. If you suspect this has happened, the cat should always see a vet, in case the ulcer, and therefore the eye, bursts. Sometimes a grass seed or thorn gets into an eye and causes it to become very swollen, with thick green pus, and the eye nearly closed. The cause may be impossible to see without a general anaesthetic.

An organism which causes very persistent conjunctivitis is called *Chlamydia psittaci*. Initially it affects both eyes, causing a watery discharge which soon turns thicker and pus-like, although the cat remains well and eating. If untreated, it may cause ulceration of the eye. It tends to be persistent and the only treatment which will cure it is oxytetracycline given for six weeks.

Constipation

(See also *Key-Gaskell syndrome*, of which constipation is often the first sign.)

Constipation seems to occur mainly in older, overweight cats and it is therefore advisable to keep weight down to prevent this condition. I find that adding one or two teaspoons of butter, or margarine, and bran to the food is better than liquid paraffin for curing the condition, but there are veterinary preparations for the really stubborn cases. Some cats, however, will need an anaesthetic and enema so, if there is no response after a couple of days, it is best to see the vet.

The symptoms of constipation are straining over the litter tray with nothing, or very little, being produced. It is more difficult to tell if the cat is constipated if it normally goes outside, until the abdomen gets so full that the cat goes off its food and starts to vomit. Occasionally constipation can result from an old fracture of the pelvis healing badly, and narrowing the exit from the abdomen.

It is important to distinguish constipation from the early stages of *diarrhoea* where a cat may well also strain after passing motions. It is also important to be sure that it is faeces that the cat is trying to pass; if he is unable to pass urine, this is an emergency situation needing immediate veterinary attention (see *feline urological syndrome*).

Coughing

The commonest reason for coughing is *cat flu* which has been dealt with above.

Most cats occasionally crouch down and cough for a minute or two with their head and neck outstretched. When they have finished, they may seem to swallow something, but this is usually just fur in the throat, and should not happen more than about once a month.

Foreign bodies in the windpipe are an uncommon cause of coughing, and very difficult to detect since the offending object is often a piece of leaf or blade of grass which does not show up on an X-ray. When this is suspected, the veterinary surgeon must do an endoscopic examination of the trachea (by putting a fibreoptic tube down the windpipe).

Asthma, or *allergic bronchitis*, causes frequent bouts of dry coughing and difficult breathing. It is often impossible to discover what sets it off; it may be pollen, paint fumes, fumes from a smoking chip pan (which can kill a cat in minutes), aerosol sprays, or even cat litter. Asthma usually responds to treatment with cortisone (acquired from the vet), but it is likely to recur unless the cause can be determined and eliminated.

In cases of coughing for which no apparent cause can be found, the vet should examine a sample of sputum or faeces for the larvae of the feline lungworm (*Aelostrongylus abstrusus*). Cats get this by eating a slug, snail, mouse or bird; they cannot get it from other cats.

Chronic bronchitis occurs in cats but the cause is not clear.

Pneumonia can result from the cat inhaling medication or food and is common in hand-reared kittens when people make the mistake of trying to feed them like a human baby. Young kittens should be placed on their stomachs to feed (as they would naturally) and a Catac kitten-feeder used.

Coughing and difficulty in breathing are the signs of *pneumonia* and sometimes one can hear crackling and wheezing noises on the chest with the naked ear. The cat usually goes off its food and is very miserable. Antibiotics and medications, such as Bisolvin (which breaks up the mucus), are given to treat this.

A teaspoonful of honey and glycerine can be given three times a day to the coughing cat until it can be taken to the vet.

Cryptorchid

A cryptorchid, or rig cat, is one in which only one testicle has descended; the other one may be anywhere from beside the kidney inside the abdomen, to next to the scrotum. Cryptorchids *must* be castrated because sooner or later the retained testicle will become cancerous.

Cystitis, see *feline urological syndrome*.

Dandruff

A certain amount of dandruff may occur twice a year at the time of the moult (cats lose hair all the time, but usually have two definite moults in autumn and spring). Excessive dandruff is an indication of something wrong. There is a mite called *Cheyletiella*, also known as 'walking dandruff', which may cause itchiness and dandruff. If some of the dandruff is brushed onto a piece of black paper, it may be possible to see some of the flakes walking about. This mite can also affect people, causing intense irritation. Wash the cat weekly, for four to six weeks, in a safe insecticide (from the vet) to clear this up.

When the cat has a chronic illness of the kidneys or liver, a lot of dandruff occurs. This condition tends to happen in older cats and the dandruff is not particularly itchy, but the coat is dull and mats easily. Veterinary advice should be sought to determine the underlying cause. Bathing in Seleen shampoo helps, but advice should be sought from the vet on the advisability of bathing an old or ill cat, as hypothermia or a chill can result.

Diabetes

Diabetes mellitus usually occurs in middle-aged and older cats. The first sign is drinking more and passing more urine. As the condition progresses, the cat loses weight and becomes less active; usually the appetite decreases although occasionally it increases. As the cat gets worse, weakness, *cataracts, vomiting* and, sometimes, *jaundice* can appear.

Diabetes is caused by a lack of insulin which is normally produced by the pancreas. Insulin is necessary to enable the glucose from the blood to get into the cells; glucose is the fuel on which animals run. Diabetes has also been associated with long-term treatment on Ovarid.

If it is thought that a cat is diabetic the vet should be provided with a sample of its urine in a *clean* container, ie not one which has sugary residues of lemonade etc. The urine can be obtained by putting only a very small amount of litter in the cat's tray and then draining the urine off. Alternatively, if the cat sprays outside, place a transparent plastic bag on the ground underneath where it sprays to try to catch a sample. If neither of these methods work, do not worry, as the vet will probably squeeze the bladder or take a blood sample.

The treatment for diabetes is daily insulin injections which your veterinary surgeon will show you how to do. Sometimes the cat will have to be hospitalised until the condition stabilises. It is very important to keep a diabetic cat on the same routine every day; half to one-third of its food is given in the morning, followed by an insulin injection, and the rest of the food eight hours later. The cat can usually stay on much the same food as before although it cannot have much milk which contains glucose, and, of course, evaporated milk, cream, etc, are also banned. They can still have fresh meat, fish, cat-treats, tinned cat-food and vegetables.

If a cat does not eat, is given an overdose of insulin, or is too active, *hypoglycaemia* can result. The cat becomes weak, staggers and may have seizures; this can be remedied by giving the cat a teaspoonful of 50 per cent dextrose solution. If symptoms persist, the vet must be contacted immediately. Once the cat has stabilised, a weekly urine sample should be checked for variations. Diabetes lowers the cat's resistance and it will be more prone to infections (especially *cystitis*.)

Diarrhoea (See also *feline infectious enteritis*)

Diarrhoea can be caused by changing a cat's diet too abruptly or by giving too much milk. In young kittens diarrhoea is quite common, and may even be severe, with blood, when cow's milk is given. Free access to fresh water should always be given.

Very often the cause of acute diarrhoea is unknown. It is not often a bacterial infection, although bacteria may take advantage of the upset state of the intestine to make the diarrhoea worse. The cause may be obvious if a cat gets acute diarrhoea after eating a certain food, although, if it is a hunter or scavenger, it may never be known what caused the problem. In a kitten it can be life-endangering, so veterinary advice should be sought immediately. An adult cat with diarrhoea should be starved for twenty-four hours and given only boiled water to prevent dehydration. After twenty-four hours only three or four small meals of boiled fish, chicken or rabbit should be given. No milk, tinned or red meat should be given for about three days, until the stomach settles. A teaspoonful of natural yoghurt with every meal helps to colonise the intestine with beneficial bacteria. A teaspoonful of kaolin (be careful *not* to give kaolin and morphine) three times a day can help.

FeLV can cause an acute form of diarrhoea, with haemorrhage and death, but it is more commonly associated with chronic diarrhoea in the alimentary lymphosarcoma form of the disease, when the tumour infiltrates the large intestine. Water is normally absorbed from the large intestine, and, when it is damaged, the water stays in the bowel contents, causing diarrhoea. This is gradual in onset and resistant to treatment. (See also *FeLV*.)

Chronic diarrhoea can also occur secondarily to another condition, such as *kidney disease* and *hyperthyroidism*, both of which occur in the older cat. Worms sometimes cause chronic diarrhoea in kittens. There is also a condition known as the *diarrhoea and third eyelid syndrome*, the cause of which is not known and where the only treatment is symptomatic.

Dislocation, see *lameness*

Ears

(See also *sun-sensitive ears*.)

Ear mites are tiny white parasites only just visible to the naked eye. They live in the external ear canal where they cause intense irritation as they move around. Oddly enough, the worse the infection the less the irritation, because a growing build-up of wax protects the sensitive ear lining. The clinical signs are a waxy ear (in the normal cat there is no visible wax at all), shaking of the head and scratching the ear, or holding it a bit flatter than usual. Canker drops (containing BHC, gamma benzene hexachloride), from a vet or pet shop, must be used daily for at least a month because the drops will kill the adult mites but not the eggs, and as the eggs hatch out a reinfection can occur. Hatching usually occurs in up to three weeks. Be careful not to exceed the recommended dose as these drops can be toxic to cats. Canker powder must *not* be used; it has caused many an abscess.

If there is any kind of secretion other than wax, eg pus, then it is not likely to be canker, but may well be *otitis externa*, or a *polyp*, and veterinary advice should be sought. Small blue tumours sometimes occur in the ear, but these are harmless. unless numerous enough to block the ear and lead to infection.

Water, TCP, etc, should *never* be put in the ear. Other than prescribed ear drops, the only safe substance to use to clean the ear is almond or olive oil. Gently wipe only around the top of the ear. Never dig into the ear with a cotton bud or anything else.

Infection in the middle ear can occur after a severe external ear infection, or for no apparent reason. At first the cat cannot get its balance, and may even not be able to stand, and the eyes dart from side to side. After several days (with treatment from the vet) this improves, but usually the cat is left with its head tilted to one side, although the ability to walk and jump return and the eyes may become still again.

An *aural haematoma* is where the whole ear flap swells up and feels squashy. It is caused by trauma, usually excessive scratching because of ear mites, which bursts a blood vessel. A small operation is needed to drain the blood.

Eczema

True eczema is actually very uncommon in the cat although many conditions may appear like eczema:

Acne On the chin or on top of the tail.
Eosinophilic granuloma Inflamed, bare orange-pink patches on the underside, back of the hind legs and lips.

Miliary dermatitis Scabs along the back plus or minus loss of hair.
Ringworm Usually a circular bald patch anywhere on the body, but most often on the head, neck and legs.
Sun-sensitive ears or *solar dermatitis* This occurs when the cat has white ears which go red and crusty at the edges due to exposure to the sun.

Reference should be made to the entries under these headings.

Eczema is a very itchy skin condition, in which the cat licks or scratches at one or more patches, or all over its body, sometimes breaking the skin. It can be caused by contact with, or inhalation of, some substance to which the cat is allergic, or can result from infection getting into a cut or scratch. Treatment with cream is often unsatisfactory because the cat licks it off, and the area must not be bathed with anything except, perhaps, Acriflavine ('Acriflex') because so many substances are toxic to cats. It can spread terribly quickly, so veterinary advice is best sought early.

Emetic

An emetic is something which makes a cat sick. It should only be used when the cat has *definitely* been seen to have eaten something toxic. Cats tend to eat grass as a natural emetic if they are feeling off-colour. The only safe and efficient artificial emetic is a crystal of washing soda, it tastes foul so should be popped right to the back of the mouth. Vomiting will occur within minutes.

Enteritis, see *diarrhoea* and *feline infectious enteritis*

Eosinophilic Granuloma

Eosinophilic granuloma, or rodent ulcer, is a condition of the skin which may be mistaken for *eczema*. The skin is inflamed, firm and orange-pink, and the cat licks it bare of fur and can make it weepy. It can occur in patches on the abdomen, or in a line on the legs. The tell-tale sign is that the cat's lips are usually affected as well and, if the cat's upper lip is lifted, the same firm, red or orange-pink marks can be seen. If left, it can eat away at the upper lip and cause deformity of the face. Vets may treat the case with Ovarid, cry-surgery or prednisolone and treatment must be given for at least a month. Recurrence is quite common.

Eyes

Black eye This is caused by fighting or other trauma. There will be fat, swollen eyelids, and if, on lifting the upper eyelid, the part of the eyeball which is usually white (the sclera) is seen to be red, then there has probably been a blow or road accident. If the upper eyelid is too painful to touch, or if there is a scab and the cat has been rather off-colour, it is quite likely that it has been in a fight and, in due course, pus will burst forth. (See *abscess*.)

Blindness Sudden blindness can occur in older cats in one or both eyes. Certain angles of light show a redness through the pupils, which are enlarged; this is caused by retinal detachment. There is no cure, but cats usually readjust quite well to loss of sight, as long as furniture is kept in the same place. Older cats do not often do much, and, with a caring owner, their quality of life can be just as good. Sometimes, however, the cause is a tumour (part of the *FeLV* complex) and the eye will begin to look bigger and bulging; unfortunately, this is always fatal.

Cataract This is when the pupil goes white. Kittens can occasionally be born with these, or they can be the result of some old injury or infection of the eye, or of old age. Sight will be lost when the cataract is completely white and sometimes the lens can then be removed.

Changing colour This is quite common in older cats in one or both eyes. Increasing amounts of pigment in the iris change the colour from green to brown. However, the iris can also change colour due to *feline infectious peritonitis* so, if this occurs, it is probably wise to have the cat checked over.

Cloudiness This is infection in the eye and the vet should be consulted immediately.

Foreign body It is not uncommon for grass seeds, grass blades and thorns to get into the eye. This is very painful and the eye will weep green pus and be closed. The conjunctivae will be inflamed.

Ulcer of the cornea The cornea is the very front of the eye. Ulcers are usually caused by trauma and are very painful initially. The cat will blink, or keep the affected eye closed. It will weep a lot from the affected eye, watery tears which will turn green and become thicker on the second day when infection gets in. The ulcer or scratch may be quite difficult to see, and it may be necessary to look at the eye at an angle to spot it. After a short while the whole or part of the eye may turn a blue-grey colour as the body begins to repair the eye. This will eventually go, but sometimes a little white scar is left. Veterinary advice must be sought since a neglected corneal ulcer may burst. It is usually necessary to use ointment for about four weeks.

Uneven pupils These can occur in infection of the iris (the coloured part surrounding the pupil); early *Key-Gaskell syndrome*; *Horner's syndrome* (in this the third eyelid protrudes, the upper eyelid droops and the pupil is small), *FIP*. Veterinary advice should be sought in all these cases.

Feline AIDS (FTLV)

Also known as *feline-T-lymphotrophic lentivirus*, feline AIDS is similar to feline leukaemia (FeLV), with symptoms such as anaemia, diarrhoea, chronic infections, abortion, and neurological signs. Whilst from the same group as human AIDs it is completely distinct and there can be *no* cross-infection from humans to cats, or vice versa.

Feline Infectious Enteritis (FIE)

This is also known as *feline panleukopaemia*. FIE usually starts three to ten days after exposure to the virus, with vomiting, extreme debility, dehydration and a high temperature. If the cat survives for two or three days, then profuse, bloody diarrhoea ensues. The virus decreases the number of white blood cells, and therefore decreases the cat's resistance to infections. This is often the case in young kittens.

If a pregnant queen is exposed to FIE virus, the virus can damage the brain of the unborn kittens, causing them to have *cerebellar hypoplasia*, a condition where the kitten cannot control its movements, falls over and has tremors.

Older cats often have some immunity and shrug off the infection with very few signs, but those that do show symptoms have only a 50:50 chance of survival.

Kittens of immune mothers are protected by her milk up to the age of about nine weeks but should be vaccinated then, and again at twelve weeks, against this. Older cats can be vaccinated at any age, but pregnant queens should not be vaccinated with a live vaccine.

Feline Leukaemia Virus (FeLV)

FeLV is a disease which can manifest itself in countless different ways. It must be at the back of the mind of every veterinary surgeon when he sees a cat, especially if the symptoms do not fit the pattern of any recognised disease.

Usually only young cats (under four months) can be infected by the virus, although a heavy dose of virus, ie very close exposure to an infected cat for a number of days, will break through the resistance of an older cat and either make it a carrier or give it the disease. The virus cannot survive for long outside the cat, so transmission does not occur via food bowls, litter trays or people: cats must be in close contact with an infected cat to catch it. If a queen is infected her kittens will be infected; the virus can cross the placenta and is found in the milk.

Once in the body, the virus makes for the bone marrow, where the blood cells are produced, and the effects differ depending on which precursor cells the virus picks on. There is one type, *FeLV-C* which destroys the precursors of the red blood cells, causing such rapid *anaemia* that the cat often dies within twenty-four to forty-eight hours of contracting the condition. However, this is very uncommon and most infections are very insidious in onset, incubating for months or even years.

FeLV is believed to be the cause of up to 70 per cent of cases of anaemia and should certainly be tested for in every case. It usually causes recurrent episodes of anaemia, increasing in severity each time (see *anaemia* for the signs). I have found that a supplement containing folic acid can extend an anaemic cat's life by months or years.

As well as damaging the cells which make the red blood cells, FeLV also lowers the resistance of the cat to *feline infectious anaemia.*

FeLV also affects the white blood cells which are the body's defence mechanism, making the cat susceptible to any of the conditions listed in this A–Z, and unable to fight illness off once it is contracted. FeLV should be tested for in any cat which has a poor health record and which does not seem to respond in the normal way to treatment.

FeLV affects the female reproductive system and causes infertility and resorption (when the kittens die and are reabsorbed); if a cat resorbs or aborts more than once, she should be tested. If kittens are born, they are invariably infected and may die before their eyes open (fading kittens), or at any time thereafter; they will not live more than three years.

The most well-known and feared result of FeLV infection is *cancer* and this can occur in *any* area of the body – skin, eye, spine, etc. However, there are three well-recognised manifestations of FeLV-related cancers.

Thymic lymphosarcoma This affects younger cats, often only one or two years old. The tumour grows in the thymus, an organ in the chest in front of the heart. As it grows it causes fluid to accumulate which gradually fills up the chest, pressing on the lungs and making it difficult for the cat to breathe. Often the symptoms are sudden in onset, such as sudden difficulty in breathing, rapid breathing, maybe with the mouth open and an inability to exercise without distress. If the tumour grows big enough it presses on the gullet and the cat may vomit back its food. FeLV can be detected in over 80 per cent of these cases. X-rays show the tumour and the cat must be put to sleep immediately if found to have this.

Multicentric lymphosarcoma This usually occurs in cats over three years old. The tumours grow in the lymph nodes. The first lymph nodes to be affected are usually the submandibular lymph nodes which are under the chin, at the top of the throat; these can get so big as to be felt even by untrained fingers. Other lymph nodes are in front of the shoulders, behind the knees, in the armpit and groin and, of course, internally, which are harder to detect. The liver, spleen and kidneys may also be affected, and *anaemia* is common in this condition. A biopsy may be needed to confirm this, as there are other possible causes of enlarged lymph nodes. However, 60 per cent of cases are FeLV positive. Sometimes these cases can be suppressed for months or even years with cortisone, and, again, folic acid seems to help. However, the cat rarely lives to six years of age.

Alimentary lymphosarcoma This is when the tumour grows in some part of the bowel, usually the small or large intestine (not the stomach or rectum). This affects cats from weeks old to eight or nine years of age and weight loss is the most striking sign. Symptoms depend on the part of the bowel affected; vomiting and diarrhoea if the small intestine is affected, as the tumour grows and narrows the lumen of the bowel; diarrhoea if the large intestine is affected, since the tumour prevents water from being reabsorbed from the digested food. Again, *anaemia* is often present and the suppression of the immune system will mean that the cat has a history of off days and minor and major ailments. The vet can often feel a lump in the abdomen in the small intestinal form, but, in the large intestinal form, the cancer cells are usually disseminated throughout the bowel wall, simply causing thickening which is hard to detect. Only 30 per cent of these cases are FeLV positive. These must be put to sleep, once diagnosed, because usually the tumours are fairly advanced by the time the diagnosis is made.

It may be wondered why only some of the cats affected by FeLV are positive on the test, whilst others are not. The reason, it is supposed, is that the virus gets into the cells and turns them into cancer cells. The body then fights off the virus and eliminates it from the bloodstream, but by then the damage is already done. Another reason is that, especially in carriers, the virus can lurk in the bone marrow and only come out into the bloodstream during periods of stress.

False positive results can occur sometimes when the ELISA (Leukassay) test is used and then a further test must be done to establish the true result. The advantage of ELISA is that it is quick and cheap, so it is routinely used first rather than doing a virus isolation test initially.

A carrier is a cat which has FeLV in its bone marrow and blood and which secretes it in its saliva, faeces, etc, but which has not succumbed to the cancer forms. The reason is that its body has developed antibodies to FeLV-related tumour cells, but not to the virus itself. The cat may not always have the virus in the blood, but it appears when it is stressed, eg by moving house, another illness, a new pet or baby, or a dose of cortisone and then the cat may be off-colour and run a temperature while the virus is in the bloodstream. A carrier may appear to be a completely normal cat although, because his immunity is suppressed, he will have had more illnesses (*cat flu, FIA, abscesses, diarrhoea* etc) than usual. If new kittens are introduced into the house, their mortality will be noticeably higher than normal. A female carrier will be more prone to abortion. It is estimated that 40 per cent of adult cats, exposed to a high dose of the virus, will become carriers.

In the United Kingdom experts generally agree that there is no risk of FeLV to humans. Surveys which have been done of the owners of FeLV-infected cats show the same incidence of cancer as in the general population, so there is no evidence of FeLV affecting people. It would, however, be wise to keep FeLV-positive cats away from immuno-deficient people, ie young babies (up to six months old), ill people, those on cortisone treatment and people with AIDS.

If a cat has FeLV, the owner *must* attempt to keep it away from all other cats; in a household where there are many cats, the chances of FeLV being introduced and causing a problem are much higher (this is why it used to be seen more frequently in pedigree cats). Multi-cat households with FeLV must, therefore, decide either to take in no more cats, or to test and euthanase all positive cats, although, bearing in mind that not all FeLV cases show up positive on the test, this might be risky. Two tests should be done, twelve weeks apart, because some cats, which have recently been exposed and show positive, may subsequently eliminate the virus and be negative on the next test. Others, which were negative on the first test, may in fact have been infected, as it takes ten days from the virus gaining entry into the cat, and appearing in the bloodstream. Some cats may be carriers which only shed virus intermittently. These will need a third test. The test is not the last word on cases and must be used in conjunction with case history and clinical signs by a veterinary surgeon experienced in dealing with FeLV.

Feline Infectious Peritonitis (FIP)
This disease is the product of a virus and the cat's reaction to the virus. The route of transmission has not been proven, but it is suspected that the cat picks it up through the nose and mouth. It seems that any age of cat can be affected, although it is found more often in young cats under two and older cats over ten years of age. Queens may repeatedly give birth to infected kittens which will not even survive to maturity at six months. The virus cannot survive more than a day outside the cat and is killed by most disinfectants, so infection can only occur through fairly close contact between cats.

It used to be found that 50 per cent of cats with FIP also had *FeLV* but now the incidence of FeLV is decreasing. It is believed that the lowering of the cat's resistance may be an important factor in its developing FIP and, of course, this is what FeLV does. When FIP is diagnosed or suspected, tests should also be made for FeLV.

When a cat catches FIP, it will often have a raised temperature and be a bit off-colour; it may sneeze or have a runny nose or eye. The next signs, which can occur days, weeks or even months later, depend on whether the cat has the dry or the wet form of FIP. In the wet form the abdomen fills up with fluid, and, in some cases, the cat feels like an old hot-water bottle when picked up. In others there is very little fluid, or none at all. Fluid can also accumulate in the chest, which makes breathing difficult.

The dry form is very hard to diagnose, but a tell-tale sign is often found in the eye where there might be distortion of the pupil or cloudiness. The dry form of FIP can affect many organs – the kidneys, the brain (it can cause fits, paralysis and loss of balance) and the liver (at the end stage it often causes *jaundice*). FIP should be suspected whenever there are odd signs such as weight loss and *anorexia*, and a blood test should be taken.

Obviously, affected cats should be kept away from other cats. Sometimes the disease can be held for a while, using tylosin and prednisolone, but no cure has been found and affected cats will die within a few months.

Feline Urological Syndrome (FUS)
FUS is when a cat gets repeated attacks of *cystitis*, ie when it strains to pass urine, passes small amounts of urine frequently, passes blood, or cannot pass any urine at all.

The reason for FUS is unknown, although many factors have been implicated, such as too early neutering, eating dry cat-food, being overweight, not taking enough exercise, urine not sufficiently acid, and the cat not drinking enough. It seems likely that a combination of these factors is to blame. The best way to try to prevent it from recurring is to avoid dry foods, keep the cat slim and lively, mash in a couple of teaspoonfuls of water with each meal and encourage drinking by leaving clean, fresh water down all the time and offering milk, gravy, cream etc.

If a cat shows any signs of *cystitis* it should be taken to the vet as soon as possible and not left to see if it gets better on its own. Cystitis is treated with antibiotics and, sometimes, urinary acidifiers. It usually responds fairly quickly but, as in people, has a nasty habit of coming back again. It is quite uncommon for cats to get stones in the bladder but these would cause repeated attacks of cystitis with blood in the urine and a poor response to antibiotics. The vet would have to operate to open the bladder and flush out the stones, and would then advise on a special diet to try to prevent recurrence.

More common is the occurrence of a sand-like material called struvite which can cause a complete blockage. This is much more likely to occur in the male than in the female because his urethra is narrower. If this occurs it is a very serious, life-endangering situation and veterinary advice should be sought immediately. The vet will try to unblock the urethra, but, if he cannot pass a catheter into the bladder, he might have to perform an emergency operation called a urethrostomy (making a new orifice for the cat to urinate through, positioned slightly above the old one).

Fits

Fortunately fits are uncommon in the cat. A fit or convulsion is when an animal loses control of itself, falls over, its legs paddling, and possibly frothing from the mouth. Owners of female cats sometimes mistake their first season for a fit; the cat (five to twelve months old and unspayed) cries out and rolls around on the ground as though in agony, holding her tail to the side.

Probably the most common cause of fits in the cat is terminal kidney or liver failure; these really mean that the time has come for the cat to be put to sleep. In these cases the cat will have been ill for quite some time.

A sudden fit, in a cat which has previously been enjoying good health, is more likely to have been caused by poisoning (see *poisons*). A large number of ordinary domestic substances are toxic to cats.

Where there has been no exposure to poison and no disease of the kidney or liver, there is the possibility that *FIP, toxoplasmosis* or a *tumour of the brain* is causing the fits. Very occasionally a cat may be epileptic, but this is rare compared to dogs and man.

Diabetic cats can have fits caused by too little sugar in the blood, or if given too much insulin, or if they have missed a meal. Too much food before the condition has been diagnosed, or if the insulin injection has been missed, can also cause fits.

A queen who is feeding a large litter of kittens may get milk fever and have a fit; this is uncommon but can be rapidly fatal (within one to twelve hours) and veterinary attention should be sought immediately.

Feeding an exclusively, or almost exclusively, fish diet can cause fits due to the destruction of the vitamin thiamin by an enzyme present in the fish. Of course, rabies causes fits but, thankfully, the United Kingdom is at present free of rabies.

If your cat has a fit, get in touch with the vet, wrap the cat in a heavy blanket or towel (leaving his head sticking out), and transport him to the veterinary surgery, remembering that he may not know what he is doing and may give you a nasty bite. Better still, put him in a secure basket. Most fits pass off in a few minutes; stimuli such as the television, noise, lights, etc, should be turned off.

Fleas

Fleas are little brown-black parasites which move very quickly through the fur and are therefore very hard to detect. The best way to hunt for fleas is to look for their droppings in the fur. The droppings are like coal dust; if put on wet cotton wool, the digested blood in them causes a red-brown stain.

Obviously, fleas cause scratching, sometimes the cat turns suddenly and bites its fur; if the cat swallows a flea it may get tapeworms.

Some cats are extremely sensitive to fleas and a single bite can set off a terrible reaction (see *miliary dermatitis*). Others seem very stoic and can be crawling in fleas without batting an eyelid!

The fleas can live away from the cat's body and it is said that, for every flea on the cat, there are seven in the house. They mostly go onto the cat to feed. They can bite people, but cannot live on them. Treatment must be relentless, and the cat must be treated once a week for at least four weeks, or all through the summer if it is meeting outside cats and getting reinfected. A veterinary preparation should be used as many fleas are resistant to the products available in pet shops. Many owners complain that they cannot spray or dust their cat, or that the cat salivates and is upset by it. In that case a Vapona fly strip should be hung in the rooms most frequented by the cat, or Nuvan Staykil should be sprayed round the rooms, particularly where the cat sleeps most. Flea collars should *not* be used as they do not work, and can cause severe reaction of the skin around the neck, and possibly be toxic to the cat. Cats should always be watched closely in the presence of insecticides in case of toxic reaction.

Fluid

The cat should always have fresh water available even though many appear never to touch it. Cats are prone to *kidney disease*, partly because they do not drink enough fluid, so moist food should be given. It is a good idea to mash water into commercial canned foods, or to pour gravy over them and, of course, to tempt cats to drink milk (unless they are prone to *diarrhoea*) along with other treats such as cream, evaporated milk and so on.

Fluid in the abdomen (ascites) can occur in some disease processes (see *FIP, kidney disease* and *heart failure*). Sometimes tumours can cause ascites. The cat has usually, but not always, been off-colour for a while. It may appear to have grown fat, and the owner may even think it is pregnant because the stomach gets larger and looks pear-shaped when the cat is viewed end-on. The abdomen may feel like a full hot-water bottle when the cat is picked up. In fact, cats with fluid in the abdomen are invariably thin, and one can feel all the ribs, and even the backbone may be prominent. A lot of fluid can impair the cat's ability to jump up. The cat will often drink more and eat less; the symptoms and treatment vary according to the cause.

Fur Ball

Fur ball tends to occur at the times of moult, twice a year, and causes the cat to be sick infrequently, perhaps only once a day or once every other day, until the fur ball comes up. Otherwise the cat is fine, although it may eat slightly less than usual. The fur often causes the cat to have bouts of a low, crouching cough, the head and neck outstretched, which can last a couple of minutes and ends in a kind of swallowing action.

Liquid paraffin can be used to shift the fur ball, but I prefer to use a knob of butter or margarine on each meal, which cats prefer. Liquid paraffin carries away vitamins from the cat's body.

Gingivitis

Gingivitis is inflammation or infection of the gums. It is normal for a kitten to have quite red, sore gums at teething (five or six months of age) and the breath will smell at this time. Other cats always have a red line along the gums, above the roots of the teeth, for no apparent reason. However, there are cats who have terribly sore and bleeding gums, so inflamed that they sometimes rise up around the teeth. This is quite a problem and one that does not

often respond to treatment. Sometimes all the teeth have to be taken out and the cat put on antibiotics and multivitamin drops. Occasionally Ovarid tablets (a hormone) may help. It is worth stopping dry cat-food for a few weeks to see if this helps, but, unfortunately, it often makes no difference.

In older cats whose teeth are deteriorating, gingivitis can be a direct result of rotten teeth and a build-up of tartar. This responds well to a clean-up, under a general anaesthetic, plus antibiotics, if necessary. Sometimes, if the gum is pressed above a brown, bad-looking tooth, pus can be seen to ooze out. Cats do not seem to show signs of toothache as humans do, but, once the dental work is done, they seem to have a new lease of life, showing that it must have been bothering them.

Grass-eating

In the wild, cats eat all of their prey, including some of the guts, which, as their prey was herbivorous, contained grass. People who keep cats in flats tend to forget that their cats miss out on this essential part of their diet and are surprised when the cats begin eating the household plants. The CPL will provide a packet of cocksfoot grass seed, on receipt of a stamped self-addressed envelope, and this may be easily grown. Many pet shops also stock the seed.

When a cat is ill or has a heavy dose of worms, it may eat much more grass than usual in order to make itself sick. If excessive grass-eating is noticed the cat should be checked over by a veterinary surgeon.

Gums, see *gingivitis*

Halitosis

(See also *gingivitis, teeth* and *ulcers.*)

Halitosis, or bad breath, is, to some extent, normal in the cat because of what he eats. It also occurs at five or six months of age when the cat is teething. If it becomes very offensive, however, it may indicate that there is something wrong with the cat. The inside of the mouth should be checked first as the cause may be obvious – bad teeth, brown, with tartar on them and maybe loose, *gingivitis* (the gums red and sore, or exuding pus if pressed), a foreign body, ie something which should not be there, such as a bone, stick or thread caught around the tongue, a tumour growing. Sometimes there are *ulcers*, redder raw-looking areas on the tongue or roof of the mouth. These put the cat off its food because they are painful.

Halitosis is not a disease in itself, but a symptom of something else wrong with the cat and in all cases, except teething, veterinary advice should be sought. In terminal *kidney failure* a foul, meaty smell is on the breath, although the cat may not have eaten for days, the saliva is thick and sticky and the mouth painful. (See under *cat flu, fur ball, kidney disease* and *vomiting*.)

Harvest Mite

This is usually only found in country areas, appearing singly, or in clusters, usually on the cat's underparts or ears where it causes a variable amount of irritation and inflammation. It is orange and about the size of a pinhead. Any ordinary flea preparation will kill the parasite.

Heart Disease

Heart disease in cats is fairly uncommon compared to the incidence in dogs and man. As in other species, kittens can be born with a faulty heart which will usually be noticeable before the cat is six months old, ie it will have difficulty breathing, will not tolerate exercise so well (reluctance to run about, or collapsing on doing so) and may even be stunted.

Most feline heart disease (or cardiomyopathy) occurs in young to middle-aged cats (three to eight years) and in three times as many males as females. It usually causes difficulty in breathing initially, due to fluid accumulating in the chest or the lungs. The cat may breathe through the mouth, may need to use its abdominal muscles to breathe and will not be keen to move much or eat because this requires too much effort. Sometimes, on picking up the cat, the heart can be felt pounding at a tremendous rate (over 200 beats per minute).

Rest is the most important part of the treatment for this, and, unless the cat can literally be kept in an area no bigger than a cage, it may have to be left with the vet so that he can enforce strict rest.

Diuretics will be given to remove the fluid from the chest; do not make the mistake of letting the cat drink as much as it likes as this will simply refill the fluid in the chest. Fluid intake should be limited to up to ¼ litre (½pt) a day and this includes milk, cream, etc, as well as water. Remember to leave a litter tray nearby, because the cat will need to urinate more frequently. Sometimes heart pills are also given; unfortunately, digitalis, with which so many humans and dogs are treated, is potentially toxic to cats. There is no total cure for heart disease in the cat, but treatment alleviates the situation and will need to be given for life, which will often be less than a year from diagnosis.

Another problem associated with heart disease in the cat is the formation of *clots* which lodge in the bloodstream, cutting off the blood supply to some organ or other (this is called a stroke in human medicine). The clot usually lodges at the end of the aorta (the major artery in the body), cutting off the blood supply to one or both back legs, causing sudden paralysis. The cat may initially howl and be in a lot of pain, unable to move one or, more commonly, both hind legs and tail. As the nerves are lost the pain becomes less and the cat may drag the whole posterior part about. The feet feel cold and are without sensation. When faeces are passed the cat is unaware of them and they stick to the tail. Most cats with this problem have to be hospitalised for days or weeks. Treatment consists of rest and something to combat the clots. Sometimes aspirin is used for this and it must be used extremely carefully because it is highly toxic to cats. No more than 25 to 50mg every forty-eight hours should be given (this is about one-twelfth of a normal aspirin).

Of course, a clot could land in and block any artery; if it blocked the coronary artery, which supplies the heart muscle itself, it would cause sudden death; if it landed in the renal artery, it would cut off the blood supply to a kidney, causing extreme pain just behind the ribs, and blood in the urine; in the brain, it would cause loss of balance and a head tilt; in the fore leg, sudden lameness and pain. Again, even with treatment, it is unlikely that the cat will live for more than a few months to a year.

Hyperthyroidism

Hyperthyroidism is a condition of older cats (over nine years) which become very thin and have a dull, greasy and often matted, coat. The cat is bright and lively however, and eats a lot. Sometimes there is a lot of scurf, and sometimes the voice changes.

The cause is a benign growth on a gland called the thyroid (in the neck). The hormones produced by the thyroid can affect the heart and the liver, causing these to deteriorate. The heart rate increases to over 200 beats per minute and sometimes there is *jaundice* due to liver damage.

Cure is effected by an operation to remove the growth; if the operation goes well a good recovery will follow.

Hyperthyroidism should be suspected in old cats whenever they lose weight for no apparent reason, especially if their appetite remains good.

Itch, see *dandruff, ear mites, eczema, eosinopholic granuloma, fleas, harvest mite, lice, miliary dermatitis* and *ringworm*.

Jaundice

Jaundice is when the mucous membranes (gums,

inside of the eyelids, etc) and the whites of the eyes look yellow. In really severe cases it is noticeable on the skin inside the ear and on the abdomen, especially if the cat has white fur.

Jaundice can result from a severe breakdown of red blood cells, such as happens in *feline infectious anaemia* (FIA) (see *anaemia*) or when the liver is affected by a *tumour, FeLV, FIP, toxoplasmosis* or *hyperthyroidism*. The prognosis is very poor in all these cases and most cats will have to be put to sleep within a few days. Occasionally one with jaundice due to FeLV, with none of the other signs, will last a few months. A cat with hyperthyroidism, which recovers from the operation to remove the thyroid, will do well, but a jaundiced candidate will have reduced chances.

Jaw
Dislocated When the jaw is dislocated the cat has its mouth stuck open and it cannot be closed. It is quite a simple job to put it back, but it requires a general anaesthetic.
Fractured The jaw of the cat is frequently fractured in road accidents and falls. The fracture is revealed by the level of the fang teeth being uneven. The vet will anaesthetise the cat, and wire the jaw together again. Soft food should be given for a few days until healing begins, and the wire removed three or four weeks later.

Key-Gaskell Syndrome
Known also as *feline dysautonomia*, this new disease only appeared in 1981; the cause is unknown and it can affect any age of cat although it seems more common in younger cats. It affects various parts of the nervous system.

Initially the cat is often brought to the veterinary surgeon because it is a bit off-colour, slightly constipated and often the third eyelids (nictitating membranes or 'haws') are slightly prominent. Some cats get no worse than this and improve, with drops, over a few weeks. Within a few days, however, many are very constipated, and one or both pupils are slightly or markedly bigger and do not constrict when exposed to light. The third eyelids are quite obvious, the mouth and nose dry up, some cats can no longer empty their bladders and there may be dilation of the oesophagus (gullet) causing vomiting or regurgitation of food. A barium meal and X-ray may have to be done to assess the amount of damage to the oesophagus; the worst cases will probably not recover. When the disease first appeared, most affected cats died, but now the death rate is only about one in four. Those with the best chance of survival are the ones which are only mildly affected.

Treatment is symptomatic; liquid paraffin or Dorbanex to relieve constipation, manual emptying of the bladder (the veterinary surgeon will do this or show the owner the procedure), and feeding sloppy fluid with the cat's head held up to make the food run into the stomach due to gravity. Eye drops are given as these not only reduce the size of the pupil and third eyelids, but also improve the tone of the gullet, bladder and rectum. The worst cases, ie those with no appetite, dehydration and all systems affected, should be put to sleep as, even if they improve a little, they never become completely normal again and will need intensive nursing all their lives. The milder cases will need good nursing and a lot of support from their families for weeks or months to recover.

Without knowledge of the cause of this disease we have no way of knowing how to prevent it or where it will strike next. Let us hope research will one day answer these questions.

Kidney Disease
Kidney disease (nephritis) is quite common in cats because they eat such a high protein diet (the breakdown product of which is urea), and they drink so little. Cats' urine is therefore very acidic and concentrated.

Kidney disease chiefly affects middle-aged to older cats; they go off their food and are a bit depressed. They may drink more, or change from drinking milk to drinking water, sometimes from puddles and ponds so that the increase in thirst is not noticed. They lose weight very quickly. Cats may seem to get over several bouts of this themselves and often they are not taken to the veterinary surgeon until it is too late and irreversible damage has been done to the kidneys. Treatment may consist of antibiotics, anabolic steroids or both. It is important to get treatment as soon as the signs start.

As the disease gets worse, urea builds up in the bloodstream and causes vomiting and ulcers on the tongue, making the breath smell meaty and horrible. The cat may drool since it becomes painful to swallow its own saliva. The cat will be very thin and very depressed, refusing all food and, probably by then, all fluids too. At the very end the urea level may affect the brain, causing fits.

There is another form of kidney disease, called the *nephrotic syndrome*, where the cat gets a lot of fluid in the abdomen, the legs and maybe the face, which looks all puffed up. Owners often think the cat has an allergy or has been stung. This swelling usually goes down with treatment but often returns later.

The vet will advise in regard to diet for nephritic

cases, most cats having to be kept on white meat (chicken and rabbit, for example) to keep the levels of protein down. They must be encouraged to drink by offering tempting fluids such as gravy, cream, etc.

Kidney disease can be prevented by feeding moist foods such as Whiskas and by regularly adding one or two teaspoons of water to the food, and mashing it in, and always having fresh water available.

Lameness

(See also *arthritis* and *paralysis*.)

Lameness is most often caused by a cat bite. The cat carries one paw, which may look swollen, and it greatly objects to the paw being touched. If the paw can be examined closely, it is usually possible to find a small puncture wound or scab. Sometimes the suppuration comes to a head and an abscess bursts out. In this case it should be bathed with salt water (one teaspoon to ¼ litre (½pt) of water). It is important that lameness is treated by a veterinary surgeon as septicaemia can result if the infection is not eliminated.

If a cat has *broken its leg*, this will be held up and will hang at an odd angle. It may be possible to feel the bones scrunch if the leg is moved. This will obviously be a sudden occurrence (whereas the condition above may appear over a couple of days) and will usually follow the pattern of the cat going out perfectly all right and returning very lame and in pain. If it has been involved in a road accident, the claws will be frayed.

Unless the break is in an obvious place and nearer the foot than the top of the leg, more harm than good can sometimes be done by splinting the leg yourself. The cat might be shocked, will be in a lot of pain, and the sooner it receives professional treatment the better. The most painful part of having a fractured bone is having it moved and the cat must therefore be kept as still as possible, perhaps by confining it to its carrying basket.

Dislocation of the hip sometimes happens to a cat. Again, it appears suddenly; the cat cannot put one of its hind legs down, and the leg will look about one inch shorter than the other if fully extended. If left untreated, the cat will gradually begin to use the leg again, although permanent lameness and arthritis will follow. The dislocated part should be moved back into position as soon as possible for the best results, and it may need to be strapped up for a week.

Occasionally a cat will get glass or a thorn in a pad and the foot should be examined carefully for this. Other uncommon causes of lameness include standing on petrol or other caustic chemicals.

Usually more than one paw is affected and they will be red, swollen and weeping (see *burns*). Sometimes a young cat will play with wasps or bees and limp in with a huge, fat paw which has been stung; this will go down within twenty-four hours.

Lice

Lice are skin parasites which are very uncommon in the cat. They are found at the roots of the hair and look like sesame seeds. If watched closely, they will be seen to move and, with good eyesight, it may be possible to spot their eggs (nits) attached to shafts of the hair. Obviously they cause itching and may also cause severe dandruff. A weekly treatment with a good insecticide (from the veterinary surgeon) will clear them in four weeks.

Lungworm, see *cough*.

Mats, see *moulting*.

Miliary Dermatitis

Miliary dermatitis usually occurs along the centre of the back, from the base of the tail upwards, although it can extend all over the body. There are lots of scabs and when you stroke the cat you can feel a horribly bumpy skin. The fur is thinner and the cat nibbles at it a lot, so it may well look cropped and in black cats the fur often looks brown.

The cause is almost invariably an allergy to flea bites and often only one or two bites will be enough to set it off, so it may be difficult actually to spot any fleas. Many will clear up with a weekly spray of a good insecticide from the vet (flea collars and most pet-shop powders, sprays and shampoos will not work). The treatment must be continued for at least four weeks, or all summer if the cat is going out and can get reinfected.

In rare cases the allergy is to something else, perhaps in the diet, eg to liver, which is very rich. Occasionally it is caused by the *Cheyletiella* mite, in which case weekly treatments with insecticidal preparations are required. Some cases respond well to Ovarid tablets but these should not be used unless regular insecticidal treatment has already been tried.

Mites, see *dandruff, ear mites* and *harvest mites*.

Moulting

Moulting takes place twice a year, in spring and autumn, although cats kept in centrally heated houses will tend to moult all the time. Longhaired cats should be groomed daily to prevent mats forming; a steel comb is best for this. When a cat is severely matted, it often needs to be anaesthetised by the vet and clipped out. The mats get so close to the skin that it is not a job to be attempted by the owner.

Mats appearing in a previously well-groomed cat can be a sign that the cat is not well, for instance, that it has *hyperthyroidism* or *kidney disease*. Mats are more common in older cats.

After the non-existent summer of 1985, there was a severe moult when some cats went quite bald along the abdomen and the inside of the back legs; this is called *telogen effluvium* and commonly happens to queens after giving birth. The hair grows back in about four to six weeks.

Obesity

Many cats, particularly those who never go out, or are on Ovarid treatment, get far too fat and this ruins their health. The heart suffers, the joints suffer due to the extra weight and *arthritis* ensues, and the coat becomes dull and matted because the cat becomes unable to bend round sufficiently to clean himself. Some cats become more prone to *constipation* and *feline urological syndrome*.

A cat's proper weight depends, obviously, on its size and bone structure. No cat, however big, should ever get to weigh as much as 9kg (20lb) and owners who encourage this sort of obesity are being very cruel. The best way to judge a cat's weight is to feel the ribs which should be easily palpable with hardly any digital pressure.

If a cat is obese, cut its daily consumption of food in half, add one tablespoon of bran to the food daily and give water instead of milk (or skimmed or diluted milk if water is unacceptable to the cat).

If a cat should suddenly look fat, it should be checked in case it is pregnant or is retaining fluid in the abdomen (ascites) (see under *fluid*). It is *very* important to make the distinction between real and apparent obesity as the latter cases may need more food, not less, depending on the true cause of the condition.

Off Food, see *anorexia*.

Paint On Fur

Emulsion paint can be washed off with plenty of soapy water. Gloss paint, however, presents more of a problem. Turpentine and Swarfega contain substances which are toxic to cats so they should *not* be used. It is sometimes best to let the paint dry and then clip off the fur, but if it is very close to the skin it may have to be removed under anaesthetic at the veterinary surgery.

Paralysis

Sudden paralysis of the back legs of a cat is not uncommon and can be due to a *blood clot* cutting off the blood supply to the hind legs.

Paralysis may also result from trauma, eg a road accident, or being savaged by a dog. An X-ray will be necessary to see the extent of the damage and, if the back is not broken, the outcome may be uncertain until a week of strict rest has gone by (to see if the nerve damage can repair itself).

Occasionally just the tail is paralysed after an accident such as a blow on the back, or being shut in a door. Again it is worth waiting a week or two before amputating because, very often, sensation and mobility return, especially if the cat can lift the first inch or two when going to the toilet. Amputation is necessary in cases which do not improve, because, without sensation, the tail can get horribly injured and soiled by faeces, and occasionally flies lay eggs in the faeces and *strike* (maggots) results.

Another form of paralysis, not uncommon after road accidents, is *radial paralysis* where a nerve in the fore leg is damaged. If sensation does not return, it will be necessary for the fore leg to be amputated.

Poisons

Fortunately cats are fastidious eaters and do not often consume poison or poisonous plants. Unfortunately, however, many substances, normally to be found around the house, are toxic to cats and these are sometimes ingested when the cat grooms contaminated fur. If a cat has eaten poison, it can safely be made to vomit with one crystal of washing soda administered like a tablet (see pictures of dosing a cat). This should only be done if the cat has been *seen* to eat the poison within the previous half-hour. Vomiting will occur within ninety seconds. The cat should then be taken, in a covered and secure box, to the vet as soon as possible, taking along, if possible, a sample of the poison concerned.

It would be impossible, in the space of this A–Z, to list all possible poisons, so only those with which the cat is most likely to come into contact are mentioned.

Alphachloralose This is a green-coloured poison for mice which causes convulsions and coma. The body temperature drops and death can result from hypothermia. A cat which has taken this should be kept warm using covered hot-water bottles, heat lamps, etc, until it can be got to the veterinary surgery.

Aniline dyes These are found in crayons, pencils, and shoe polish, and cause depression, vomiting, convulsions and difficulty in breathing.

Anti-freeze This causes loss of balance, depression, convulsions and sometimes coma and death.

Aspirin This should only be used on veterinary advice, at a dose of no more than 25–50mg every other day. An excess will damage the liver, and it should never be given if the liver is impaired. Aspirin poisoning causes vomiting and diarrhoea with blood, panting, convulsions, collapse and death.

Bleach This causes burning of the skin if walked on and ulceration of the tongue when the cat tries to clean it off. There is salivation and loss of appetite. The contaminated area should be washed in water and the cat given a teaspoon of olive oil if it has been licking itself and might have swallowed some bleach.

Flea Collars These cause depression and loss of balance.

Iodine This causes depression, vomiting and diarrhoea, hypothermia, coma and death. If ingested, give one or two teaspoons of olive oil.

Paracetamol This causes pallor, anorexia, depression, then cyanosis (the mucous membranes look blue), facial swelling, coma and death.

Rat Poison Warfarin, a blue poison. See *bleeding*.

Slug Pellets (metaldehyde) This causes fits, loss of balance, salivation, twitching (especially if touched) and the eyes dart from side to side. If treated promptly by a vet this can usually be cured.

Smoking Chip Pan This can cause death in under five minutes. The cat should be rushed to the vet immediately or the lungs will fill with fluid and the cat will drown in its own secretions.

TCP/Dettol These cause vomiting, diarrhoea and coma.

Turpentine This causes vomiting, diarrhoea, fits, depression and death.

Wood Preservative This causes drooling, vomiting, sometimes loss of balance, exaggerated response to stimuli, then convulsions, coma and death.

Pox

Cat pox produces one or several itchy, red, moist areas on the skin which can go septic, ulcerated, or scabby. They usually go away in four to six weeks. Under *no* circumstances should cortisone be put on them because it is a viral infection which could spread right through the body. Handle an infected cat with rubber gloves and use strict hygiene precautions.

Pregnancy

A female cat reaches puberty at around five or six months of age and can become pregnant at any time from then on. It is not safe for a young queen to conceive and she should be at least nine months old before mating.

Pregnancy lasts about sixty-three days, ie nine weeks, and the nipples look more obvious in the pregnant queen three or four weeks after mating. In the last half of the gestation period she will obviously gain weight and look pot-bellied. In the last third of the pregnancy she should eat twice as much as usual.

If you want your cat to bring up her kittens in a kittening box she should be encouraged to become accustomed to it as soon as possible, and well before they are due. Otherwise she will seek out some quiet corner of her choice. Cats like to have their kittens in private and she should be left well alone to get on with it; too much interference may cause her to delay and the kittens may die.

Most cats give birth easily unless mated too young. If a kitten has appeared but is not out in less than twenty minutes, the queen should be taken to the veterinary surgery. A couple of hours' gap between kittens is quite safe, but if the queen is straining for more than two hours and nothing comes, again she should be taken to the vet.

Check that an afterbirth is delivered with each kitten; if one is left inside, an injection should be given to bring it out. It is always a good idea to have the queen checked the day after giving birth in case any kittens or afterbirths remain. The mother will probably eat the afterbirth which is quite normal.

Leave the queen to bite through the umbilical cord herself, although, if a kitten is delivered in its bag, you should burst the bag and clear the mouth and airways, then let the mother lick the kitten to stimulate it to breathe. If, after ten minutes, she has not bitten the cord, tie it off 7cm (3in) from the body with a piece of sterilised (boiled) cotton thread.

The kittens should begin to suckle very shortly after birth, and when she is finished the queen will lie down and sleep with all her kittens.

Cats can have three or four litters a year, but to let them do so is cruel as they will soon become exhausted.

Pyometra

Pyometra is when the womb fills up with pus. It is relatively uncommon in the cat as most non-breeding cats are spayed. It usually occurs when a pregnancy has gone wrong, but can also occur when *FeLV* has lowered the cat's resistance to infection. The cat is sometimes, though not always, a bit miserable and lethargic, may vomit, have a high temperature, be off food and may drink more. There may be a discharge of pus from the vulva.

Although thinner (one can easily feel the ribs) she may appear to have gained weight and the abdomen may look pot-bellied because of the pus-filled womb inside. A complete hysterectomy should be done as early as possible if her life is to be saved.

Ringworm

Ringworm is not actually a worm but a fungus. The cat usually catches it directly from another animal (not necessarily a cat; it might be a dog, horse, cow or human) or indirectly, via a contaminated cage, brush, hands, etc.

It usually causes a round area of hair loss which expands in a circle although there are several types of the fungus which can show different appearances. The commonest type will fluoresce under ultra-violet light (the vet will have a special lamp to diagnose ringworm); in other cases a sample of infected hair has to be taken for a laboratory test. The cat often spreads the infection by scratching it and, if the head is affected, the front paws become infected too when the cat washes itself. On people, ringworm causes a red, itchy circle, but most pharmacists can supply a cream to cure it.

The cat needs at least a month's treatment of daily Griseofulvin tablets and if there is more than one cat (or a dog) in the house, all should be treated or infection will spread back and forth between them. Avoid too much handling of an infected animal and wash your hands carefully after touching the pet. Ringworm can be difficult to eradicate.

Sometimes bacteria get into the damaged skin and it can get red, weepy and sore; then antibiotic treatment is also needed.

Road Accident

Waste no time in getting the cat to the vet if it is known, or even suspected, of having been involved in a road accident. A sure way of telling is by looking at the claws; they will be frayed if the cat has been knocked down.

If you find it lying on the road, ie it is unable to stand up, move it gently onto a stiff board and then put this in a box to transport it to the veterinary surgery. The cat will be in a state of shock, so try to keep it warm and use gloves to pick it up as it may bite.

If it is bleeding, try to stem the flow by applying a clean cotton or linen pad or paper tissues to the area and holding this on. The pad should not be changed; if the blood seeps through an extra pad should be applied on top. If the cat vomits, its head should be tilted downwards and care taken to ensure that the airways are clear, especially if it is unconscious.

Rodent Ulcer, see *eosinophilic granuloma*.

Roundworm

All kittens are infected with roundworms (*Toxocara*) from their mother's milk as soon as they have suckled, and they should be wormed at four, six, eight, twelve, twenty and twenty-four weeks and thereafter, as adults, twice a year. In kittens, roundworms can cause diarrhoea, a pot-belly after feeding, and vomiting. A bad dose can kill a young kitten. The worm looks like a thin, small (6–7cm, 2–3in) piece of spaghetti. In adults they are rarely a cause of illness although they will, occasionally, be vomited up. Any pet shop or veterinary surgery will supply a good roundworm tablet.

Salivating

Salivating, or drooling, can occur temporarily when the cat feels upset or sick, such as after being sprayed with flea spray, or travelling in a car. Some cats drool with pleasure when they are being petted. It can occur for longer if the teeth are bad, the throat sore, a foreign body is stuck in the mouth or throat, or the tongue is ulcerated. When the teeth are bad this is fairly obvious (see *teeth*) and the vet must deal with it. Sometimes, on opening the mouth to find the reason for salivation, the cause is obvious – a stick or bone stuck across the teeth, or big ulcers on the tongue (see *ulcers*). At other times the cat needs an anaesthetic to find the cause, for instance when there is a growth or foreign body in the throat. A common cause is cotton or elastic around the base of the tongue and down the throat, and needles are frequently found embedded well into the soft tissue of the mouth.

Cats also salivate when exposed to certain poisons, eg a house which has recently been treated with wood preservative, such as creosote, or painted, and also to disinfectants and rat or slug poisons. Since salivation is usually the first sign, it is important to seek veterinary advice and to remove the cat from the source of the fumes or poison immediately.

Shock

Cats can easily be shocked after a road accident, fall, dog attack or similar trauma, and shock can kill. For this reason veterinary advice should always be sought after an accident. The signs of shock are pale mucous membranes (gums and inside of eyelids), a fast heart rate and, sometimes, mouth breathing. The cat should be kept warm; place a hot-water bottle, wrapped in a blanket, beside him and talk to him.

Kittens sometimes chew cables and get electric

shocks. If this does not kill them outright, they may be unconscious and, in this case, a few drops of brandy or whisky should be put under the tongue and the kitten rushed off to the vet.

Stings

Cats are quite prone to stings because of their habit of playing with anything that moves. They usually come in from the garden with a fat paw, two or three times its usual size! It happens more towards the end of summer when wasps and bees are dying and are easier to catch.

If the cat seems to be in pain, it should be taken to the vet for an injection, but most are not apparently bothered by the sting and the swelling should go down in under twenty-four hours. The foot should be examined closely in case the sting has been left in it. This will indicate if it was a bee, rather than a wasp, which stung the cat.

A stung foot should be differentiated from a bitten paw. In the latter case the cat will be much iller and in pain which will affect it for much longer than a few hours. Bites must receive veterinary treatment.

Stings in the mouth are serious and, if suspected, must have veterinary attention straightaway because, in swelling up, the cat's airways may be blocked.

Stud Tail, see acne.

Sun-sensitive Ears

Some cats with white ears get very sore ear edges after being out in the sunlight. They look red, may be scabby or bleed and the cat washes them a lot. Since this can, over the years, lead to cancer, it is wise to let such cats out only on cloudy days, or to apply sun-tan oil to the ears before letting them out, to filter the harmful ultra-violet rays from the sunlight. Glass also filters ultra-violet rays, so it is safe for the cat to sun itself in the window.

Tapeworm

The only way to be sure that a cat has a tapeworm is to see a white segment on its fur or faeces. The white segment is an egg packet and sometimes it wriggles out of the cat's bottom; if the cat has an itchy bottom and keeps licking it, this could be the reason. The cat catches a tapeworm by eating an infected intermediate host, such as a flea, louse, rat or mouse. They cannot be passed directly from cat to cat, nor can people pick one up from a cat.

It is rare for a tapeworm to cause any clinical signs in a healthy adult cat except, possibly, an increased appetite. If a cat with tapeworm has marked weight loss, diarrhoea or vomiting, it is likely that there is also something else wrong with it and it should have a check-up from the veterinary surgeon.

The head of the tapeworm is well embedded in the intestinal wall and tablets should be given only after twelve hours' starvation if the head is to be killed. The tablet should be given whole and the cat fed three hours later. If the head is not killed, it will grow another tail and segments will reappear a few weeks later. There is now an injection, available from the vet, which is much more effective than tablets for difficult cases. Cats with tapeworm should also be treated for fleas and, if reinfection keeps occurring because of hunting, a collar and bell might help – although puss is usually wily enough to move without ringing the bell!

Temperature, High, see abscess, cat flu, FeLV, FIA, FIP.

Testicle, Not Descended, see cryptorchid.

Teeth

(See also gingivitis.)

Cats do not often show signs of toothache (pawing at the mouth, difficulty in chewing and salivating), so it is a good idea to check the teeth periodically to see if everything is all right. One sign of bad teeth, often noticed by owners, is bad breath (halitosis).

Cats change their teeth at six months of age, sometimes the breath smells during teething and the gums look red and sore, but this soon passes.

Older cats develop tartar on their teeth. This is a brown deposit and, if left, can become so bad that the teeth appear almost to have doubled in size. It is usually only when a tooth is actually loose that the cat will begin to paw at its mouth and when matters get to this stage the cat will need to have a general anaesthetic to have the teeth extracted or scaled.

The problem of tartar arises largely because of the mainly meat diet of the cat; feeding a dozen or so Munchies, Go-Cat or similar hard cat-treats daily can help prevent tartar formation. Fresh water must always be available when dry food is given.

Third Eyelid

The third eyelid, haw or nictitating membrane, is a flesh-coloured structure which comes from the side of the eye nearer the nose. Sometimes it protrudes onto the eyeball when the cat is unwell, most noticeably in Key-Gaskell syndrome, the diarrhoea and third eyelid syndrome and in cases of conjunctivitis or cat flu. If the third eyelid is more noticeable than normal, it would be wise to have the cat checked over.

Ticks

A tick is a parasite which only occurs in the countryside. The cat picks it up as it wanders around in a field and it usually attaches itself to the cat's head or legs. At first it looks like a small wart which grows rapidly over about a week. It is greyish or brown in colour and, on close inspection of the embedded end, it is possible to see little black legs which move. *Never* try to remove the tick by force as this will result in the head being left in to go septic. It can be killed with a spray of good veterinary insecticide (eg Nuvan Top), or by holding cotton wool, impregnated with methylated spirit or whisky, over it. It will then take quite a while to relax its grip by this method. Ticks do drop off, in any case, about ten days after they latch on. Once it is off it usually leaves a small wart-like area which takes two to three weeks to go away. If the head is left in it may fester and need antibiotics if septicaemia is not to result.

Toxocara, see *roundworm*.

Toxoplasmosis

Toxoplasmosis is a protozoal infection which the cat acquires by eating raw meat, birds or small rodents. It usually causes no symptoms in a healthy cat although, in a debilitated cat (eg with *FeLV*), it can be responsible for a variety of problems, such as *vomiting, diarrhoea, abortion, anorexia, raised lymph nodes, pneumonia* and *hepatitis* and it can affect any body tissue.

Occasionally it can cause a condition like a dose of flu in a person, but, if it infects a pregnant woman, it can affect the baby. For this reason it is important for pregnant women to wear gloves when cleaning the litter tray, or, better still, that the husband does it.

Ulcers

(See under *eye* for ulcers on the surface of the eye.)

Ulcers in the mouth cause difficulty in eating, *anorexia, halitosis* (bad breath) and *salivation*. If an ulcer is suspected, the inside of the mouth should be examined when it may be possible to see red, raw-looking areas, the ulcers, on the roof of the mouth or on the tongue.

Little circular ulcers on the tongue and palate are usually caused by *feline calicivirus* (see *cat flu*). Large ulcers round the edge of the tongue may be caused by chemical burning, ie the cat walks in petrol or some other chemical and then licks it off, burning the tongue. The coat and feet should be checked for signs or smell of chemicals, and, if these are present, they should be washed off. In this case the cat, although otherwise quite bright, will be in too much pain to eat. It may drool and, if it has ingested any of the chemical, it may become ill (see *poisons*). A teaspoon of olive oil should be given and the cat taken for a check-up. Large ulcers round the edge of the tongue are also caused by severe, usually terminal, *kidney disease*.

As well as veterinary treatment, care should be taken that the cat drinks, if necessary giving fluid by means of a dropper. The cat can go without food for two or three days without harm, although, after twenty-four to forty-eight hours of starvation, it should be tempted with liquidised food, perhaps a chicken stock, boiled fish or tinned baby food, again given by dropper.

Vitamin A Toxicity, see *arthritis*.

Vomiting

Cats have a strong vomiting reflex, evolved to protect them in the wild, so that anything bad which was eaten was returned quickly before it could do any harm. They may vomit because they have gobbled their food too quickly, or because the food has been in the fridge and not allowed to reach room temperature before being fed. A heavy worm burden will cause a cat to vomit, when one or two roundworms may be seen together with a piece of grass and some saliva or bile.

Fur ball will also cause the sporadic vomit, with returned food on two or three occasions and, perhaps, the offending fur ball. A knob of butter will help this to pass through. Cats, in these cases, are bright and want to eat; if the cat is off its food and listless then it is not fur ball or worms and no treatment should be given until the cat has been seen by a vet.

The following cases of vomiting are all very serious and veterinary advice should be obtained immediately. Until the cat is taken to the vet, it should be starved and offered (not forced to have) a tablespoon of boiled and cooled water, every hour.

Pyloric dysfunction Here the pyloric sphincter at the exit of the stomach fails to open correctly to allow food through, and this stimulates the vomiting reflex. It is apparent at weaning when the kitten is going on to solid food although, depending on the severity, it may not be really noticeable until five or six months of age. A small operation to loosen the sphincter can sort out the problem. The cat is bright and otherwise healthy, wants his food and may do all right on liquidised or mashed food, fed at a slight height, eg off a pile of books.

Foreign body Again this tends to occur in young animals which have been known to eat string and plastic bags with which they have been playing.

Small bones should *never* be given to cats since they, too, can cause an obstruction. If the foreign body is in the stomach, the cat may remain quite bright. There will be no diarrhoea; indeed, no faeces may be seen since little or nothing gets past the foreign body. The cat may want to eat, but food will be vomited back, usually up to twenty minutes later. When the foreign body moves into the small intestine, then the situation becomes dangerous and may well be fatal; the cat can go into shock. The abdomen may be painful, the vomiting becomes more frequent and consists only of bile. The cat is dull and does not want to eat. An *intussusception* (when the bowel turns into itself like a telescope) also causes these signs and it is very painful and dangerous. It is usually seen in young kittens and necessitates immediate treatment. A vet may be able to feel the foreign body or intussusception and may want to do an X-ray to confirm it; an operation will have to be performed immediately.

Alimentary lymphosarcoma Part of the *FeLV* complex, this is a tumour in the small intestine which can cause vomiting.

Key-Gaskell Syndrome In this condition the food does not get as far as the stomach, the gullet becomes distended and food is brought back undigested, without the usual amount of contraction of the stomach muscles associated with vomiting. Also there is frequently *constipation*, protrusion of the third eyelid and dilation of one or both pupils.

Kidney disease Cats which drink a lot, vomit and lose weight may be suffering from kidney disease. If this is suspected, veterinary advice should be sought quickly since the longer it continues the more of the kidney will be damaged. People often make the mistake of leaving it because the cat seems to get over bouts after a few days.

Waxy Ears, see *ear mites.*

Weight Loss, see *diabetes, kidney disease, FeLV* and *hyperthyroidism.*

Worms, see *roundworm, tapeworm.*

Below *The correct way to give a cat a pill. This is not as difficult as it looks, provided you have two people*

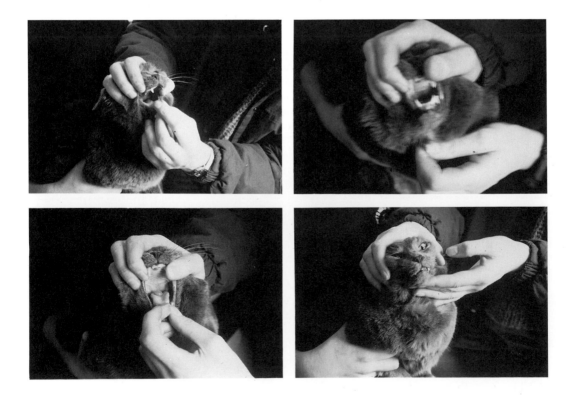

Cat Quiz

1 Who gave his cat an occasional feast of oysters?
2 What is the nictitating membrane?
3 What is the name of the breed of cat with short wavy and curly coats which appeared in the Westcountry in the 1950s?
4 Which cat is commemorated in a window in Westminster Abbey?
5 What is polydactylism in cats?
6 What is a feral cat?
7 Which Act of Parliament controls the operation of boarding catteries?
8 Why do a cat's eyes shine in the dark?
9 Who was the creator of Tom Kitten?
10 Which aromatic garden plant is very attractive to cats?

Answers

The answers to the questions may all be found in the book but are, for convenience, summarised below.

1 Dr Johnson
2 The cat's so-called 'third eyelid'
3 Cornish or Devon Rex
4 Dick Whittington's cat
5 Extra toes in addition to the normal five at the front and four at the back
6 One which was domesticated but which has taken to living in the wild or one which was born in the wild although its immediate ancestors were domesticated
7 The Animal Boarding Establishments Act 1963
8 Because of the tapetum, a reflective layer in the eye, which acts like a mirror
9 Beatrix Potter
10 Catmint (*Nepeta mussini*)

FURTHER READING & USEFUL ADDRESSES

Day, Christopher, *The Homoeopathic Treatment of Small Animals* (Wiemore Publications 1984)

Eliot, T. S., *Old Possum's Book of Practical Cats* (Faber & Faber 1939 and many reprints)

Hamilton, Elizabeth, *In Celebration of Cats* (David & Charles 1979)

Hunter, Francis, *Homoeopathic First Aid Treatment for Cats* (Thorsons 1984) (Also published under the title *Before the Vet Calls*)

Lane, D. R. (Editor), *Jones's Animal Nursing*, 4th edition (Pergamon Press 1985)

McClinton, K. M., *Antique Cats for Collectors* (Lutterworth Press 1974)
In spite of the title covers figurines and many other cat items up to comparatively recent times.

Pond, Grace (Editor), *The Complete Cat Encyclopaedia* (Heinemann 1972)
A lavishly illustrated volume dealing with every aspect of the pedigree cat.

Sillar, F. C. and Meyler, R. M., *Cats Ancient and Modern* (Studio Vista 1976)

Tabor, Roger, *The Wildlife of the Domestic Cat* (Arrow Books 1983)
The standard work on the feral cat.

Wright, M. and Walters, S. (Editors), *The Book of the Cat* (Summit Books, New York 1980)
A comprehensive study of the cat with many diagrams and photographs.

British Association of Homoeopathic Veterinary Surgeons:
    Chinham House, Stanford in the Vale, Faringdon, Oxon SN7 8NQ

Cat Action Trust:
    1 Coldharbour Close, Thorpe, Egham, Surrey

Cat Fanciers Associated Inc
    1309 Allaire Avenue, Ocean, New Jersey, USA, 07712

Cats Protection League:
    17 Kings Road, Horsham, West Sussex RH13 5PP

Department of Agriculture and Fisheries for Scotland:
    Chesser House, 500 Gorgie Road, Edinburgh EH11 3AW

Feline Advisory Bureau:
    350 Upper Richmond Road, Putney SW15 6TL

Governing Council of the Cat Fancy:
    4–6 Penel Orlieu, Bridgwater, Somerset TA6 3PG

Midland Counties Cat Club:
    Nilgiris, 4 Orchard Lea, Naunton Beauchamp, Pershore, Worcestershire

Ministry of Agriculture, Fisheries and Food:
    Hook Rise South, Tolworth, Surbiton, Surrey

National Cat Club:
    The Laurels, Rocky Lane, Wendover, Bucks HP22 6PR

Northern Counties Cat Club:
    56 Tudor Avenue, North Shields, Tyne & Wear NE29 0RX

People's Dispensary for Sick Animals:
    South Street, Dorking, Surrey RH4 2LB

Royal Society for the Prevention of Cruelty to Animals:
    Causeway, Horsham, West Sussex RH12 1HG

Scottish Cat Club:
    85 Ormonde Drive, Glasgow, Strathclyde G44 3RF

Southern Counties Cat Club:
    Littlecroft, Willow Grove, Chislehurst, Kent BR7 5DA

ACKNOWLEDGEMENTS

The Cats Protection League reached its sixtieth anniversary in 1987, and this book was created to commemorate this milestone in the League's history. The CPL has, over the years, produced a series of authoritative pamphlets on various aspects of cat welfare, but until this book was published, there was no one readily available source where all the distilled wisdom of the CPL could be found. The Diamond Jubilee year seemed an appropriate time at which to record it all in a permanent form.

The CPL has many friends whose help is sought when the occasion demands, and this book is no exception. The result can be seen in the impressive variety of material contained in the book. The CPL, and the editors, wish to thank everyone who contributed to the book in any way – from Desmond Morris and Beryl Reid who so kindly contributed their thoughts to the short personal stories of many CPL members. We are most grateful to everyone who has helped make this book such a success.

To avoid repetition and generally meet the overall requirement, some contributions have inevitably been shortened and edited and the editors and publishers alone are responsible for the final product. Those who wrote pieces that are the basis of what is included in these pages include:

Diane Addie, for the section The A-Z of Cats' Ailments and Diseases

Phillipa Bryan and Tony Bryan for the stories of inn signs

D. J. Davies for setting out the (often obscure) position of the cat in the eyes of the law

Eric Delderfield for his stories, taken from *Eric Delderfield's Book of True Animal Stories*, and *Eric Delderfield's Second Book of True Animal Stories*

Margaret Ellis for her research into cats and churches

Lorna Gulston for her account of cat welfare work at the front line

S. M. Hamilton-Moore for the information on the efficient running of boarding catteries

Elizabeth Hamilton for kind permission to quote several excerpts from her book *In Celebration of Cats* (David & Charles) including *Church Cats*

Francis Hunter, 'Alternative Medicine for Cats'

Marc Henrie, ASC, for his guidance on the elusive art of cat photography as well as his photographs

D. R. Lane for his clear account of just how a cat is put together

Grace Pond for her chapters on 'The Pedigree Cat' and 'Breeding, Show Preparation and Care'

Roger Tabor for the fascinating account of feral cats

David St John Thomas for 'Making the Most of a Cat', and his obituary of his beloved Siamese

British Rail and Miss June Watson for details of the Paddington Cat

Contributors to *Cats of Character* are Fiona M. Wilkie (*Jane on Top*), the late Eileen R. Taylor (*My Cat Richard*), Margaret Bevan (*Benson . . . a live wire*), Josie Smith (*Requiem for Coleby*) and David St John Thomas (*A Publisher's Cat*).

In addition, many pieces were taken from various issues of *The Cat*. It was not always possible to find the names of the authors, who are all CPL members, past or present, but we are indebted for the personal touch their words have given the book.

Mollie Caborn for *Trophies*

Lorna Gulston, *Rescued Cats, We Help If We Can*

Alexis Charles, *Down came a Spider*

Ute Williams, *The Icing on the Cat*

Heather Smith, *Tabitha*

W. Girt, *The Night Cat*

Diana Berlow, *Cat-in-the-Snow*

M. Calder, *My Name's Henry*

E. S. White, *Just one Point of View* and others

M. Foster, *Memories*

Miss Drummond, *Clever Cat*

Louise Simpson, *Charlie No Nose*

Geraldine Cox, *Thoughts from a Foster Mum*

Grace Sykes, *The Good Old Days*

the late Barbara Joyce, *Ode to the Common Cat*

Apart from the identifiable contributors, a helping hand has been received from various sources, and thanks are due to Joyce Caldwell of Victoria, BC for her recipe for Canadian Cat Relish, John Hall of the Anderson House Hotel, Wabasha, Minnesota, for the account of the unusual facilities offered to guests, Peter Fairlie of the Glenturret Distillery, Crieff, for the remarkable story of Towser, the Post Office for information on the official feline employees. Caroline Smith for help with illustrations, Alison Swann for the splendid drawings on physiology, Kathleen Wood for her recipe for Crunchies.

Many of the photographs were selected from entries for the CPL's annual photographic competition, and have not been previously published. The entrants are too numerous to thank individually, but The Cats Protection League is most appreciative of their contribution to the book.

Finally, my grateful thanks to the staff at the CPL Headquarters in Horsham, and especially to the Director, Group Captain H. E. Boothby, OBE, who not only read the manuscript and made many helpful suggestions, but who also dealt with my often abstruse problems cheerfully and effectively, and made what sometimes seemed impossible achievable after all. *Philip Wood, The Cats Protection League.*

PICTURE CREDITS

Tony Bryan p 84. **British Museum** p 81. **The Cats Protection League** p 10 (Mrs E. V. Price), 15 (Mrs L. P. Hicks), 20, 23 (Mrs E. V. Price, Joan Fowler), 24, 25 (Mrs I. P. Rothera), 29 (A. D. Williams), 31 (Dorothy Lancaster), 32, 42, 46 (M. C. Whittall), 48 (Sandra Thirtle), 53 (Mrs L. McClay), 55 (Philip Wood), 58 (M. N. Foster), 64, 70 (Jane Skinner), 71 (E. W. Harper), 72, 73, 74 (Karin Ingram, Joan Fowler), 76 (J. R. Richards), 80 (Mrs Cathie Toner, Miss V. A. Wilkerson), 82 (Hon Sally Plummer), 83 (Sue Greaves), 86 (Mrs C. James), 90 (Sue Hagon), 91 (Mrs C. James), 96 (Mrs B. Birkby), 97 (P. S. Silver, P. C. Docherty), 103 (Mrs S. Blamire), 104 (R. Hannam), 114 (Karin Ingram), 123, 126, 139 (R. Willbie), 153 (Miss A. Banneville), 154, 158 (Grace Officer), 170 (Mrs June Nelson-Tomsen), 173, 174 (N. Green), 179 (Mrs S. Ferns, F. McGuiness), also Caroline Smith for work on black & white photos. **Bruce Coleman** p 14, 22, 75, 111, 115, 127, 138, 159, 162, 167. **Ian Cox** p 21, 39, 44, 68, 72, 119, 120, 122, 123. **Anne Cumbers** p 22, 23, 134. **Don Griffiths** p 9. **Marc Henrie** p 3, 13, 30, 47, 63, 87, 94, 98, 100, 126, 144, 146, 148, 149, 151, 152. **Howard Loxton** p 21, 34, 38, 39, 111, 117, 129, 181. **Oxford Scientific Films** p 10. **Shuel** p 57, 125. **Tony Stone** p 2. **Roger Tabor** p 134, 135. **Sally Anne Thompson** p 2, 14, 22, 30, 51, 71, 95, 99, 147, 150. **Noman Tozer** p 36, 37, 61, 75, 77, 110, 112, 113, 118, 143, 157, 178. **June Watson** p 92.